Hiking
Maryland and Delaware

David Lillard and Chris Reiter

American Hiking Society

FalconGuides help support
the American Hiking Society

FALCON®

HELENA, MONTANA

A FALCON GUIDE®

Falcon® Publishing is continually expanding its list of recreation guidebooks. All books include detailed descriptions, accurate maps, and all the information necessary for enjoyable trips. You can order extra copies of this book and get information and prices for other Falcon® books by writing Falcon, P.O. Box 1718, Helena, MT 59624 or calling toll free 1-800-582-2665. Also, please ask for a free copy of our current catalog. Visit our website at www.Falcon.com or contact us by e-mail at falcon@falcon.com.

All black and white photos by David Lillard unless otherwise noted.
Cover photo by Laurence Parent.

Project Editor: Jay Nichols
Maps by Kenneth L.Graham
Page composition by Darlene Jatkowski
Book design by Falcon® Publishing, Inc.

Cataloging-in-Publication Data is on file at the Library of Congress.

CAUTION

Outdoor recreational activities are by their very nature potentially hazardous. All participants in such activities must assume the responsibility for their own actions and safety. The information contained in this guidebook cannot replace sound judgment and good decision-making skills, which help reduce risk exposure, nor does the scope of this book allow for disclosure of all the potential hazards and risks involved in such activities.

Learn as much as possible about the outdoor recreational activities in which you participate, prepare for the unexpected, and be cautious. The reward will be a safer and more enjoyable experience.

♻ Text pages printed on recycled paper.

Contents

Land between the Bays

Appendices

Dedication

For all the volunteers who build, maintain, promote, advocate, and otherwise act as the stewards of our trail systems, and for the ever underappreciated staffs of trail managing and planning agencies—together, they make sure the rest of us have places to enjoy the outdoors.

Acknowledgments

Thanks to Ed Talone, who has walked more than 30,000 miles, for helping to find many of the hikes in this book, which are previously unpublished in any source, and to Ann Hall for use of her extensive library. Thanks to the agency staffs in Delaware and Maryland who took the time to help ensure the accuracy of information contained in the guide, and to Joe Reiter, who produced the draft maps for the guide. Thanks to Jayson Knott, to Ceil Petro and Lisa Gutierrez of the Maryland Department of Natural Resources for help with photographs, and to Kitty Clark for fact checking and Nelson Pressley for proofreading the manuscript. A big thanks to Lauren Clingan for navigating the road to many trailheads.

Overview Map

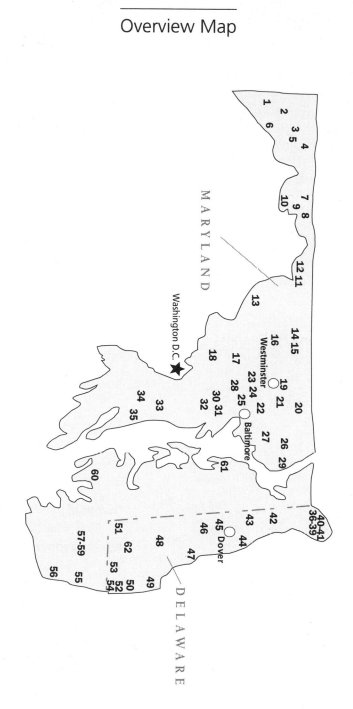

Legend

Interstate		Field	
US Highway		Bridge	
State or Other Principal Road		Tunnel	
		Campground	▲
Interstate Highway		Picnic Area	
Paved Road		Powerline	
Dirt / Gravel Road		Marsh	
Trailhead	○	Overlook/Point of Interest	
Main Trail(s)		Building	■
Alternate/Secondary Trail(s)		Mine	
Railroad		Boundary	
River/Creek (Branch, Run)		Parking Area	Ⓟ
Falls		Cemetery	†
Boardwalk		Summit/Hill	
Town	○	Private Property	
Locator Map		Scale	

0   0.5   1
Miles

Introduction

You would not think it could be such a secret to residents, but here it is: Delaware and Maryland are wonderful day-hiking states. It is true that remote backpacking experiences are rare in both states, with the rugged mountains of western Maryland and the open beaches of Assateague offering the only real places to disappear into the landscape for a few days. But if you are looking to spend a day wandering through hardwood forests, along meandering creeks, or through the mixed scent of salt water and beach pines, both states have plenty to offer.

Although housing development exploded in the Washington, D.C., to Wilmington, Delaware, corridor in the 1980s and 1990s, both states have invested heavily in conserving land for outdoor recreation. Two examples illustrate the types of hiking lands found most often in both states. White Clay Creek State Park, in Delaware's New Castle County, offers hikers a wild woodland experience, despite its proximity to thousands of homes. Likewise, the Gunpowder Falls State Park system in Maryland, a collection of separate recreation areas connected by the riverway, preserves within minutes of one of America's largest cities the "fall zone" and piedmont stream valleys that attracted settlers to the region more than three centuries ago.

There are three facts about hiking Del-Mar that every hiker must face. First, it can be hard to escape the sound of cars or airplanes. Interstates 68 and 70, for example, certainly have made getting to the trailheads of western Maryland a lot easier, but the same highways take thousands of other motorists within earshot of your hike. There are few hikes where this intrusion interferes with an entire hike, but there are many otherwise splendid places that are sometimes overwhelmed by the sounds of cars. This is such a consideration that we have included an entry about "car sounds" in the Trail Finder section of this book.

Second, most of the hiking trails in these states are only a few miles in length, with the average being 3 to 5 miles. For many hikers, a hike of that length does not make a destination in and of itself. The truth is, few out-of-staters travel to either of these states just for the hiking, except those hiking the Appalachian Trail, the Chesapeake & Ohio Canal Towpath, or the Allegheny Mountains in Allegany (yes, they are spelled differently) and Garrett Counties of Maryland. Thankfully, there is a lot to see and experience that offers a perfect complement to hiking.

Often, it is a small town or crossroads near the trail that rounds out the hiking day. This is especially true of the hikes on Maryland's Eastern Shore and in Delaware "below the canal," known collectively as the Delmarva Peninsula (taking into account a tip of Virginia at the bottom). The same is true for western Maryland as well. It is hard to think about hiking Snavely Ford Trail in Antietam National Battlefield without considering the ice cream that follows in Sharpsburg.

Finally, the majority of trails in both states is managed to accommodate bicycles and horses as well as human feet. Sometimes this can put a damper on the attempt to find solitude, especially when you have hiked several miles into a lonely wood only to have a bicycle whiz past. However, relations among so-called user groups in these states are good for the most part, in no small part due to the education efforts of mountain bicycling groups in the area. Both states do restrict bicycle and horse traffic on a portion of their trails, allowing hikers to find the narrow, quiet footpaths they crave.

THE HIKING REGIONS

This book is divided into three hiking regions: West from Catoctin, West of the Chesapeake Bay and Susquehanna River, and the Land between the Bays.

West from Catoctin. Just west of Frederick, Maryland, the rolling piedmont gives way to a series of northeast-leading ridges. Catoctin Mountain is home to a national park, two state parks, and a municipal forest—all strung together to provide plentiful day-hiking opportunities. The Catoctin Trail, a pathway winding along the length of the mountain, makes possible a short but sweet backpacking trip.

Although the border between Maryland's western, mountainous counties lies atop South Mountain, Catoctin Mountain serves as the mental demarcation line between mountain hiking in Maryland and everything to the east. The farther west you go, the taller and more remote the mountains you will find. Green Ridge State Forest, at about 38,000 acres, and Savage River State Forest, at 53,000 acres, are the two largest land areas devoted to recreation. The backpacking options are limited even in these areas, but there are plenty of trails to take you into the woods where you can find a quiet place to spend a night. Call them "overnight hikes"—wonderful places to hike, enjoy the evening, and hike back the next day.

In this West from Catoctin region, you will find the mountainous terrain, waterfalls, and tumbling streams beneath hemlock groves that capture the spirit of any hiker.

West of the Chesapeake Bay and Susquehanna River. The content of our second hiking region, east of Frederick, Maryland, and west of the Susquehanna–Chesapeake waterscapes, is grouped together here as much for its proximity to Baltimore and Washington, D.C., as for any topographic or geologic similarities. From the almost lunar surface of the serpentine grasslands in Soldier's Delight, to the rolling agricultural lands of Baltimore and Carroll Counties, to the brackish, still-water creeks of the Chesapeake's western shore, this region has all the physiographic complexity of a small country. There are few trailheads in this region that cannot be reached within 90 minutes on a weekend morning. And the region happens to be home to some of the most overlooked hiking trails in the east. Residents of the Baltimore–Washington metropolis will be amazed at how much hiking there is so close to home.

Most remarkable about hiking in this region are the surprises in store on every hike, such as the open countryside viewed from the Northern Central Trail and the old carriage road that follows a narrow ridge above Big Pipe

2

Creek in Carroll County. When you watch a blue heron grab a fish dinner out of the ponds at Patuxent River Wildlife Area, you have to remind yourself you are hiking within 30 miles of 5 million people.

Land between the Bays. This region encompasses two distinct areas essentially east of the Chesapeake Bay and Susquehanna River. First is Cecil County, Maryland, and northern New Castle County, Delaware, two counties that were transformed from mostly rural to mostly suburban in 20 short years beginning in the 1970s. But for residents, even the workaday routine need not be an impediment to hiking. With Lums Pond, the White Clay Creek State Park, and Brandywine Creek State Park nearby, you can stow a pair of boots in the trunk and hit the trail whenever the gift of an extra two hours presents itself.

Below the Chesapeake and Delaware Canal is the Delmarva Peninsula. Here, hiking opportunities are found in the salt marsh wildlife preserves, the pine-covered state forests, and the shores of inland bays. Mountain snobs, who believe the quality of the hiking experience is directly proportional to the elevation above sea level, will be amazed to lose themselves amid the tall shore grasses and backwaters. One winter hike in Delmarva is all it will take to turn any hiker into a cool-weather lowlander.

HOW TO USE THIS GUIDE

We have selected the hikes for this book with a phrase in mind: easy to find, easy to follow. Few things are more frustrating than spending an hour trying to find a trailhead to a two-hour hike or spending half your time trying to match the trail before you to a map in your hand. We have assembled this guide with you busy Easterners in mind.

We have selected not only the best day hikes in Delaware and Maryland, but also ones that even novice hikers can navigate. This book is for hikers of all abilities and interests. If you have never hiked before, this book will put you on the trail in safe, beautiful settings. For seasoned hikers, this book will help you discover new destinations.

To put this book to work for you, start with the **Overview Map.** Each hike is numbered, and its location is represented on the map by its number. Then go to the **Trail Finder** to find a hike that matches your plans for the day—for example, a hike for kids, a walk along the water, a snowshoe hike. Then, find your hike listed by number in the table of contents. Go to that hike's pages and read about what you will see.

Be sure to read the entire entry for a hike before you go, in case there is anything special you need to know to enhance your enjoyment of or safety for the trip. For example, in the hike description for Paw Paw Tunnel, you'll find a suggestion to bring along a flashlight. In another example, the trails in Herrington Manor and Swallow Falls State Parks are groomed for cross-country skiing. In other hikes, under the heading "Special considerations" we tell you which trails pass through lands managed for hunting in autumn and winter. That is important to know! Read the entire hike before you leave.

To really make use of this guidebook and discover the best trails in Maryland and Delaware, keep a copy of this book in your car, right next to that extra pair of boots or running shoes in the trunk. Delaware's moniker as the "Small Wonder" holds true for hiking trails in both states. There are many, many fine short hikes that you may never make a destination of but will be glad you visited when you had a chance.

Maps in this guide

Because all of the hikes in this book are accessible by primary and secondary roads and because few of the hikes involve major elevation changes, the maps in this book are all you will need to find your way along the trail. For further research on regional topography, you can consult the U.S. Geological Survey maps for each hike. In the beginning section of each hike description, we have noted the USGS topo map for the quadrant or quadrants for each hike's area.

LONG-DISTANCE HIKING AND BACKPACKING

There are only a handful of truly worthy backpacking trips in Maryland, and none in Delaware. By worthy, we mean hikes that will keep you on the trail for more than 25 miles and longer than a couple of days—and that do not include a great deal of road walking. Those few hikes are adequately documented in other sources and are therefore not the subject of this book. Contact information for those sources is available in the appendices of this guide.

Among the most notable backpacking trips in Maryland are the 40-plus miles of the Appalachian Trail in the Free State. The majority of those miles traverses South Mountain from the Potomac to the Pennsylvania line. While there are many opportunities for day hikes along the AT, most involve either a two-car shuttle or hiking in and hiking out. Because of the narrow corridor preserved for the trail by the State of Maryland, the number of loop hikes utilizing the AT and side trails does not compare to, for example, the Virginia sections of the trail.

Like most of the trails in the United States, the AT is maintained by volunteers. The Appalachian Trail Conference in Harpers Ferry, West Virginia, is a nonprofit organization charged with overall management responsibility of the "longest national park," under a unique partnership arrangement with the National Park Service. The volunteers of the Potomac Appalachian Trail Club perform the on-the-ground work that keeps the trail open and safe in Maryland.

The longest trail in Maryland is the 184-mile Chesapeake & Ohio Canal National Historical Park. Begun in 1828 as a transportation route between the commercial centers in the East and the frontier resources of the West, the C&O Canal stretches along the Potomac River from Georgetown in Washington, D.C., to Cumberland, Maryland. Remnant canal locks, lock houses, and other historical features along the way interpret the past along the waterway known widely as the "Nation's River." The trail is the former towpath followed by the mules that pulled the cargo barges downriver. It also provides incredible, up-close contact with the Potomac for many miles, while traveling through woodlands and small towns.

It is a wonderful trail, but like the AT in Maryland, there are few opportunities for loop hikes. Most of the day hikes on it are "in-and-out" walks, and all but one of the backpacking trips along it require a shuttle or two cars. This book does contain a loop hike over part of the C&O Canal, one which travels through Paw Paw Tunnel. The trail is managed by the National Park Service and is supported by the nonprofit C&O Canal Association.

A very special backpacking trip covers 25 miles of Atlantic shoreline and inland bays south of Ocean City, Maryland. The best-known attraction here on Assateague Island is the wild ponies that inhabit the island. This hike offers such a unique experience that we included it in this book.

Three other backpacking trips bear noting. There is a 25-mile loop created from trails in Maryland's Savage River State Forest and New Germany State Park. It requires a longish stretch of road walking but is otherwise an enjoyable and very popular hike. The Green Ridge Hiking Trail covers some 19 miles as it climbs from the Potomac River and winds its way north to Pennsylvania, where it connects with Pennsylvania's Mid State Trail to make a hike of more than 200 miles. It is a lovely hike but also one requiring a shuttle arrangement. Finally, there is one loop that utilizes portions of the C&O Canal Towpath and the Green Ridge Hiking Trail to assemble a very nice 50-plus-mile hike. To obtain information on these hikes, contact the Potomac Appalachian Trail Club.

That is the best of it for backpacking. But, again, that does not mean that other "day hikes" in this book do not offer splendid spots for an overnight in the woods, even if you are hiking only several miles.

BEING PREPARED: SAFETY AND HAZARDS

Here are a few basic planning strategies and precautions to keep you safe on the trail. For a thorough understanding of backcountry travel and safety, consult *Wilderness First Aid* and Will Harmon's excellent *Wild Country Companion*, both published by Falcon.

Planning and preparation

The two easiest ways to stay safe when hiking the trails in this book are to plan ahead and to stay on the trail. When you head out for a hike, especially to a backcountry location that is new to you, take a few precautions. Pack a little extra food, warm clothing, rain gear, and anything else you may need if you are forced to rough it for the night. We are not talking about packing a tent and sleeping bag every time you go out for a day hike, but, when hiking in the West from Catoctin region, it is a good idea to know what you need to survive for a night, even uncomfortably, if you are forced to do so.

A second precaution is to always tell someone where you are going, your basic itinerary, and when you plan to return. If you have told a spouse or roommate that you will be home by noon on Sunday, then you know someone will be looking for you if you do not come home. This is especially important when hiking in western Maryland, where the woods are wonderfully deep. Remember, most tragedies start out simply. All it takes is an unexpected slip on a rock to break an ankle. If you have not left word about where you are, no one will be looking for you.

Although Maryland and Delaware are not known as states with vast wilderness areas, anyone can get lost in the woods by straying from the trail. Experienced hikers can and do get lost. If you do unwittingly leave the trail you are supposed to be on, follow your footsteps back until you find the place where you went astray.

If you are totally lost and you have taken the precautions outlined above, the worst that will happen is that you will spend an uncomfortable night in the woods. Stay put, eat your extra food, find shelter, and wait until morning. If you have left word with someone of your whereabouts, someone will be searching for you soon. Whatever you do, do not go scrambling around in the darkness; that is an easy way to get hurt.

An essential precaution is to carry a first aid kit. The **Hiker's Checklist** in appendix D lists some of the items any hiker should carry. Your personalized first aid kit should contain a couple of days' worth of any prescription medications you take, a bee-sting kit if you have a known allergy, your eyeglasses if you are hiking in contact lenses, and other similar items. When hiking in the West from Catoctin region of this guide, a snakebite kit is also recommended.

Animals and critters
When hiking in the mountains of western Maryland, if you are very lucky you will see a black bear or a rattlesnake. There is no need to be afraid of either if you keep your distance. In general, black bears stay clear of humans, but if cornered or hungry, their behavior can be unpredictable. Keep your distance. If you happen upon a bear, make sure you leave it an escape route so that it will not feel threatened. Back away slowly and it will go about its business. For an excellent, short book on bear behavior, read Falcon's *Bear Aware.*

Rattlesnakes are most often seen sunning themselves on rocks or stretched out across a trail where the sun is poking through the trees. Give the snake plenty of room when you walk by. When hiking in the mountains, make a habit of stepping onto rocks or logs and then over them. Do not stretch to put your foot down just beyond the rock or log where you cannot see the ground. The two most common snakebite incidents involve reaching around a rock or tree or stepping into rocky crevices where you cannot see. Watch your step.

Rather than describe every critter, hazard, and remedy in this book, again we refer you to the two comprehensive resources *Wild Country Companion* and *Wilderness First Aid.* Carry the latter in your day pack.

A word about water
First, a note about what is safe to drink. Your best bet is to assume that no stream or spring you encounter is safe to drink without treatment, with the exception of protected springs emerging from the ground or pipe before your eyes. In both the West of the Chesapeake Bay and Susquehanna River and the Land between the Bays regions, agricultural runoff and suburban

nonpoint source pollution compromise water safety. In the agricultural areas, the problem is a parasite called *Giardia lamblia,* a protozoan which, when ingested, can cause "backpacker's diarrhea," a mild name for the intense abdominal cramps brought on by the illness.

In the West from Catoctin region, in addition to the *Giardia* from farm and wild animals, streams in the Allegheny Mountains suffer from the presence of heavy metals leaching into the waterways from mining operations.

Because this book consists primarily of day hikes, let us assume that you will either bring your water with you or get it at the trailhead. In the chapter covering each hike, there is a heading called "Trailhead facilities." If water is available at the trailhead, it is noted there.

Now a word about how much to drink. Without getting too technical, drink a lot, especially in summer. In the heat and humidity of Maryland and Delaware summers, plan for about a quart for every 90 minutes you will be on the trail—assuming you have downed at least that much just before hitting the trail. *Wild Country Companion* will give you the precise details about figuring your body's need for water at various altitudes and temperatures, but here is an easy guideline for the day hikes in this book.

1. Drink a lot of water during the day leading up to your hike; take every opportunity to stop at a water fountain or force an extra glass down while standing in the kitchen. Do not make coffee the only beverage you consume before starting out on a summer hike.

2. Pack at least two quart-size water bottles and make sure they are full when you start hiking.

3. Have an extra quart bottle or more in the car with you to drink while lacing up your boots and checking your gear. Just before you start your hike, drink whatever is left in the bottle. The best way to avoid thirst-related problems is to drink before your body is crying for it.

4. Invest in a simple water purification system and carry it with you just in case. A bottle of iodine tablets stowed in your day pack will usually get you through a one-day water emergency.

Trail etiquette

Go gently. Observe the Zero Impact Hiking guidelines outlined below.

Go courteously. Because most of the trails in Maryland and Delaware are used by hikers and bicyclists—and many by equestrians as well—a few rules of the trails help ensure enjoyment by everyone. Hikers should yield to horses. Yes, horses are big and their dung is dropped right on the trail, but they have to deal with you, too. Bicyclists are supposed to yield to hikers, but there are times when it is easier for hikers to step aside. Work it out courteously. In Maryland, most of the trails open only to hikers are designated as such because of a wildlands designation or the fragility of the ecology. Report trail use violations to park officials.

Being courteous also means not hogging the scenery. If you have made it to the top and there is limited space from which to enjoy the view, do not bring a crowd to spend a day in the way of everyone else trying to get a look.

Get there, savor it, and then let others enjoy it. It is annoying to hike a few miles to a popular feature and then be made to feel like you are an intruder.

Go quietly. If you can be heard from more than a few feet away when hiking, you are talking too loudly. Not only are you destroying the quiet for other hikers, but you are scaring off the deer, the owls, and all the other wildlife that are seen only by those who go quietly.

SEASONS AND WEATHER

Bug season

If you live in Delaware or east of Allegany County, Maryland, you know that summer means heat and humidity. It also means mosquitoes in the woods and marshlands. In the section that introduces each hike in this guide, there is a heading for "Best months." You will notice a number of hikes that omit summertime from their best months. In general, this is an effort to spare you the misery of mosquitoes. If you are prepared for the annoyance or have a high tolerance for these pests, take the necessary precautions (use repellent) and hike away.

By far the most treacherous creature on Delaware or Maryland trails is the deer tick. The best precaution against ticks is to hike in long pants with the cuffs tucked in. A pair of polyester-nylon blend pants will protect you from the elements without making you uncomfortably hot. After the hike, be sure to check your legs, torso, and head for these little spiders.

To repel mosquitoes and ticks, there is, unfortunately for naturalists, nothing as effective as the chemical compound DEET, found in most insect repellants. But never put DEET directly on your skin, and never on the skin of a child. If you use a DEET-based product, apply it to your clothing, especially around the ankles and wrists. Some hikers spray a little on the outside of their hats.

There are now many products on the market that contain no DEET. Instead, they contain everything from citronella oil to complex concoctions of other organic compounds. These are the ones to use on your skin. Natrapel is a popular brand.

Stormy weather

Another summer phenomenon in most of the United States is the afternoon thunderstorm. Always check local weather forecasts before heading out. By all means, think twice about starting a hike when electrical storms are forecast. In case you are caught in an electrical storm, here are a few basic precautions. Find shelter in a low-lying area. Take shelter amid the shorter trees and shrubs in the area. If you are hiking on a ridge when the storm hits, move off the ridge into a hollow. If possible, move to the side of the ridge opposite the side from which the storm is approaching.

Do not run for cover under tall trees; they act as huge lightning rods. The lightning that strikes any tree in the area causes a charge known as ground current that momentarily electrifies the very ground where you are standing. In fact, most people who are killed by lightning are not actually struck by lightning; they are electrocuted by ground current.

If you are carrying a pack constructed with a metal frame, ditch it at least 50 yards away and seek the low ground. Avoid standing water or getting too close to a water source. In short, do not be on the high ground and do not be in the water. Then just hunker down. Thankfully, most afternoon storms do not last long. And if you can find adequate shelter, a storm on the trail can be beautiful.

Let it snow

Western Maryland is blessed with snowy winters. This is great for hikers. Because the Maryland mountains are not prone to the avalanches of the western United States, and because the trails covered in this book travel fairly moderate terrain, snow time is a great time for hiking on snowshoes.

Snowshoe hiking is one of the fastest-growing outdoor pursuits. And for good reason. Hiking in snowshoes can take you into winter wonderlands you have never been able to access. The popularity of snowshoeing, along with several technological advances in the materials used in the construction of snowshoes, has resulted in much lower prices for the gear.

However, one note of caution. Snowshoes are not magical antigravity devices. Walking on a narrow snowpacked ledge on a trail you are not intimately familiar with should be left to the experts. A good guideline for beginner snowshoe hikers is to snowshoe on trails you have already hiked in snow-free months. In the **Trail Finder,** there is a heading for hikes where snowshoes can provide winter access without traversing questionable terrain. For example, the hike through Green Ridge Forest's Fifteenmile Creek Canyon may be suitable for experienced snowshoe hikers, but the terrain will present special challenges to novice snowshoers. Therefore, it is not a highlighted snowshoe hike in this book.

There are a few hikes in this book on trails that are managed for cross-country skiing or snowmobiling in winter. Those instances are noted in each hike under the heading "Special considerations."

BACKCOUNTRY ESSENTIALS

Many of the hiking areas in Maryland and Delaware are managed primarily for day use. For these areas, the only permitting requirement may be an entrance fee payable at a contact station.

However, some of the state parks do provide developed campsites for tent camping and recreational vehicles. The fees and facilities vary widely. Check with the appropriate managing agency listed in appendix A.

Most of the hikes in the West from Catoctin region allow backcountry camping. They are listed as day hikes in this guide because they are short enough to be hiked in a day. Camping is permitted in Maryland state forests provided a backcountry permit is received from the area's managing agency, for which information can be found in appendix A. Primitive camping also is permitted on Assateague Island.

ZERO IMPACT HIKING

The increased popularity of hiking has put added pressure on the natural resources that draw us to the trail. Many new hikers, bicyclists, and others have taken to the trail without learning how to protect the natural environment. You can help protect trails and become a knowledgeable steward of the land. To begin, here are seven basic steps. These are only an introduction, however. Consult Falcon's *Leave No Trace* for further information.

1. Plan ahead, prepare well, and prevent problems before they occur.

2. Keep noise to a minimum and strive to be inconspicuous.

3. Pack it in, pack it out.

4. Properly dispose of anything that cannot be packed out.

5. Leave the land as you found it.

6. In popular places, concentrate use.

7. Avoid places that are lightly worn or just beginning to show signs of use.

If you can become an evangelist for only one example that encapsulates the Zero Impact ethic, perhaps it should be the care with which you hike along streams, marshes, and shorelines. Everyone loves a water feature. We want to get as close as we can, to dip our hot feet into cool waters, to see the shorebirds dancing and feeding their chicks. Responsible hikers always resist the urge to get too close.

The trees along these streams play an enormously important role in the health of a stream, not the least of which is to prevent erosion of the fragile stream banks that are the habitat for riparian life. The forest cover over the Maryland and Delaware streams began to disappear long ago when the landscape was cleared for farming and timber. Unwitting hikers can do more damage by stomping down the vegetation around streams and ponds. In the marshlands in southern Maryland and Delaware, shorebirds and aquatic animals mate and inhabit these riparian zones. Stand clear and observe from a distance.

HIKING WITH CHILDREN

Courtesy of the gentle terrain over the two eastern regions covered by this guide, Delaware and Maryland are wonderful places for hiking with children. Several books have been published that provide detailed information about planning extended outings with kids and instilling in them a love of the outdoors. Leaving you to do your own further research suitable to your own parenting, here are a few basic things to remember.

Kids enjoy the world differently than do adults. Many adults expect their kids to like the same things about hiking that they do. You may enjoy getting to the wide open view of a valley. Well, that may be your mission, but it may not be your kid's. Young hikers are often more smitten with the idea of lingering to play in creeks and springs, watching the antics of insects, or just hanging out. Take along a hand lens, so that they can see things up close, and a picture book that identifies the plants and bugs they see.

Kids often talk and enjoy themselves more loudly than do adults. Most adults enjoy the squeals of delight that kids emit. However, remind the children you are hiking with that there are others on the trail seeking peace and quiet. Tell them that they will see more wildlife if they can hike along talking only in a whisper.

Kids cannot walk as far and as fast as adults. We should not need to say too much more on this topic, but one hint is useful. If you are planning a three-hour hike, pack a light blanket or sleeping bag so that you can all enjoy a post-lunch siesta. Also, there are a number of quality "kid packs" on the market, which enable you to carry a child as you would a backpack. For your own enjoyment, when you first start hiking with kids, start with short outings and work them up to longer day hikes.

TRAIL FINDER

Use the table below for a quick glance at the special features of each hike.

Water features: has a waterfall, significant contact with creeks and streams, or nice views of water.

Open vistas: has either an open view from a summit or hill, or a broad open view of the landscape—not just a view across a field.

Primitive camping: allows you to find a place to camp along the trail.

Campground or cabins: has developed campsites, car camping, or cabins available for rent; may require you to drive from trailhead to campground.

Snowshoeing: places where annual snowfall is above average for the region and where snowshoe hiking is permitted and safe for novices. Nearly every hike in both the West of the Chesapeake Bay and Susquehanna River and the Land between the Bays regions is open to, and safe for, snowshoe hiking; however, snowfalls here tend to be only a few inches at a time.

Suggested for kids: hikes of moderate distance, with a minimal degree of difficulty.

Autumn colors: has nice views of deciduous trees displaying foliage, even if the views are across a field; more than just a quick glance from one place.

Little or no car sounds: except at the beginning of a hike, where the trail may be near a roadway, or when crossing a road. In general, these are hikes in which the sounds of cars do not intrude on a quarter or more of the hike.

Trail Finder Table

	Water Features	Open Vistas	Primitive Camping	Campground or Cabins	Snow shoeing	Suggested for Kids	Autumn Colors	Little or no Car Sound
1 Herrington Manor State Park Loop	•	•				•		•
2 Swallow Falls State Park Loop	•	•		•		•		•
3 Deep Creek Vista	•	•	•	•	•	•	•	
4 Poplar Lick Run	•	•		•	•	•		
5 Monroe Run Trail	•	•	•	•	•			•
6 Lostland Run Loop	•	•		•	•			
7 Rocky Gap Canyon to Evitts Summit		•	•	•	•			
8 Green Ridge Hiking Trail North Spur Loop		•	•			•	•	•*
9 Fifteen Mile Creek	•	•	•	•			•	•
10 C&O Canal Towpath—Paw Paw Tunnel			•	•	•		•	•
11 Fort Frederick State Park Nature Trail				•				•
12 C&O Canal Towpath—Fort Frederick to Little Tonoloway	•	•				•		•
13 Snavely Ford Trail	•	•			•	•	•	•
14 Blue Ridge Summit—Hog Rock		•	•	•	•		•	
15 Wolf Rock—Chimney Rock Loop			•	•	•			
16 High Knob—Catoctin Mountain			•		•		•	
17 Little Bennett Loop	•	•		•		•	•	•
18 Schaeffer Farm Trail						•	•	
19 Hashawha Loop			•			•	•	•
20 Northern Central Railroad Trail	•	•	•			•	•	
21 Gunpowder Falls, North and South Loop	•	•					•	•
22 Oregon Ridge Park Loop		•					•	•
23 Soldier's Delight, East Loop						•		•
24 Soldier's Delight, West Loop		•				•		•
25 Sawmill Branch Trail	•	•		•		•		
26 Sweet Air Loop	•	•				•	•	•
27 Wildlands Loop	•	•					•	
28 McKeldin Area	•	•				•		•
29 Susquehanna State Park Loop		•	•	•		•	•	•
30 Wincopin—Quarry Run Loop	•	•				•		
31 Savage Park River Trail		•				•		
32 Cash Lake Loop	•	•		•		•		•
33 Jug Bay Natural Area Loop	•	•	•			•	•	•
34 Cedarville State Forest Loop		•				•	•	•
35 American Chestnut Land Trust Loop		•				•		•

*Some road walking, but otherwise quiet

	Water Features	Open Vistas	Primitive Camping	Campground or Cabins	Snow shoeing	Suggested for Kids	Autumn Colors	Little or no Car Sound
36 Possum Hill Loop				•		•	•	•
37 Earth Day Trail		•				•	•	
38 White Clay Creek Preserve Loop		•				•	•	•
39 Whitetail Trail			•			•	•	•
40 Hidden Pond Trail		•	•			•	•	•
41 Rocky Run Trail		•					•	•
42 Swamp Forest Trail	•	•	•	•			•	•
43 Blackbird State Forest Loop						•	•	•*
44 Bombay Hook National Wildlife Refuge Loop	•	•	•					
45 Norman G. Wilder Wildlife Area Loop								•*
46 Killens Pond Loop	•	•	•			•	•	•*
47 Prime Hook National Wildlife Refuge Loop	•	•	•			•	•	•
48 Redden State Forest Loop								•
49 Cape Henlopen State Park Loop	•	•	•	•		•		•*
50 Delaware Seashore State Park	•	•	•	•		•		•
51 Nanticoke Wildlife Area Loop		•				•	•	
52 Fenwick Island State Park	•	•	•			•		
53 Seahawk Nature Trail	•	•	•			•	•	•
54 Burton's Island Loop	•	•	•			•		•
55 Ocean City Boardwalk	•	•				•		
56 Assateague Island Loop	•	•	•	•				•
57 Paul Leifer Nature Trail						•	•	•
58 Pocomoke State Forest Hiking Trail					•	•	•	•
59 Milburn Cypress Nature Trail					•	•		•
60 Blackwater National Wildlife Refuge Loop	•	•	•					
61 Eastern Neck National Wildlife Refuge Loop	•	•	•	•		•		•
62 Trap Pond State Park Loop	•	•	•	•		•	•	•*

*Some road walking, but otherwise quiet

13

West from Catoctin

1 Herrington Manor State Park Loop

Highlights:	A woodland stroll through a pine grove, a forgotten cemetery, and the mixed hardwood forest surrounding Herrington Lake. The hike finishes at the lake's beach.
Location:	Herrington Manor State Park is located in Garrett County, Maryland, near the West Virginia border. It is about 200 miles west of Washington, D.C.
Type of hike:	Loop; day hike.
Total distance:	4.2 miles.
Difficulty:	Moderate.
Elevation gain:	Minimal.
Best months:	April–October.
Maps:	USGS Oakland, Maryland.
Permits:	None; $2-per-car entrance fee.

Finding the trailhead: From Oakland, Maryland, in Garrett County, travel 6 miles north on State Park Road, which becomes Herrington Manor Road. The park entrance is on the left. Bear right at the gate and proceed half a mile to the trailhead parking, just past the lake.

Trailhead facilities: Snack bar, water, restrooms.

Key points:
- 0.0   Trailhead
- 0.4   Pine grove
- 0.7   Cemetery
- 2.0   Junction with unblazed trail
- 3.5   Herrington Lake

The hike: This leisurely walk follows ski trails near Herrington Lake. The beach, concession, and kayak rentals make the park an ideal spot to spend the day hiking and enjoying the lake.

Start the hike by walking back up the park road 0.3 mile. Go left, following the yellow blazes; the trail here is identifiable largely by mowing. Enter the woods, and go right at the fork near a giant oak.

Begin circling a pine grove at 0.4 mile. The straight, evenly spaced trunks here are wonderfully reminiscent of Ansel Adams. Enter a clearing at an old family cemetery at 0.7 mile. Of particular interest are a series of markers for Uphold, the spelling of which is modified over three successive generations and illustrated by adjacent headstones.

To continue, return to the point at which you first entered the cemetery clearing and go left following the yellow blazes. Through the grove, especially

Herrington Manor State Park Loop

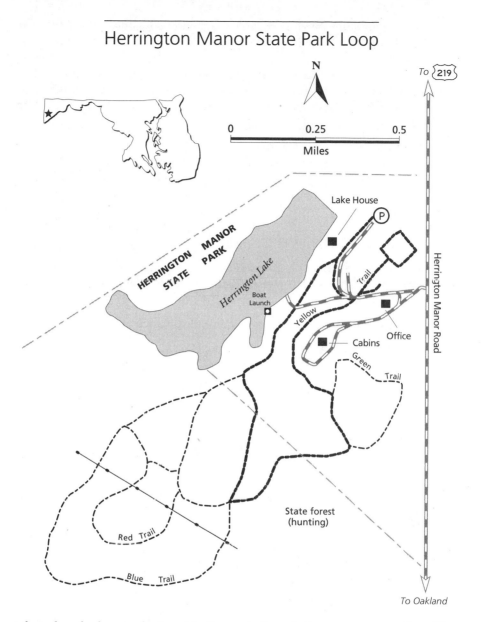

where hemlocks are clustered to the east, there is the strong scent of conifers. In May and June, bluets carpet the pathway in places, shimmering all around. At the junction, go right to retrace your steps to the park road; cross here and stay with the yellow blazes.

Stay with the yellow blazes until a T intersection with the green trail. Go right and walk below black oak and blue spruce with an understory of American hornbeam. At 2 miles, go right at the T intersection with an unblazed trail; a small spring flows to the right of the trail. Continue straight at the clearing, where a sign marks the beginning of the managed hunting area; enter the woods.

At the next junction, go right (power lines will be visible 100 yards to the left). This is the blue-blazed trail, but you may not see a blaze for the first 100 yards or so.

At the next junction, the blue and red trails go left. Turn right and follow a narrower footpath with the lake on your left. At 3.5 miles, emerge from the woods at the boat launch; then follow the paths beside the lake back to the trailhead.

Options: For an additional 1.5 miles of meandering, go left at the blue–red junction, continuing on the blue trail at the next fork. Then turn left at the next junction onto the red trail and follow it on a loop that circles back to the blue–red junction. Continue straight with the lake on your left and emerge at the boat launch.

The trails in the state park are designed for cross-country skiing. There are several color-coded trails in the park.

Special considerations: When snow is on the ground, plan to visit these trails only on skis. The hike passes through areas managed for hunting; inquire at the park office.

Camping: Cabins are available for a fee with advance registration.

For more information: Swallow Falls State Park.

2 Swallow Falls State Park Loop

Highlights:	An easy circuit hike in Swallow Falls State Park through a mature hemlock forest along the scenic Youghiogheny River to Maryland's tallest waterfall.
Location:	Swallow Falls State Park is located in Garrett County, Maryland, near Deep Creek Lake, about 200 miles west of Baltimore.
Type of hike:	Loop; day hike.
Total distance:	1 mile.
Difficulty:	Easy.
Elevation gain:	Minimal.
Trailhead elevation:	2,300 feet.
Best months:	April–November.
Permits:	None; entrance fee $2 per person on weekends from Memorial Day to Labor Day, $2 per car at other times.
Maps:	USGS Sang Run, Oakland, Maryland–West Virginia.

Finding the trailhead: From Interstate 68, take exit 14A and drive 19 miles south on Maryland Highway 219, passing Deep Creek Lake; turn right onto Mayhew Inn Road. Drive 4.3 miles north, and then turn left onto Sang Run Road. In 0.25 mile, turn right onto Swallow Falls Road (Garrett County 20), which leads west to the park entrance in 4.7 miles.

Swallow Falls State Park Loop

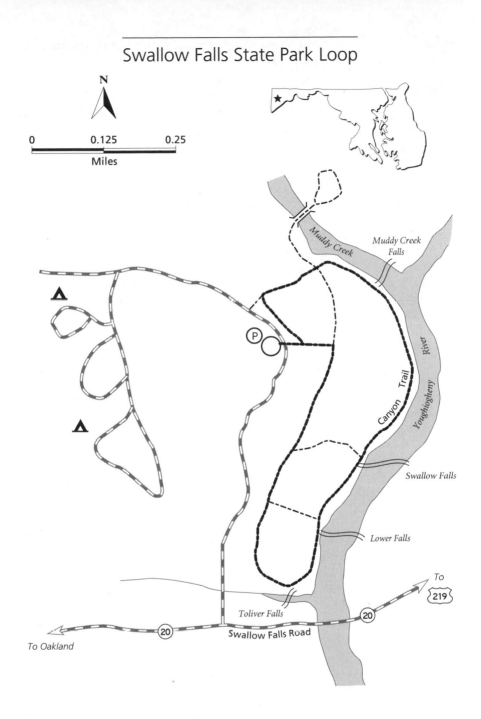

N

0   0.125   0.25
Miles

Muddy Creek

Muddy Creek Falls

Youghiogheny River

Canyon Trail

P

Swallow Falls

Lower Falls

Toliver Falls

To 219

20

To Oakland

20

Swallow Falls Road

Trailhead facilities: Restrooms, water fountain, soft drink vending machine, picnic pavilions and tables.

Key points:
- 0.0   Trailhead
- 0.4   Toliver Falls on Toliver Run
- 0.6   Swallow Falls; Swallow Rock and Lower Falls
- 0.7   Muddy Creek Falls
- 0.8   Bridge; junction with short loop trail
- 0.9   Historic marker

The hike: This is a delightful short hike that packs into a small package some of the outstanding features of hiking the Allegheny Front, including a stretch along one of the eastern United States's most notable whitewater rivers, the Youghiogheny. It is also a perfect hike for getting an outdoor fix when traveling with small children or with friends or family who take the outdoors in small doses. There are picnic tables and a pavilion, so a prehike picnic makes for a real kid pleaser.

The trailhead is just beyond the comfort station and kiosk at the north end of the parking area. Traveling southeast (right) from the kiosk, immediately find yourself in a stand of huge, ancient hemlocks and white pines. To protect these 300-year-old trees and their ecosystem, the 40-acre grove is designated a Sensitive Management Area, which means the grove is managed as a wilderness. Trees are allowed to fall or burn as nature wills; only trees blocking trail access are cleared.

At 0.4 mile, descend east to the first of four waterfalls on the hike, Toliver Falls on Toliver Run. Here the hemlock boughs slant nearly into the run, creating a dense shade over a low cascade, a nice spot to spend time splashing about in the ripples a hundred yards above Toliver Run's confluence with the north-flowing Youghiogheny or, as it is known to whitewater runners everywhere, the "Youck."

Scampering over wet boulders to the mossy Canyon Trail heading north along the Yough, you will be just out of earshot of Toliver Falls when Swallow Falls appears on your right—the second of four falls on the hike. The hemlock and pine are accompanied by mountain laurel and rhododendron, and the granite outcrops in and near the water call out for further exploration. As a point of Zero Impact Hiking ethics, follow the established passages to the river. So many enthusiastic hikers have trammeled new paths leading to the water that in places the bank is losing its protective trees. The trees keep the waters clean and cool enough for trout and other cold-water-loving fish.

Another 200 yards downriver is Swallow Rock and the Lower Falls, popular spots to capture this scenic hike on camera. Below the falls, boulders strewn into the river provide access for getting a great angle on the cascade from the middle of the river. At 0.7 mile, Muddy Creek drops into the Yough to create a rare type of river confluence. Muddy Creek flows southeast, anticipating a wash into a south-flowing river. But with the Yough flowing north, Muddy Creek seems to be headed in the wrong direction when it spills into the river. Instead of a smooth junction, the clash creates quite a stir of water and mist.

Just beyond the confluence is Muddy Creek Falls, at 63 feet the highest waterfall in Maryland. To the left, steps lead to the top of the falls, and you will want to take plenty of time to explore it from every angle. Prime photography opportunities here are during midday, when the sun is high.

From the top of the falls, follow Muddy Creek to a junction with a footpath leading over the creek and into the forest. For an additional ramble of less than half a mile through dense rhododendron, go right at the junction and over the footbridge. On the other side of the creek the trail makes a circuit.

From this junction, it is 0.2 mile back to the car, but on the way, be sure to stop at the overlook and historical marker commemorating a camping trip of four notable Americans: Henry Ford, Thomas Edison, John Burrows, and Harvey Firestone.

Maryland's tallest waterfall, Muddy Creek Falls, in winter.
PHOTO BY JAYSON KNOTT

Special considerations: In winter, the trail is designated for skiing; hikers without skis should avoid this hike when snow is on the ground. When there is not enough snow for skiing, this is a terrific winter hike.

Camping: The park has a developed campground; permits and information are available from the park office. For reservations, call Maryland's statewide reservations line for state parks and forests: 888-432-2267.

For more information: Swallow Falls State Park.

3 Deep Creek Vista

Highlights:	The trail climbs to the flattop ridge of Meadow Mountain for a stunning view of Deep Creek Lake. On the way down, stop at an abandoned mine site for an insight into mountain cultural history.
Location:	Deep Creek Lake State Park in Garrett County in western Maryland, 200 miles northwest of Washington, D.C.
Type of hike:	Out-and-back day hike.
Total distance:	2.9 miles.
Difficulty:	Moderate.
Elevation gain:	400 feet.
Best months:	April–May, October–November.
Permits:	$4-per-car entrance fee into park, Memorial Day through Labor Day.
Maps:	USGS McHenry, Maryland.

Finding the trailhead: From Frederick, Maryland, drive west on Interstate 70 to I-68 West in Hancock. Go 69 miles and then exit south on U.S. Highway 219 to Deep Creek Lake. After crossing the lake on US 219, pass through the Thayerville commercial area and turn left onto Glendale Road. After crossing the next bridge, take an immediate left onto State Park Road. Cross a small bridge and turn left at the T junction, following signs for the beach area. Inside the entrance station, turn right and proceed to lot 3. The trailhead is at the far end; the hike begins by crossing back over State Park Road.

Trailhead facilities: Water and privy inside park.

Key points:
- 0.0   Trailhead
- 0.4   Junction with end of Old Brant Mine Trail
- 0.9   Junction with beginning of Old Brant Mine Trail
- 1.5   Vista access trail junction
- 2.3   Junction with beginning of Old Brant Mine Trail (on return)
- 2.5   Meadow Mountain Trail junction

The hike: Most of the people who hike in the park never get to a good view of Deep Creek Lake; they content themselves with a terribly obstructed peep from the fire tower. Too bad. It is the view from the wooden platform specially constructed for the purpose that is the main objective of this hike.

From the parking area, cross State Park Road and ascend the 0.1-mile connecting path. Turn left onto the white-blazed Meadow Mountain Trail, an 11-mile trail that follows the ridgeline. Hiking west in a slow ascent, see striped maple saplings that dot the understory, easily identifiable by the dark green stripes on a smooth, olive green bark.

At 0.4 mile, pass the red-blazed Old Brant Mine Trail on the right, which will be used for the descent at the end of the hike. Then, switchback east for a steep

Deep Creek Vista

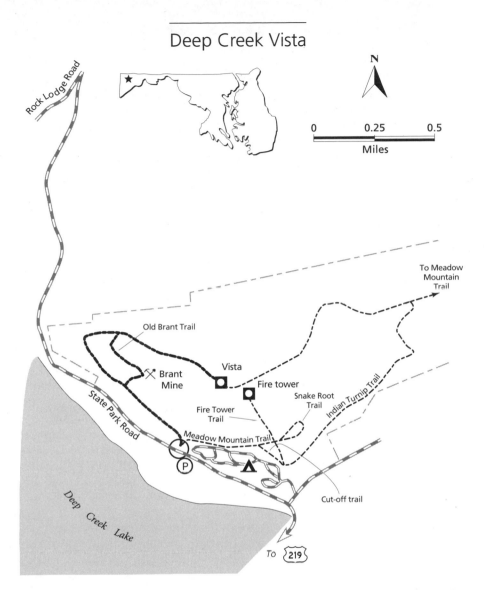

climb of 200 feet over a quarter of a mile. Just as the climb becomes a chore, the trail levels off at the top end of Old Brant Mine, at 0.9 mile. You could take Old Brant Mine Trail directly to this spot, but it is a much steeper climb.

Continue east along the ridge. Here it is apparent why this ridge is called Meadow Mountain. Its flat, wide top holds water like a rimmed plate. The ground is carpeted in ferns and mushrooms. Wildflowers typically found in bottomlands flourish in small pockets.

At 1.5 miles, turn right at the vista access trail; a sign marks the way. The vista is about 175 yards south of the main trail. From the platform, there is a dramatic view south over the lake and into the West Virginia Alleghenies. In summer, the sound of motorboats makes its way to the top of Meadow Mountain, so you might want to save this hike for late September. Then the leaves have already fallen from the ridgeline trees, but the lower reaches are ablaze in color.

Return to Meadow Mountain Trail by retracing your steps, and turn left back onto the white-blazed trail (at 1.7 miles, including the jaunt to the vista). At 2.3 miles, turn left onto the red-blazed Old Brant Mine Trail; the blazes may disappear for a hundred yards or so. At the mine site, take some time to examine the fine reconstructed camp there. The mine operated only for a few years in the 1920s, when Garrett County was practically still a frontier. Unfortunately for the mine's owners, both contracted illness caused by their work and were forced to abandon the mine.

Continue descending on the red-blazed trail to a junction with Meadow Mountain Trail at 2.5 miles. Turn left and follow the white blazes to the access trail; then turn right to return to the trailhead.

Options: For a loop of 3.9 miles, continue east on Meadow Mountain Trail after visiting the vista. In 0.9 mile, or 2.4 miles from the trailhead, turn right onto Indian Turnip Trail and descend. At Fire Tower Trail, 3.2 miles from the trailhead, turn right and then immediately left onto Meadow Mountain Cutoff Trail, which ascends 150 yards to Meadow Mountain Trail. The starting trailhead is 0.5 mile farther west.

Special considerations: For those seeking quiet enjoyment of the natural setting, this hike should be avoided from Memorial Day to Labor Day. The continuous sounds of outboard motors on the lake may be a distraction.

Camping: Developed campsites are available in the park; registration and a fee are required.

For more information: Deep Creek Lake Recreation Area.

4 Poplar Lick Run, New Germany State Park

Highlights:	Following wide, color-coded cross-country ski trails, this is a pleasant walk along Poplar Lick Run, a babbling stream offering many opportunities to stop and enjoy the woods. There is an interlude to a cool pine grove. Because the hike covers mostly wooded areas, there are few opportunities for long views of the landscape.
Location:	New Germany State Park in Garrett County, about 180 miles west of Washington, D.C.
Type of hike:	Loop; day hike.
Total distance:	5 miles.
Difficulty:	Moderate.
Elevation gain:	Minimal.
Best months:	April–November.
Maps:	USGS Bittinger, Barton, Frostburg, Grantsville.
Permits:	$2-per-person entrance fee on weekends, June–August.

Finding the trailhead: From Frederick, Maryland, drive west on Interstate 70 to Hancock. Then go 65 miles west on I-68 to Grantsville, Maryland, and take exit 19 north onto Bittinger Road. In half a mile, turn right (east) on Alternate U.S. Highway 40. In 3 miles, turn south (right) onto Chestnut Ridge Road, which will end in 2 miles at New Germany Road. Turn left. In 2 miles, proceed past the Savage River Complex headquarters on the right. Just beyond, turn left into New Germany State Park. Proceed to lot 5; the trailhead is at the far end of the lot behind the information board. (Note: Directions are from the Grantsville exit to provide an opportunity to obtain provisions; you can also exit directly from I-68 onto Chestnut Ridge Road at exit 22.)

Trailhead facilities: Water is available from a spigot used by campers, located just past the turnoff to lot 5. There are restrooms at the park meeting facility, which is walking distance from the trailhead.

Key points:
- 0.0   Trailhead
- 0.6   Fork in Yellow Trail
- 0.9   Bridge to Three Bridges Trail
- 2.6   Pine grove loop
- 3.6   Stream

The hike: Hemlocks, mountain laurel, azaleas, and the sound of tumbling water await you on this woodland hike. From the information board, follow the green blazes on the park road for 150 yards; then turn right (west), following the yellow blazes. Cross the bridge and stay left with the blazes.

Poplar Lick Run, New Germany State Park

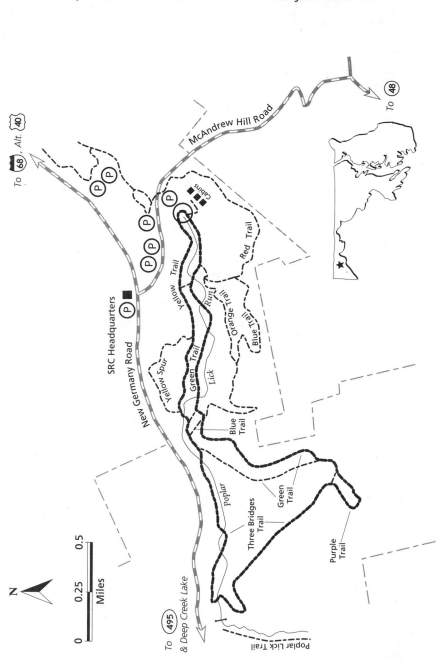

Rhododendrons and ferns form the understory beneath the hemlocks shading the stream on your left.

Pass through an old picnic area and water treatment facility, and then duck into woods and climb a small knob with Poplar Lick Run on your left. Continue past the yellow spur that breaks west at 0.6 mile and move along a wooded ledge; a wooded knoll rises to the right, and the landscape drops left toward the stream.

At 0.9 mile, enter a garden area planted with native species. A bench and small waterfall make for an inviting rest stop. Cross the bridge and turn right onto the green-blazed Three Bridges Trail. In 150 yards, stay right, now following the blue blazes. Over the next 0.8 mile, the trail weaves near and over the stream and into and out of small patches of sunlight. A small waterfall near the third bridge (not counting the one in the garden area) drops into a small pool teeming with small fish that will hypnotize young hikers.

Reaching the gate at Poplar Lick Trail, at 1.7 miles, turn left and cross the creek. Poplar Lick Trail descends toward the Savage River. Although the trail is open to motorized trail use, there are several quiet places to camp near the stream. Ascend on Three Bridges Trail, a wide ski trail that is steep in places. Climb almost 400 feet over the next half a mile, pausing for rests to look behind you to Meadow Mountain. These are the only open views on the hike. Reaching a stand of hemlock and cedar on your left, at 2.6 miles, watch for the purple blazes leading right just as the trail reaches the top of the hill.

The pine grove is a short detour into a dark, swampy world. It offers a striking difference from the lush vegetation only half a mile back. There is almost no ground cover or understory, only straight, fragrant conifers living in a soupy soil created by the small bowl at the top of this knoll.

Emerging from the pine grove, go straight at the junction to rejoin the blue trail. This is a tricky spot. The trail to the left is the blue trail you ascended on; the gated trail to the right descends into the forest. You will actually see the gated trail first, so the junction with the blue trail will feel like a left turn. Stay straight on the blue trail. Just below, at 3.1 miles, reach the top of the green trail loop. Go right, but either spur will lead to Poplar Lick. (If you want to spend a little more time following the stream, despite having to retrace your steps for a few hundreds yards covered earlier in the hike, go left at the fork.)

Taking the right fork, descend to a junction with the blue trail, just above the stream. Take the soft left (the hard left leads back to Three Bridges Trail) and reach the stream, at 3.6 miles, just northeast of the garden area that you passed at 0.9 mile. Follow the green trail as it crosses Poplar Lick Run four times over the next mile on its route back to the trailhead. Watch for wildlife, especially deer, near the stream in the late afternoon hours.

Options: The color-coded trails offer many options for shorter and longer hikes through the woods, including backpacking down Poplar Lick Trail. For a 2-mile stroll along Poplar Lick Run, turn left onto the green trail after crossing the bridge at 0.9 mile.

Special considerations: Pets are not allowed on the New Germany trails. Trails are designated for cross-country skiing when snow is present.

Camping: Within the park, cabins are available; advance registration and a fee are required. In the forest surrounding the park, there are developed sites and backpacking opportunities. Registration is required for both; there is a fee for the developed sites. For reservations, call Maryland's statewide reservations line for state parks and forests: 888-432-2267.

For more information: New Germany State Park.

---

5 Monroe Run Trail

Highlights:	A creek-side hike into a very remote, wild stream valley covered in a canopy of hardwoods and hemlocks. There are 22 stream crossings, some on bridges, many by rock hopping. On an autumn weekday in late afternoon, you are as likely to see a black bear as another person.
Location:	Monroe Run Trail is located in Savage River State Forest in Garrett County, Maryland, about 185 miles west of Washington, D.C. The trail begins in the state forest and ends in Big Run State Park.
Type of hike:	Shuttle; day hike or overnighter.
Total distance:	5.2 miles.
Difficulty:	Moderate due to stream crossings.
Elevation gain:	1,100-foot descent.
Best months:	April–November, winter on snowshoes.
Permits:	None.
Maps:	USGS Bittinger, Maryland.

Finding the trailhead: From Frederick, Maryland, drive west on Interstate 70 to Hancock. Then go 65 miles west on I-68 to Grantsville, Maryland, and take exit 19 north onto Bittinger Road. In half a mile, turn right (east) onto Alternate U.S. Highway 40. In 3 miles, turn south (right) onto Chestnut Ridge Road, which will end in 2 miles at New Germany Road. Turn left. In 5 miles, reach the Monroe Run overlook and trailhead on the left. (Note: Directions are from the Grantsville exit to provide an opportunity to obtain provisions; you can also exit directly from I-68 onto Chestnut Ridge Road at exit 22.)

Trailhead facilities: None.

Key points:
- 0.0 Trailhead
- 1.1 First crossing of Monroe Run
- 2.0 Hemlock grove

Monroe Run Trail

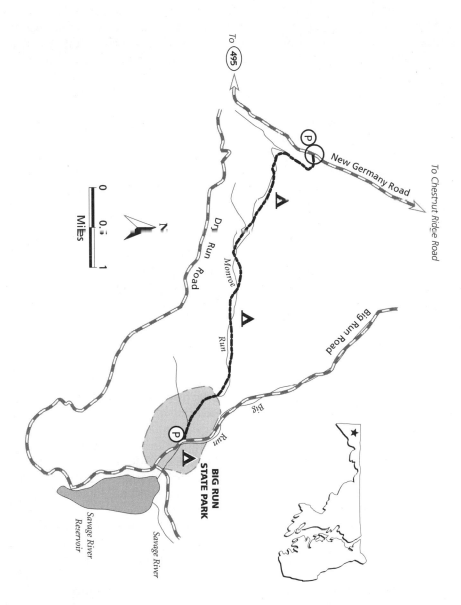

The hike: With the casual terrain of the trail, this hike can be covered in a couple of hours of walking. To truly enjoy it, however, plan on at least twice that long. This is one of the wildest stream canyons in Maryland, and because it offers no loop options without a road walk, one of the quietest. Because the trail descends into the canyon, there is no intrusion of noise from outside activity.

This hike is especially suited for an overnight hike, either by creating a loop (see "Options" below) or by hiking in to a favorite spot along the stream and then out the same way. Before hiking, take a few minutes to gaze at the canyon from the overlook.

Begin by descending on a wide path, remnants of an old road built by the Civilian Conservation Corps in the 1930s as a connector between camps atop and below Meadow Mountain. The wooden guardrails on the downhill side at sharp turns were placed by the CCC crews. There are a few openings in the canopy near the top, with views west up the mountain and south toward Savage River Reservoir.

The terrain eases as the trail approaches Monroe Run; then at 1.1 miles, come to the first of more than 20 crossings (the precise number depends on the weather). Near the stream here are several good campsites, back under tall oaks and tulip poplars. The understory leading from the trail is dense with rhododendron, at times so thick that even on sunny days it is nearly nighttime on the ground.

At 2 miles, reach a large hemlock grove. The temperature here seems to drop by several degrees. In fact, it is the cooling effect of hemlock groves that stave off evaporation on headwater streams like Monroe Run. Scientists are battling a blight that threatens to destroy the hemlocks of the southern Appalachians, a potentially calamitous event that would alter the entire ecosystem of these mountains.

Several stream crossings further on, beginning at about 2.6 miles, is a series of secluded campsites. If you plan to camp along Monroe Run, use one of the sites that have already been tended. There are enough sites along the run to provide solitude, but any more such sites would threaten the wild experience of the canyon. If forced to camp in a new site, be sure to exercise Zero Impact camping by eliminating any sign of your presence before leaving.

The canyon narrows to barely wider than Monroe Run at 3.2 miles and stays that way for about half a mile. Then, in a wider flatland, the run divides into two, and at times three, streams, creating small isolated islands. In rainy periods, these areas form a washed-out delta of alternately fast-moving and stalled water. Take great care if crossing in these conditions.

The final crossing comes at 3.9 miles, where the run reaches wide bottomland. As you approach the bottom, you are more likely to encounter hikers venturing uphill from the developed campsites near Big Run Road. Still, except on weekends in summer, a lonesome, remote feeling dominates the trail.

Monroe Run canyon is prime black bear habitat.

At 4.6 miles, reach Big Run Road, which closely parallels the trail to the trailhead. Car camping at the developed sites through this area affords a quiet spot for launching day hikes to the surrounding mountains.

Options: You can make a loop hike by turning left onto Big Run Road at the bottom of the trail and then turning left onto New Germany Road, for a round trip of 8 miles. Although this is a road walk, it is very scenic and sees little automobile traffic.

Special considerations: This trail has many stream crossings that are subject to flooding, and there are no constructed bridges (there are a few simple log bridges). Most of the time, all of the crossings can be managed with the only consequence being an occasional wet boot. In high water, especially in spring, a few of the crossings may require wading in shallow water. Fast-moving water, even knee deep, should be crossed only by or with the assistance of experienced hikers.

Camping: Camping is permitted; a permit is required for primitive camping, and a fee is required for developed sites at the bottom of the trail. For reservations, call Maryland's statewide reservations line for state parks and forests: 888-432-2267.

For more information: Savage River Complex.

6 Lostland Run Loop, Potomac State Forest

Highlights:	A hike through a hemlock–laurel canyon, following Lostland Run en route to the Potomac. There are stream crossings on footbridges, a waterfall, and many opportunities to view wildlife.
Location:	Potomac State Forest is in Garrett County in western Maryland.
Type of hike:	Loop; day hike.
Total distance:	7.4 miles.
Difficulty:	Moderate.
Elevation gain:	Lose 650 feet and then gain 650 feet on road walk.
Best months:	April–November.
Permits:	None.
Maps:	USGS Gorman, Maryland–West Virginia; Deer Park, Maryland; Mt. Storm, West Virginia.

Finding the trailhead: From Frederick, Maryland, drive west on Interstate 70 to I-68 West in Hancock. Go 69 miles on I-68, exit south on U.S. Highway 219 toward Deep Creek Lake, and go 26 miles to Oakland, Maryland. Stay on US 219 when it turns left in Oakland; when US 219 turns right outside of town, go straight onto Maryland Highway 135. In about 2 miles, turn right onto MD 560 just outside of Mountain Lake Park. In 2 miles, turn left onto Bethlehem Road (staying right at the fork at 2 miles). In 1.4 miles, turn left onto Combination Road, then in half a mile, turn left onto Potomac Camp Road. The forest headquarters is about a mile further on the left. To find the trailhead from the parking area, cross the road and walk 75 feet back up the road; look for a wooden marker.

Trailhead facilities: There is a water spigot behind the headquarters office.

Key points:
- 0.0   Trailhead
- 0.9   South Prong bridge crossing
- 1.3   Steep steps; log bridge
- 1.5   South Prong bridge crossing
- 2.1   North Prong bridge crossing
- 3.0   Cascade Falls
- 4.0   Potomac River parking area

The hike: You can lose your cares amid the hemlock and laurel along the swift Lostland Run and forget the time gazing at Cascade Falls deep in the gorge. The trail crosses the run several times, and there are several scenic falls.

There are a few areas of rough and rocky terrain, and a couple of places where the trail seems to disappear, but with little effort you will steer the course toward the cliffs of the Potomac River at the bottom of the run. The river is reached at 4 miles, after a hike that is largely downhill. The return to

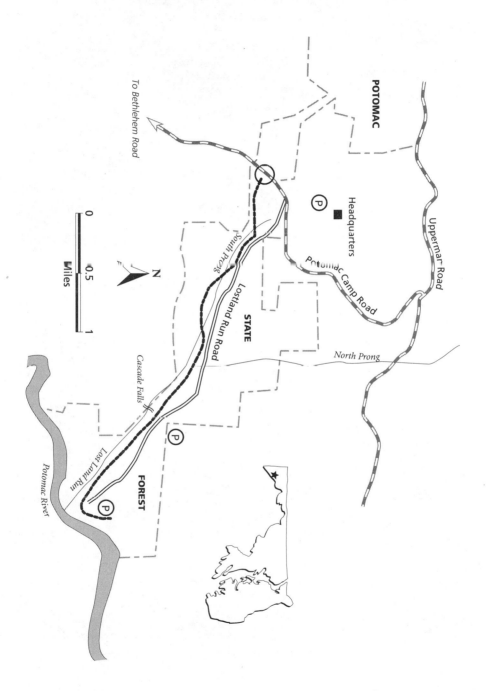

Lostland Run rushes toward the Potomac River. PHOTO BY JAYSON KNOTT

the trailhead is via the gravel Lostland Run Road, which serves the camping area. It is mostly uphill from the river, but the grade is not overly challenging and is plenty wide enough to walk side by side with a companion.

From the trailhead, the path and white blazes are easy to follow, tracing the drainage of a seasonal run on the north side of South Prong Lostland Run (you will follow the South Prong until its confluence with the North Prong at 2.1 miles). At 0.6 mile, the trail passes close to the creek and the road. The intermittent clanging of steel you will hear is a lime dozer; these are installed on several streams in western Maryland to restore the pH balance after the destruction left by mining operations. Just beyond is a rocky section, followed by the footbridge to the south side at 0.9 mile.

Turning right after the bridge, follow a footpath above the run, with hemlocks and red pine overhead and rhododendron below the ledge. A steep stairway of carved logs drops to the run at 1.3 miles, where the trail crosses back to the north side on a log bridge forged from a tree that happened to fall in the perfect place.

At 1.5 miles, cross the South Prong Lostland Run on a nifty swinging bridge constructed by the Maryland Conservation Corps, a youth program responsible for many good works in Maryland forests. Ascend to the ledge above the run, which now enters a steep gorge. Watch for blazes here because the trail is not always obvious and it is easy to get distracted by beautiful foliage in the cool, dark gorge.

At 2.1 miles, the trail breaks left away from the run and crosses North Prong Lostland Run just before the confluence of the two prongs. If you miss the break, the path will end at the confluence. From there, you will see the bridge 100 feet to the left.

Follow a wide cart path that keeps to the high road as the run drops to the right. A quarter of a mile later, watch for a switchback descending right—a false trail continues straight ahead. The next 0.5 mile is a delightful stroll down in the gorge, up close to the fast-flowing water. This is prime habitat for black bears and nocturnal hunters such as bobcat and owls.

Hugging a narrow ledge at stream level, the trail passes under a dense canopy, dark even at midday. Cross several small knobs and then reach Cascade Falls at 3 miles. A viewing platform provides an excellent prospect. If you are lucky enough to have the falls all to yourself, you will want to linger here. Then, climb wooded stairs following blue blazes that lead to a trailhead serving the falls. At the top of the bluff, follow the white blazes right; the blue blazes continue straight to Lostland Run Road.

The final mile below the falls is the most remote and solitary. The path alternates from ledge walking on the bluffs above to close, intimate contact with the stream. Just before the trail emerges at the Potomac River parking area at 4 miles, a footbridge leads across the run.

Before heading up Lostland Run Road for the return walk, follow the path at the end of the parking area to the cliffs above the Potomac and take in the splendid views.

Options: With a second car stashed at the bottom, you can shorten the hike to 4 miles, eliminating a 3.4-mile walk along the gravel camping road.

Special considerations: In the first mile of the hike, there are two sections of rough and rocky terrain. They are passable by hikers of most abilities, but they make for slow going for a time.

Camping: The gravel Lostland Run Road serves primitive car campsites, which may be reserved for a fee through forest headquarters. Despite the fact that some of the campsites are literally adjacent to the road, the place has a remote quality. For reservations, call Maryland's statewide reservations line for state parks and forests: 888-432-2267.

For more information: Potomac State Forest.

7 Rocky Gap Canyon to Evitts Summit

Highlights:	A challenging walk through the dark and lush Rocky Gap Canyon followed by an ascent over an old woods road to a monument marking the Mason–Dixon Line high atop Evitts Mountain, where there are expansive views. Along the way, visit the historic homestead of the first white settler in the rugged Allegheny Mountains.
Location:	Rocky Gap State Park in Allegany County, Maryland, is 12 miles east of Cumberland, Maryland.
Type of hike:	Out-and-back day hike.
Total distance:	5.2 miles.
Difficulty:	Moderate.
Elevation gain:	1,200 feet.
Best months:	Year-round.
Permits:	None.
Maps:	USGS: Evitts Creek, Maryland–Pennsylvania–West Virginia.

Finding the trailhead: From the junction of Interstates 70 and 68 in Hancock, Maryland, drive 30 miles west on I-68 to exit 50, Rocky Gap State Park. Go straight at the junction with the park road, following directions to the lodge. Bear left at the lodge and continue past it 1 mile to the trailhead parking on the left.

Trailhead facilities: Water, restrooms at park headquarters at park entrance, other refreshments at lodge.

Key points:
- 0.0 Trailhead
- 0.2 Canyon Overlook Trail junction
- 0.3 Left at fork
- 0.5 Rocky Gap Run footbridge

Rocky Gap Canyon to Evitts Summit

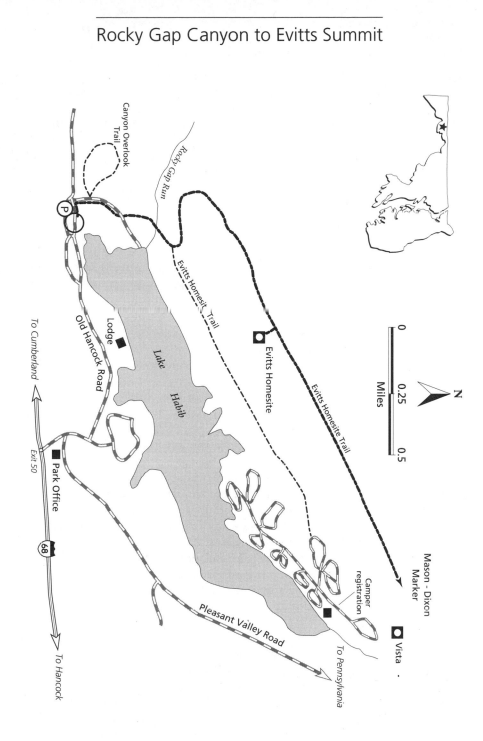

The hike: This hike begins with a visit to an enchanting hemlock canyon and climbs to the summit of Evitts Mountain, where there are endless views of the Allegheny Mountains and a Mason-Dixon line marker that is placed, as most were, in the middle of nowhere. From Rocky Gap Run in the canyon, you will climb 1,200 feet over 2 miles, but the majority of the ascent is over a wide dirt road that provides a stable surface and plenty of rest spots. The 0.5-mile walk through the canyon is rocky and steep at times, but hikers comfortable sliding down a couple of boulders on their backsides will fare just fine.

From the nature trail parking area, walk through the gate on the paved road; do not follow the gate onto the gravel road at the left. One hundred yards beyond a trailhead for Canyon Overlook Trail, at 0.2 mile, follow a footpath left into the woods at a sign marking the Evitts Homesite Trail. Immediately, you will forget you are in a resort area only 400 yards from the lodge. Rhododendron and azalea abound under a dense canopy.

Follow the white blazes left at the fork at 0.3 mile; the trail straight ahead leads to the dam. Descend for 75 feet over boulders and outcrops, only a couple of which require hand maneuvers. In the canyon, the trail follows a ledge on a narrow footpath surrounded by hemlock, table mountain pine, and giant oaks and pignut hickory.

Just as the trail begins a final dip into the canyon, a side trail leads 50 feet straight ahead to a view of Rocky Gap Run below. Towering above are scarlet oaks, marked by their smooth vertical stripes on the bark. Below, a thicket of rhododendron leans over the creek. To the left, the canyon walls reveal the layered shale of the Alleghenies.

Descend into the canyon and, at 0.5 mile, cross Rocky Gap Run on a footbridge. Then begin a steep ascent that pauses enough to catch a breath. Emerge onto an old farm road at 0.9 mile, which is Evitts Homesite Trail. Follow the trail left and ascend. The pleasant walk under many white oak, Maryland's state tree, is marred only by the sounds of trucks a mile away on the highway rising on the wind, but, as the trail slabs around the hill, you will leave the noise behind. The climb to the top from here is steady but offers plenty of pauses in its bends, where the road is level for a short stretch.

A short trail at 2 miles leads 75 yards right to the Evitts Homesite. A man whose first name seems forgotten by all, Mr. "Everts" (the spelling varies among local sources) escaped to these rugged mountains in 1801 to live out his life as a hermit. Some accounts cite bad business deals; others, failure at love. Only a stone well and a few stone fences remain.

Back on the trail, climb steadily on the woods road another 0.6 mile to an aviation signal tower. The Mason-Dixon marker is a dozen steps farther on the left; the views another dozen farther into Pennsylvania. The wonderful view of the rugged Allegheny Mountains reveals why, to this day, the area remains rather remote, except for the city of Cumberland a short distance west.

Return to the trailhead by retracing your steps. At the bottom, just before you reach the trailhead, a side trip onto the 0.25-mile Canyon Overlook Trail is recommended.

Options: After visiting the canyon and reaching Evitts Homesite Trail, you can turn right for a mile-long stroll along Lake Habib.

Special considerations: The wide dirt road of Evitts Homesite Trail makes an especially fine trail for snowshoe hiking.

Camping: A developed campground is available in the park. For reservations, call Maryland's statewide reservations line for state parks and forests: 888-432-2267.

For more information: Rocky Gap State Park.

8 Green Ridge Hiking Trail North Spur Loop

> **Highlights:** A pleasant walk on trails and dirt roads through ridgetop forests and bottomland meadows.
> **Location:** Green Ridge State Forest is in Allegany County, Maryland, just off Interstate 68, about 140 miles northwest of Washington, D.C.
> **Type of hike:** Loop; day hike.
> **Total distance:** 4.8 miles.
> **Difficulty:** Moderate.
> **Elevation gain:** Minimal.
> **Best months:** April–November.
> **Permits:** None.
> **Maps:** USGS Artemas, Maryland.

Finding the trailhead: From the junction of Interstates 68 and 70 in western Maryland, go west on I-68. Take exit 62 to Fifteenmile Creek Road/Maryland Highway 40 and travel northeast. At 0.5 mile, follow Fifteenmile Creek Road as it splits to the left, becoming a dirt road (paved MD 40 continues east). Proceed on Fifteenmile Creek Road 0.8 mile. You will see a trail marker on the right. Cross a narrow stream on a culvert to the trailhead parking on the left.

Trailhead facilities: None.

Key points:
- 0.0   Trailhead
- 1.2   Green Ridge
- 2.0   Camp and picnic site
- 2.4   Old Cumberland Road
- 2.5   Double Pine Road
- 4.6   Fifteenmile Creek Road

Green Ridge Hiking Trail North Spur Loop

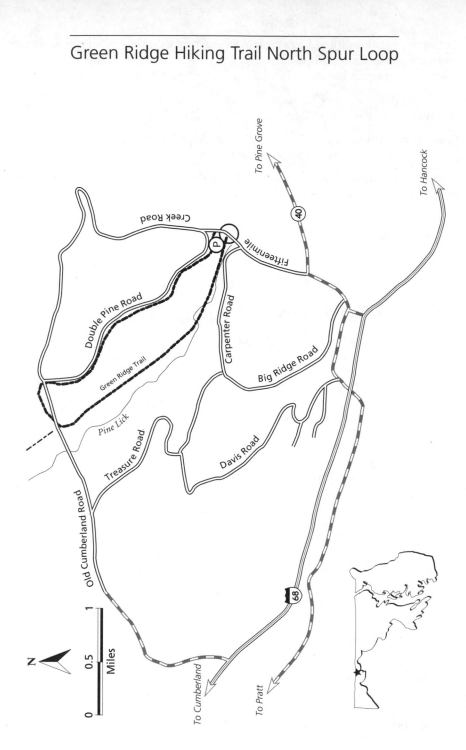

The hike: Located in the ridge and valley region of the Allegheny Mountains, Green Ridge Hiking Trail North Spur Loop gives you a taste of both. The trail begins in the bottomland woods and meadows along Pine Lick, a shallow meandering stream, and continues up into mature oak–hickory stands along a narrow ridge. In the hollow you will find sun-dappled creek banks, spring wildflowers, and vernal ponds. On the ridgeline, although the uniformly deep forest allows no spectacular views, its groves provide a wonderfully shady, refreshing place to walk. Though there are some harvested areas of forest along the dirt road section of the hike (about two-thirds of the way through), most of the woodlands are mature and healthy, and the walk is not greatly diminished by the clearings.

The trail begins on the west side of Fifteenmile Creek Road on the bank of Pine Lick, just a few paces south of the trailhead parking area. The path, a section of the 24-mile Green Ridge Hiking Trail, is well marked with white blazes. For the first 1.2 miles, the footpath meanders through Pine Lick Hollow, crossing the narrow stream several times. None of the crossings are difficult—there are well-placed rocks in the stream—but in the spring or after heavy rains you may be in for a wet crossing. Even in the muddy season, walking the creek banks among the hollow's hardwoods and mayapple meadows is quite pleasant.

At 1.2 miles the trail climbs steeply up Green Ridge, clearing the ridgeline at 1.3 miles. Under the shade of big oaks, the path continues through the woods to a clearing at 1.8 miles. Grassy openings in the forest canopy like this one do not naturally occur in the woodlands of the eastern states, but the state forest maintains them to provide much needed food for wild turkeys, grouse, deer, and squirrels. The trail bends around the clearing and, at the far edge, reenters the woods. Be careful here. Look for the white blaze and continue straight on the narrow hiking trail where a wider, grassy path breaks to the right.

After the clearing, the trail descends a bit into hardwood stands that remain dense and shady but are here mixed with white, Virginia, and shortleaf pines. At 2 miles pass a camp and picnic site on the right and soon begin a descent to Old Cumberland Road, at 2.4 miles. On the way, get a glimpse of a neighboring ridge on the left and pass through a stand of white pines in an area cleared of oaks to make room for the regeneration of the once plentiful native conifer.

Turn right onto Old Cumberland Road at 2.4 miles. This was the first road constructed west from Hancock to Cumberland. Proceed 0.1 mile and turn right onto Double Pine Road at 2.5 miles. Double Pine Road is a dirt access road that cuts through the forest 2.1 miles back to Fifteenmile Creek Road. Except for the narrow harvested areas—beginning on the right at 2.9 miles and continuing intermittently to 3.4 miles—the road passes through beautiful, mature stands of oak and hickory, winding along like a wide trail or an unpaved country road. At 4.5 miles, the road bends to the left, descending through a stretch wonderfully lush with dogwood blossoms in the spring, and meets Fifteenmile Creek Road at 4.6 miles. Turn right and continue 0.2 mile back to the trailhead.

Options: Green Ridge Hiking Trail runs 24 miles through the state park, from the Chesapeake & Ohio Canal at lock 67 to the Pennsylvania line. Crossing roads several times, the trail is accessible for many short hikes and longer circuit hikes.

Special considerations: During the spring, be prepared for muddy conditions along Pine Lick. The area is managed for hunting; check with rangers for season dates.

Camping: Yes; a permit and a fee are required.

For more information: Green Ridge State Forest.

---

9 Fifteenmile Creek, Green Ridge State Forest

Highlights:	One of Maryland's best hikes for getting away from it all, this is a circuit hike in and above the remote canyon of Fifteenmile Creek.
Location:	This trail is in Green Ridge State Forest in Allegany County, Maryland, 140 miles northwest of Washington, D.C.
Type of hike:	Loop; day hike.
Total distance:	5.4 miles.
Difficulty:	Moderate.
Elevation gain:	380 feet.
Best months:	April–November; wildflowers abundant in May and June.
Permits:	None.
Maps:	USGS Artemas, Maryland–Pennsylvania–West Virginia.

Finding the trailhead: From the junction of Interstates 70 and 270 near Frederick, Maryland, drive west 29 miles to I-68 in Hancock, Maryland. Take I-68 26 miles west to exit 64, Flintstone. Go south (right) at the end of the exit ramp. Cross over I-68 and then, in 0.3 mile, turn right into the state forest headquarters. The trailhead, marked with a white diamond, is beside the restrooms.

Trailhead facilities: Water, restrooms at comfort station; visitor center has displays.

Key points:
- 0.0   Trailhead
- 1.1   Green Ridge Hiking Trail junction
- 1.3   Ford of Fifteenmile Creek
- 1.9   Deep Run, Wellesley Hollow Trail junction

Fifteenmile Creek, Green Ridge State Forest

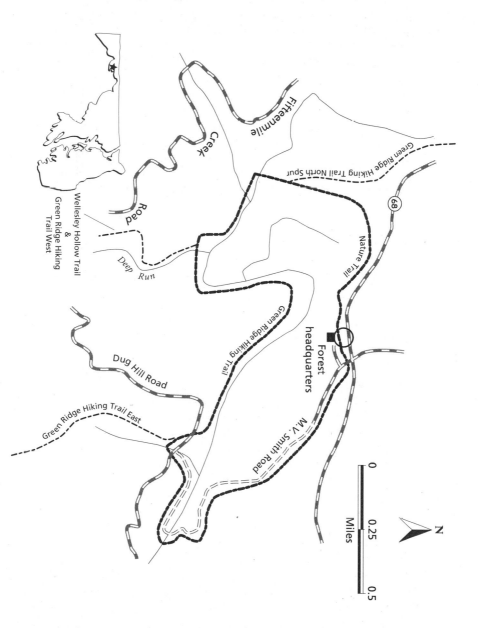

3.6   Dug Hill Road
3.8   M. V. Smith Road
4.2   Creek crossing

The hike: Fifteenmile Creek slices a 200-foot gorge between Green Ridge and Town Hill on its way to the Potomac River. The 38,000-acre Green Ridge State Forest provides a sense of the wild backcountry, only two-and-a-half hours from Washington, D.C. Considering the hike begins only a few hundred yards from the interstate and then spends the first 0.3 mile in close proximity to it, this ramble offers surprising solitude. It also presents a nice opportunity to combine hiking with fly fishing in one of several shaded holes down in the gorge. The hike travels south on Green Ridge Hiking Trail, spending about 3 miles within sight and sound of tumbling water.

Starting at the state forest visitor center, the first 0.5 mile is an unremarkable scamper through conifer and maple as the trail makes its escape from the intrusion of I-68, sitting practically astride the trail. Completed in the 1980s to provide a high-speed route west over the rugged Allegheny Front, the highway has succeeded in bisecting key forests and hiking lands. After the trail breaks south away from the road at 0.5 mile, it ascends into eastern cedar and pine along an old forest road. Soon the highway is easily forgotten.

Following the ridgeline at about 1,000 feet, the trail enters a stand of towering chestnut oaks and scattered eastern hemlock, signaling a more mature forest of more hardwoods and fewer pines that the trail will follow along the creek. Just beyond a remnant pine grove, the trail passes the ruins of an old cabin, unremarkable except for the tin shard implanted deep into the trunk of an ash tree and high above the ruins, another sign of the hardwoods reclaiming a forest stripped clean a century ago for charcoal and tanning bark.

The pathway ends at a T intersection with Green Ridge Hiking Trail North Spur at 1.1 miles, the high point on the hike at 1,060 feet. To the north (right), it is 6.3 miles to the Pennsylvania border and the southern terminus of the Mid State Trail, a 187-mile path through the heart of the Keystone State. To the south, it is 13.7 miles to the Potomac. Looking in that direction, in the leafless months you can catch a revealing view of the regional topography with the view to the left of Town Hill.

The descent to Fifteenmile Creek, at 690 feet, is steep but not overly challenging. It is made more enjoyable by the rock formations lining the trail, reminders of the volcanic activity that built the mountains. On a typical summer's day, fording the creek, at 1.3 miles, is an easy task of rock hopping or splashing across the stream. In spring or after heavy periods of rain, the narrow crossing might be a few feet deep and moving swiftly enough to warrant all the standard precautions. The steel lines that are still in place since the 1996 flood that destroyed the bridge provide a cable bridge for the surefooted. If fording, be sure to unbuckle your pack so that if you are thrown into the water you will not be facedown with a pack on your back.

Following the crossing, the trail cuts sharply left and then travels 0.5 mile of up and down, but none of the climbs are challenging for more than 50 yards. The sound of falling water and songbirds, coupled with sightings of deer and wild turkey, will be remembered long after the climbs. In its 3 miles along the river—at times down in the gorge astride the river and at times a hundred feet above—the trail passes one of the more wild, remote landscapes you can find in Maryland.

If you have brought rod and reel along, Deep Run, at 1.9 miles, is the place to find a spot where the water runs fast and cool. This is the end of the Green Ridge Hiking Trail North Spur as well as the junction with the main Green Ridge Hiking Trail. To the south (right), Wellesley Hollow Trail and Green Ridge Hiking Trail climb a saddle of Town Hill up the headwaters of Deep Run and then descend along Big Run to the Chesapeake & Ohio Canal. Straight ahead, Green Ridge Hiking Trail heads east.

Crossing Deep Run, Green Ridge Hiking Trail stays left of the hill for about a hundred yards and then veers subtly right up the ridge on an old woods road. Follow the markings carefully through the next 0.5 mile because a couple of false trails and old roads veer from the trail. With the sandstone cliffs and the hemlock stands capturing your attention, it would be easy to stray down a dead-end. After crossing an unnamed run, the trail enters a long, lazy curve where the bottomlands offer prime campsites and swimming holes. Even during the summer months, it is possible to move downstream and find an out-of-the-way spot for a quiet lunch and a dip. The best swimming hole, but one you will not enjoy alone, is at about 3 miles, just before the middle of the creek bend. It sits beneath sandstone towering a hundred feet from the gorge.

From here the trail climbs amid oak and hemlock, offering occasional views of the gorge and back to Green Ridge, until passing under a sparkling

Endless ridges of Allegany County, Maryland. PHOTO COURTESY OF MARYLAND DNR

cool cascade at 3.4 miles. The waterfall seems to emerge from the side of the rock face, a fine place to shower off the early miles of the hike if you can stand the chill. The climb from here takes the trail away from Fifteenmile Creek and then through oak and hickory stands, where there are remnant chestnut trees—they will grow to a dozen feet or more before succumbing to the chestnut blight that decimated this once all-American species early in the twentieth century.

The trail emerges onto the dirt-and-gravel Dug Hill Road at 3.6 miles and goes left. There is no sign here. Follow the road 350 yards and turn left onto M. V. Smith Road at 3.8 miles, which is marked by a gate. Green Ridge Hiking Trail continues on Dug Hill Road. The road is public, but the property along it is private, so hikers should stick to the road as it passes old hunting camps en route to a creek crossing at 4.2 miles. Exercise judgment here and know your own skills. When the water is a foot or more deep, it can be surprisingly swift. If it looks too challenging for your level of experience, your best choice is to retrace your steps and enjoy a return along the creek.

From the other side of the creek, you are 1.2 miles from the visitor center via M. V. Smith Road.

Special considerations: The forest is open to hunting from November through February; check with the state forest headquarters for details.

The trail is well maintained for foot travel and is passable by hikers of most abilities, with three minor exceptions on the circuit hike: The cable bridge at Fifteenmile Creek has been damaged by a storm; in high water you will have to either look upstream for a safe crossing or, as many hikers do, gingerly make your way across the damaged bridge using cables for handholds. Also, in two places the trail follows a narrow ledge that makes for careful going with young children or novice hikers. Finally, there is no bridge crossing Fifteenmile Creek at 4.2 miles, where "high water" usually means about 24 inches at a moderate flow. Consider bringing an old pair of sneakers for this crossing.

If there has been heavy rain in the days before your hike, drive down to the creek crossing before setting out on your hike. That way, you will know long before reaching the final crossing whether your return to the visitor center will be an uneventful uphill road walk or a return by the way you came.

Camping: Primitive sites are available along the river; contact the visitor center for information on developed campsites in the forest. For reservations, call Maryland's statewide reservations line for state parks and forests: 888-432-2267.

For more information: Green Ridge State Forest.

10 C&O Canal Towpath—Paw Paw Tunnel

Highlights:	A walk along the Chesapeake & Ohio Canal towpath through a tunnel more than half a mile long, followed by a scenic walk near a remote stretch of the Potomac. The return hike is over a shoulder of the mountain on the Potomac side, offering stunning views of the West Virginia mountain landscape.
Location:	Paw Paw Tunnel on the C&O Canal is about 100 miles northwest of Washington, D.C., and 15 miles southeast of Cumberland, Maryland, just across the Potomac River from Paw Paw, West Virginia.
Type of hike:	Loop; day hike.
Total distance:	3.1 miles.
Difficulty:	Moderate.
Elevation gain:	360 feet.
Best months:	April and May for flowering trees and wildflowers.
Permits:	None.
Maps:	USGS Paw Paw, West Virginia; map and guide available from C&O National Historical Park (see appendix A).

Finding the trailhead: From the Capital Beltway, go north on Interstate 270 to I-70 West. At Hancock, Maryland, take I-68 west to Cumberland, exiting onto Maryland Highway 51 south. Follow MD 51 about 25 miles to the tunnel trailhead on the left. The trailhead is at the far end of the parking area.

Trailhead facilities: Portable privy and water pump at trailhead.

Key points:
- 0.0   Trailhead
- 0.5   South tunnel entrance
- 1.1   North tunnel entrance
- 1.4   Tunnel Hill Trail junction
- 2.1   Junction with footpath
- 2.4   Views of Potomac River, Paw Paw, and West Virginia
- 2.6   Junction with towpath at south end of tunnel

The hike: You could take longer getting to the trailhead than hiking this delightful section of the C&O Canal towpath, but you will find you want to savor every moment out there. Take a flashlight along to better explore the tunnel walls and the several places where brick courses have been removed back to stone.

To get on the towpath, which passes through the parking area, follow the signs to the tunnel. Black cherry, serviceberry, and redbud line the path, putting on quite a flower show late in April and early May. To the right is

C&O Canal Towpath—Paw Paw Tunnel

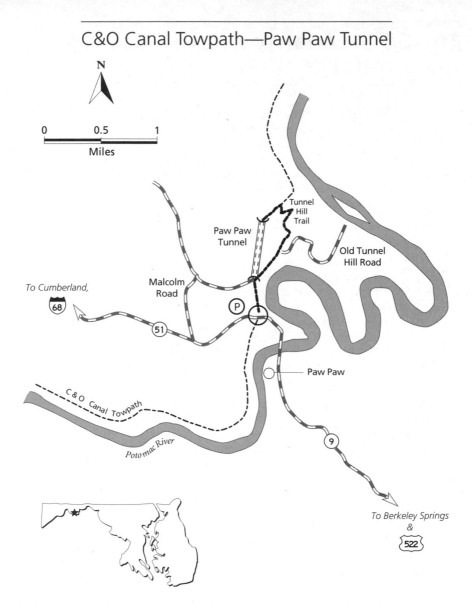

the former "section house," which served as home and office for the tunnel's area superintendent.

The tunnel entrance is at 0.5 mile (the pathway emerging from the right just before the entrance is the over-mountain return route). Note the natural arch of the shale above the tunnel opening, a contributing factor in the choice of this location for the tunnel. Climbing the stairs to examine the exterior tunnel closely, you will see a ceaseless dripping water through the shale. If you have ever stood by a river and wondered how the water just keeps flowing, the answer is revealed here. All over the mountain, gravity is slowly pulling water through the earth and toward its drainage.

Enter the tunnel, and for the next 0.5 mile wander through the darkness on the 4-foot-wide path. The only light inside comes from the openings at either end of the tunnel. You can rely on the handrail for support and guidance; it is the same rail followed by canal men and mules until the canal's closing in 1924. The rail is as smooth as a wood floor from the action of the tow ropes gliding over it between mule and barge for so many years.

Most people prefer to hike through with flashlights off, except to examine features here and there, but you may find the surface too uneven for that. In either case, two points of Zero Impact Hiking apply: Keep your flashlight to the floor, except when exploring features, so as not to disturb the darkness for others. And keep your conversation to a whisper because part of the experience is the utter silence of the tunnel.

Exit the tunnel at 1.1 miles and continue north, first on a boardwalk and then back on the towpath. In spring, at your feet you will find wild pink. Above, water cascading over the shale walls of the tunnel gorge splashes into the canal channel. To head back over the mountain, watch for a trail sign on the right at 1.4 miles. The trail breaks to a hard right switchback. Before ascending, take as much time as you can to wander down the canal. You will find the remains of three canal locks, once used to raise and lower the water level for barge passage. You also may see signs of beaver plying their trade in the canal waters or at the Potomac River shoreline.

At the cutoff trail for the return hike, begin a steady ascent on a woods road, staying with the orange or red blazes (both are called orange, but some appear red). You will climb for nearly half a mile, gaining more than 350 feet, but there are several places to stop and enjoy the landscape. Two hundred yards into the ascent is a wonderful view west of Green Ridge Mountain, the eastern shoulder through which the tunnel passes.

At 2.1 miles, reach the upper prominence and junction with another woods road. One path makes a hard left back behind you, one goes straight, and another is a soft left. Take the soft left and descend. The trail becomes a narrow footpath that slabs around the shoulder of the hill and then descends on switchbacks. Stay on the trail here; the switchbacks protect the hillside ecology.

Still a hundred feet above the river, at about 2.4 miles, is an open spot offering long views of the Potomac, the town of Paw Paw, and West Virginia. From here, you can see the wide bends in the river, known as Paw Paw Bends, that prompted canal builders to blast a tunnel through Green Ridge rather than build the canal around so many curves.

Reach the towpath at the tunnel's south end at 2.6 miles, and continue south back toward the trailhead. Just before the trailhead, a footpath diverges left to lead past the old section house, allowing a close-up view of the structure.

Camping: There is a campsite on the trail 1 mile north of the tunnel; registration with the National Park Service is required.

Special considerations: Bring a flashlight for walking through the tunnel.

For more information: C&O National Historical Park.

11 Fort Frederick State Park Nature Trail

Highlights:	An easy walk through a young forest in an area that was previously logged. A good hike for children on a family outing to the park or for a field study of forest succession.
Location:	Fort Frederick State Park is located in Washington County, Maryland, about 80 miles northwest of Washington, D.C., and 12 miles southeast of Hancock, Maryland.
Type of hike:	Loop; day hike.
Total distance:	1.2 miles.
Difficulty:	Easy.
Elevation gain:	Minimal.
Best months:	April–November.
Permits:	None.
Maps:	USGS Clear Spring, Maryland.

Finding the trailhead: From Interstate 70 in western Maryland, take exit 12 (Big Pool–Indian Springs) and travel 1.1 miles east on Maryland Highway 56 to the entrance of Fort Frederick State Park. Turn right into the park; bear left in 0.1 mile and follow the road 0.4 mile to Fort Frederick National Historic Monument. Turn left just past the fort, and travel 0.5 mile to the parking at the picnic area.

Trailhead facilities: Water; restrooms at the park visitor center.

Key points:
- 0.3   Pine Plantation Area
- 1.0   Tulip tree grove

The hike: Because it is very short and not entirely pristine, Fort Frederick State Park Nature Trail is not a "destination hike." Nevertheless, a walk on the 1.2-mile loop could be a nice part of a family outing to the park or a field study of forest succession. In addition to the nature trail, the park boasts Fort Frederick, the national historic monument that played a role in the French and Indian, Revolutionary, and Civil Wars. The historic Chesapeake & Ohio Canal towpath passes through the park, as does, of course, the Potomac River. With the picnic area by the trailhead, it is a great place to spend a day exploring the human and natural history of the area.

On the white-blazed nature trail, climb a hill from the parking area, passing through the dense thickets and saplings common to recovering forests, and then bend into an older forest of pines and mixed hardwoods. The pine duff path descends to a wash, crossing the narrow stream on a primitive log footbridge, and then switchbacks up a hillside. At the crest of the hill, cross another small clearing overgrown with thickets. Leaving the clearing, reenter

Fort Frederick State Park Nature Trail

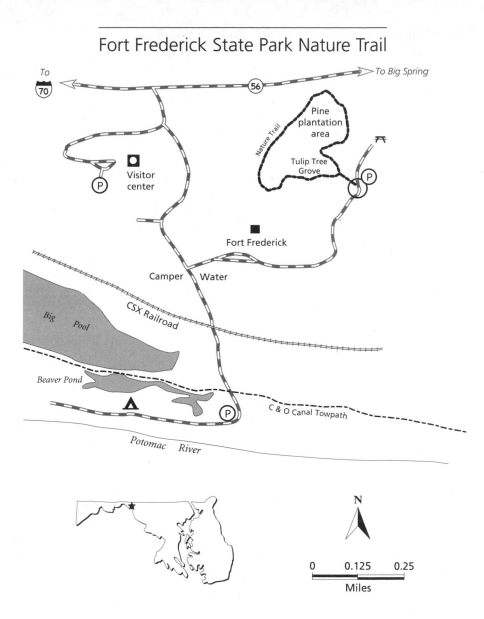

the woods—a mix of pines and the young oaks, hickories, and black walnuts that will one day succeed the conifers.

Already you will have a sense of why this part of the park is called the pine plantation area. The marks of logging are everywhere, but so are the signs of recovery. As you walk the woods here, note the different stages a forest passes through on its way from clearing to thicket to pine forest to an ever increasing mix of hardwoods.

Continuing through the woods, follow the trail as it bends to the left and then cuts through a clearing and back into the woods by a stone pile on the right. The navigating gets a little tricky here. Though an Eagle Scout is making preparations to repair and maintain the trail, there are places on the path where its thin log borders can be hard to see. This is one of those areas. Turn right into the woods by the stone pile, then quickly left, and follow the trail for 25 yards to the next clearing. At the clearing, look downhill and to the right for a post marked with the number 6. Cut through the clearing to the post and then turn left, following a white blaze into the woods.

The trail now travels through a more mature woodland. Still young by forest standards, there are nevertheless some big pines along with sturdy oaks, maples, and sweet gums. There are also grassy meadows where deer browse. After passing through the meadows, turn left into even bigger hardwoods—mostly tall, straight tulip trees on their way to being stately giants. In the shade of the poplars, the trail bends through another meadow—first right, then sharply left—and continues through a stand of pines back to the trailhead.

Options: You can also hike on the C&O Canal towpath or the park's other short nature trail, the Wetlands Trail.

Special considerations: Pets are not permitted at Fort Frederick State Park.

Camping: Yes; at the park's riverfront campground.

For more information: Park Manager, Fort Frederick State Park.

12 C&O Canal Towpath—Fort Frederick to Little Tonoloway

Highlights:	A long, easy walk through the woods along the Potomac River on the Chesapeake & Ohio Canal towpath, with a return by bicycle on an adjacent rail-trail. With Interstate 70 nearby, this is not the quietest section of the towpath. However, we have included it here because it offers a rare opportunity along the towpath to make a loop by bicycle back to the trailhead. Adding in a lunch at Hancock's historic Park 'N Dine will make a day of it.
Location:	This route is located in Washington County, Maryland, 12 miles southeast of Hancock and about 100 miles northwest of Washington, D.C.
Type of hike:	Shuttle; day hike.
Total distance:	12 miles hiking plus 12.4 miles biking.
Difficulty:	Moderate (easy hike, long distance).
Elevation gain:	Minimal.
Best months:	April–November.
Permits:	None.
Maps:	USGS Big Pool, Cherry Run, Hancock, Maryland; National Park Service brochure.

C&O Canal Towpath—Fort Frederick to Little Tonoloway

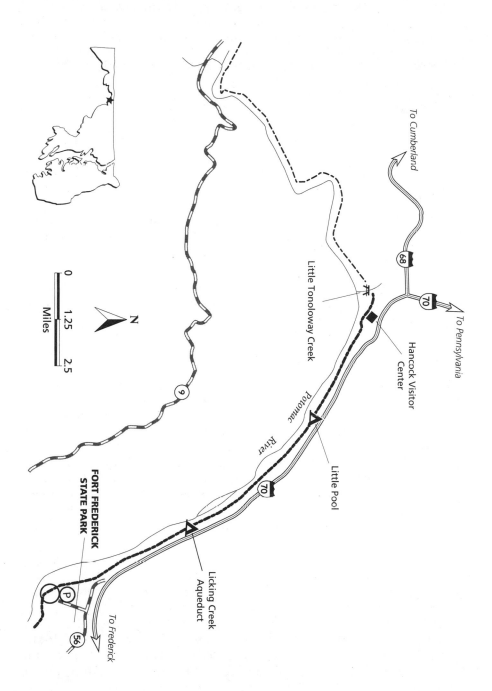

To Cumberland

Little Tonoloway Creek

68

70

To Pennsylvania

Hancock Visitor Center

Potomac River

Little Pool

70

9

FORT FREDERICK STATE PARK

Licking Creek Aqueduct

P

56

To Frederick

0
1.25
2.5
Miles

N

Finding the trailhead: From Interstate 70 in western Maryland, take exit 12 (Big Pool–Indian Springs) and travel 1.1 miles east on Maryland Highway 56 to Fort Frederick State Park. Turn right into the park, bear left at the fork at 0.1 mile, and continue on the road 0.6 mile past Fort Frederick National Historic Monument to the parking on the right at the C&O Canal towpath.

Trailhead facilities: Restrooms and water are available in the park.

Key points:
- 0.0   Trailhead
- 3.5   Licking Creek Camp
- 6.0   Potomac River views
- 7.8   Little Pool Camp
- 10.3 Two locks; ruins of stone canal house
- 11.8 Hancock
- 12.0 Little Tonoloway

The hike: The C&O Canal towpath runs nearly 185 miles along the Potomac River from the mouth of Rock Creek in Washington, D.C., to Cumberland, Maryland. The path was originally built for mules to pull barges loaded with coal and other goods up and down the river. Today, the towpath provides great hiking along the Potomac. Like much of the towpath, the straight, level 12-mile section between Fort Frederick State Park and Little Tonoloway travels through a lush floodplain forest, along the edges of cornfields and on the ridge above the shallow, slow-moving river, giving a walk on the trail the feel of a nineteenth-century country stroll.

From the parking area in Fort Frederick State Park, cross the bridge over the canal and turn right onto the towpath, heading northwest. The trail is wide, level, and two-tracked, with ample room for walking side by side or for the occasional cyclist to pass. For just over the first mile, the towpath follows the edge of a long, narrow pond on the right and a border of trees on the left. At 1.4 miles, as the pond gives way to swamp, cross under an old iron bridge and proceed through lush forest with the canal on the right.

You might expect the towpath to run right along the river's edge, but for much of its length it is separated from the Potomac by a forested border; along this section, it is separated by both woods and cornfields in the floodplain. Views of the river are ahead, but for the next 4.5 miles you will continue in the shade of sycamores, oaks, poplars, and hickories. Look for wildflowers along the trail, and listen for songbirds and the screech of hawks in the high branches. With the cornstalks visible through the trees and the sunlight spilling onto the peaceful path, this stretch can feel a lot like walking a country lane.

Except for the sound of traffic. As you proceed on the towpath to Licking Creek Camp at 3.5 miles, the rush of cars from I-70 will begin to drift in and in places it will be a steady companion. The landscape and the walking remain very pleasant, but an occasional loud truck does tear through the bucolic setting. For some, this might ruin the hike. Others, especially city folks accustomed to traveling through a busy world, may not be bothered by the parallel pathways of the nineteenth and twenty-first centuries. At Licking Creek Camp there is a water pump and a chemical toilet.

Beyond Licking Creek Camp, at 6 miles, look left for the nearby Potomac. From here to Little Pool Camp, at 7.8 miles, the towpath runs close to the river, providing views of its easy bends and grassy banks, clear shallows and wooded shores. At Little Pool Camp, in the shade of a big, double-trunked sycamore, you can leave the towpath, walk down to the water's edge, and watch turtles sunning on snags. You'll find a water pump and chemical toilet here.

At 10.3 miles, the towpath leaves the woods and travels past two old locks and the preserved ruins of a stone canal house. Just past the second lock, the path crosses a footbridge built on a rocky ridge above the river, providing a nice view out over the green water to the hillsides on the far shore. At 11.5 miles, the loud, refreshing sound of rapids overwhelms the rush of I-70 traffic.

The towpath rolls through Hancock at 11.8 miles. Continue to Little Tonoloway at 12 miles, where you can cross into town on Pennsylvania Avenue and catch a shuttle back to Fort Frederick State Park. Pathfinders Canoe and Bicycle Livery operates the shuttle service. (To make a reservation or for more information, call 301-678-6870.) The picnic area on the river at Little Tonoloway is a good place to rest and snack before catching your ride back to the trailhead.

Options: This hike works best if you stow a bike near Little Tonoloway and cycle back to Fort Frederick on the Western Maryland Rail Trail, which runs between I-70 and the towpath to Little Pool, 0.5 mile from the entrance to the park. At Little Tonoloway, look for signs to the trail. The bike path makes for a nice ride, but it is a little noisy as a hike.

Special considerations: As mentioned, the sound of traffic will be an off-and-on companion for the final 0.25 mile of the hike. If you are looking for a quieter hike along the C&O Canal, walk west a short distance from Little Tonoloway—a short walk from Hancock is a nice accompaniment to a day exploring western Maryland.

Camping: Yes, in the state park. There is a fee. For reservations, call Maryland's statewide reservations line for state parks and forests: 888-432-2267.

For more information: C&O Canal National Historic Park.

13 Snavely Ford Trail, Antietam National Battlefield

Highlights: A pleasant circuit walk along the surprisingly wild Antietam Creek, one of three fronts in the Battle of Antietam, the bloodiest day of the Civil War. Wild turkey, beaver, barred owls, and other wildlife inhabit the stream valley. Cows can often be seen grazing on the other side of the creek.

Location: The hike is in Antietam National Battlefield, located in Washington County, Maryland, about 75 miles northwest of Washington, D.C.

Type of hike: Loop; day hike.

Total distance: 2.5 miles.

Difficulty: Easy.

Elevation gain: Minimal.

Best months: October–May.

Permits: None.

Maps: USGS Keedysville, Maryland.

Finding the trailhead: From the Capital Beltway, drive north on Interstate 270 to Interstate 70 West. In 25 miles, exit onto Maryland Highway 65 South. The Antietam National Battlefield visitor center is 10 miles on the left. To reach the trailhead, continue 1 mile to the town of Sharpsburg and turn left onto Maryland 34. In about half a mile, descend from a hill and turn right into the park. At the bottom of the next hill, just after crossing a road bridge, turn left. (Turning right leads to Harpers Ferry Road, the route you will take to exit the park.) Parking for Burnside Bridge is at the end of the road. The hike begins at the bottom of the steps leading to the bridge.

Trailhead facilities: None; water and restrooms are available at the visitor center.

Key points:

0.0	Trailhead
0.5	Georgians Overlook cutoff
1.4	Snavely Ford
1.6	Battle road
2.0	Hilltop

The hike: The lovely bucolic countryside belies the carnage that took place along the creek on September 17, 1862. The Battle of Antietam (also known as the Battle of Sharpsburg) took place in three phases over 12 square miles. Down by the creek, Union General Burnside tried to move his army over the bridge and into Sharpsburg. The streamside trail preserves the landscape that saw the deaths of thousands. Now it is alive with towering oaks and maples, blackberries on the edges, and the scent of paw paws by the bank.

From the parking area, descend the walk to Burnside Bridge and turn right onto the narrow footpath next to the creek. Pass a small dam that

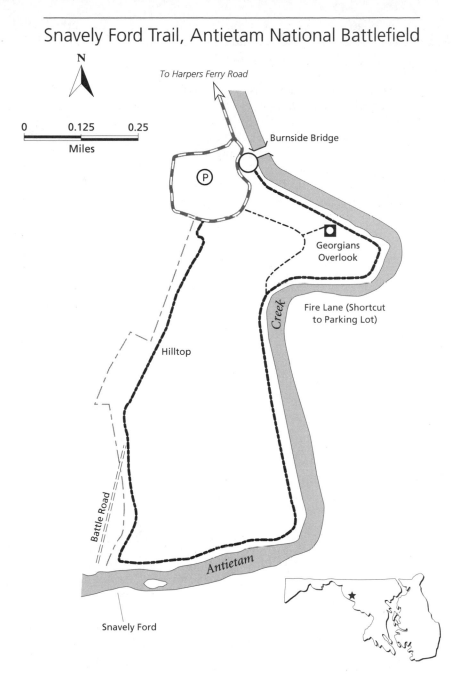

Snavely Ford Trail, Antietam National Battlefield

N

0   0.125   0.25
Miles

To Harpers Ferry Road

Burnside Bridge

P

Georgians
Overlook

Fire Lane (Shortcut
to Parking Lot)

Creek

Hilltop

Battle Road

Antietam

Snavely Ford

creates enough of a waterfall to give paddlers a thrill. Ancient beech line the creek and uplands, while the bottomland is still thick with the lower story of second-generation forest. The pathway leading right, at 0.5 mile, ascends steeply to Georgians Overlook; from there southern troops trained their rifles on federal troops approaching the bridge.

The river bends sharply west at about 1 mile. The hillside to the right is home to wild turkey, barred owls, and deer. In spring, there are Dutchman's britches flapping in the breeze; in fall, the paw paws give the forest a banana smell.

At 1.4 miles, reach Snavely Ford, the crossing point for several divisions of Union soldiers on a flanking maneuver. They made their way up the hill toward Sharpsburg here; the road they traveled is still visible to the left beginning at about 1.6 miles. Uphill, the forest cover changes to thick red cedar. On early evening hikes, you may see several deer leaving the cedar cover to follow the trail down to the creek.

At the top of the hill, at 2 miles, a dirt road to the right leads to an old homestead. To the left, the parking area is 0.5 mile down a dirt cart path.

Options: For a shorter hike of 1.6 miles, walk the route in reverse and take the Georgians Overlook cutoff trail. It is not marked, but it will be the only trail leading left from the creek.

Special considerations: The creek is stocked with trout in spring; licenses are available at a store near the park. The rest of the battlefield and the charming town of Sharpsburg make a fine conclusion to the hike. A hiking ritual: Stop at Nutters in Sharpsburg for ice cream.

Camping: None.

For more information: Antietam National Battlefield.

14 Blue Ridge Summit—Hog Rock

Highlights:	A ramble through hardwood forests and over ridges of Catoctin Mountain, with views of the Blue Ridge and the Monocacy Valley. In spring, dogwoods and other flower trees are abundant.
Location:	Catoctin Mountain Park, a unit of the National Park Service, is located in Frederick County, Maryland, about 50 miles northwest of Washington, D.C.
Type of hike:	Loop; day hike.
Total distance:	5.1 miles.
Difficulty:	Moderate.
Elevation gain:	700 feet.
Best months:	September–May.
Permits:	None.
Maps:	USGS Blue Ridge Summit, Pennsylvania; "Catoctin Mountains," National Park Service; and topo map sold in National Park Service visitor center.

Finding the trailhead: From the Capital Beltway, drive north on Interstate 270 about 32 miles and exit onto U.S. Highway 15 North. In 17 miles, head

56

Blue Ridge Summit—Hog Rock
Wolf Rock–Chimney Rock Loop

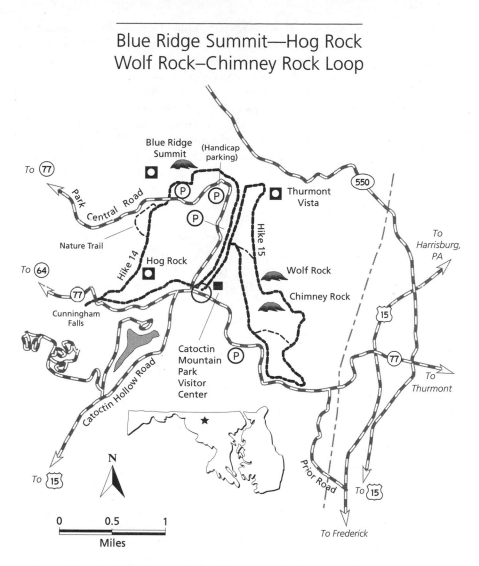

west on Maryland Highway 77 (at Thurmont). Catoctin Mountain Park visitor center is 3 miles on the right. The trailhead is at the far end of the lot.

Trailhead facilities: Water fountain outside visitor center; bookstore, museum, restrooms, and water fountain inside visitor center.

Key points:
0.0	Trailhead
0.6	Wolf Rock Trail junction
1.0	Thurmont Vista Trail junction
1.7	Blue Ridge Summit
2.1	Hog Rock Nature Trail
2.2	Park Central Road
2.5	Hog Rock
3.5	Cunningham Falls

The hike: In about two hours, you can visit a splendid waterfall, enjoy a spectacular view of the Monocacy watershed, and find an intimate cross ridge at Catoctin's summit and South Mountain, all while wandering through a second-growth, almost old-growth-again, hardwood forest. But what is the rush? The hike is short enough that extended stays are in order at each highlight.

Starting at the trailhead at the visitor center, begin ascending toward Hog Rock and Thurmont Vista. The first 0.25 mile is a rude start to automobile-weary legs, but leveler ground is found soon enough. The dogwoods and spicebush, scattered here and there with mountain laurel, are reason enough to take it slow and get your lungs working. This is a scenic hike any time of year, but spring on Catoctin Mountain is a world of flowering trees.

At 0.6 mile, Wolf Rock Trail leads east to Wolf Rock, a formation of Weverton quartzite named for its resemblance to the snout and mane of a wolf. You can detour to Wolf Rock without backtracking to this junction: from Wolf Rock, hike north past Thurmont Vista to rejoin this hike at the 1-mile key point (Thurmont Vista trail junction) shown above. It will add about 1.6 miles to the hike and a fair amount of up and down.

Following the ridgeline north from the junction with Wolf Rock Trail, to the left is Charcoal Trail, which tells the story of the charcoal industry that, along with leather tanning, supported the mountain settlers in the nineteenth century. The bark was gathered and sold to leather tanners, and the trees were felled to make charcoal as a fuel for nearby iron furnaces. The mountain people effectively worked themselves out of an existence, however, because their livelihoods were hardly sustainable once they had denuded Catoctin Mountain of every tree. The story is true for many of the nearby mountains of the Blue Ridge. Still, the process of charcoal production is fascinating, worthy of a detour to Charcoal Trail.

At 1 mile is a junction with the Thurmont Vista Trail, leading right. The left trail leads 250 yards to a trailhead. Go straight toward Hog Rock and descend into a small hollow. Pass through a boulder field of Catoctin greenstone, a basalt rock made from compressed lava flows. Then begin a long, slow ascent toward Blue Ridge Summit Overlook, passing another boulder field, where rock has tumbled down the mountainside. A section of level ground prepares you for a short, intense rise of about 100 feet over only 200 yards.

Another brief respite from ascending follows, then a quick final ascent to Blue Ridge Summit Overlook, at 1.7 miles. A short trail leads to the view over the ledge. From here, you can almost reach out and touch Catoctin's summit, at 1,880 feet about a half mile away on the other side of a narrow hollow. On a clear day, you can also spy South Mountain between the ridges, part of the jumbled collection of peaks and hollows that make up the Blue Ridge. In places, the Blue Ridge runs southwest to northwest in one clearly defined ridge. In many others, the naming of one mountain as a separate summit seems almost arbitrary.

From here, follow the ridge and gently descend amid mature chestnut oak and beech. On a damp day particularly, the scent of sassafras fills the air. At the Hog Rock Nature Trail junction, at 2.1 miles, there are picnic tables and privies. Crossing Park Central Road, follow Hog Rock Nature

Ridgeline of Catoctin Mountain.

Trail on a casual ascent. Mature sugar maples and basswood line the trail. The crosscut wounds on the maples that resemble closed lips are the handiwork of woodpeckers and other insect-loving birds. They cut a horizontal gash in the trunk, which gets the sap running. When the insects come to feed on the sap, the birds arrive for their own feeding.

Several interesting rock formations of Catoctin greenstone abut the trail; shagbark hickory rise above them. The nuts, once favored by swine turned loose to roam the woods, now attract legions of squirrels and chipmunks. To this day, hickory is a choice wood for tool handles. Before the mountain was cut for bark and charcoal, the hickory here was prized for hammer mauls.

Hog Rock, at 2.5 miles, is a fine rest stop. A huge, flat outcrop of greenstone, it is also the place for a nap, especially on weekdays when you stand a good chance of having the place to yourself. As was the custom throughout much of the Blue Ridge, mountain farmers let their swine run wild through the woods, allowing them to graze on nuts and seeds and whatever else they could find. In autumn, the hogs typically ended up at the base of this rock, feasting on hickory and chestnuts. The farmers would retrieve the fattened animals here at Hog Rock.

From Hog Rock, begin a slow 1-mile descent toward Cunningham Falls. There are a few stream crossings and boulder fields amid the towering, misnamed tulip poplars and the occasional, aptly named musclewood tree. The tulip poplar, known by its excellent upright posture, light-gray bark, and distinctive mitten-shaped leaves, actually is not a poplar at all. It is a member of the magnolia family. The musclewood's small stature belies its strength, so tough it was once used to make ox yokes.

Descend more steeply for the final 200 yards to reach the junction with the short trail to Cunningham Falls, at 3.5 miles. To see the falls requires a short detour. Cross MD 77 into Cunningham Falls State Park, and follow the boardwalk another hundred yards to the falls. Early in the morning or late in the afternoon are the best times to find some solitude there—winter is a great time to visit. The 0.1-mile detour to the falls puts you back at the main trail, at 3.7 miles.

On the main trail, the final 1.4 miles is an easy ramble under tulip poplars and beech, with two short ascents over low knobs. The bookstore and museum inside the visitor center make a good finish to this hike.

Options: For a short hike to Cunningham Falls, start at the visitor center and hike west, reversing the final 1.6 miles of this hike.

Special considerations: This hike is described as moderate because most of the climbing is done in two short stretches: the first 0.25 mile and the 0.3 mile approaching Blue Ridge Summit Overlook. Most of the rest of the hike is a mixture of level ground and gradual ascents and descents. This is a beautiful hike in winter, especially in snowshoes after a winter storm.

Camping: In Catoctin Park and adjacent Cunningham Falls State Park, camping is available in campgrounds only; several locations have multiple sites. Cabins are also available.

For more information: Catoctin Mountain Park and Cunningham Falls State Park.

15 Wolf Rock–Chimney Rock Loop

See map on page 57

Highlights:	This is a somewhat rugged hike to two outstanding vistas and a fascinating rock formation known as Wolf Rock, traveling through immense stands of hardwoods and abundant mountain laurel.
Location:	Catoctin Mountain Park, a unit of the National Park Service, is located in Frederick County, Maryland, about 50 miles northwest of Washington, D.C.
Type of hike:	Loop; day hike.
Distance:	4.8 miles.
Difficulty:	Strenuous.
Elevation gain:	500 feet overall, a lot of up and down.
Best months:	April–November.
Permits:	None.
Maps:	USGS Blue Ridge Summit; Cunningham Falls State Park Map.

Finding the trailhead: From the Capital Beltway, drive north on Interstate 270 about 32 miles and exit onto U.S. Highway 15 North. In 17 miles, head west on Maryland Highway 77 (at Thurmont). Catoctin Mountain Park visitor center is 3 miles on the right. The trailhead is at the far end of the lot.

Trailhead facilities: Water and restrooms are in the National Park Service visitor center; books on local natural history are for sale.

Key points:
- 0.0 Trailhead
- 0.8 Fork to Chimney Rock
- 2.2 Chimney Rock
- 2.7 Wolf Rock
- 3.6 Thurmont Vista

The hike: Starting at the trailhead at the visitor center, begin ascending toward Hog Rock and Thurmont Vista through dogwoods and spicebush. In spring, these blooming trees teem with mountain laurel and rhododendron to create quite a flower show.

At 0.6 mile, turn right (east), following the sign to Wolf Rock. Ascend by switchback to a junction, at 0.8 mile. Go right, toward Chimney Rock. Begin a long descent, steeply at times, amid a field of huge boulders. Stay left when, at 1.7 miles, the trail drops right to the national park headquarters. Ascend again below Chimney Rock, a huge group of outcropping composed of Weverton quartzite.

The trail levels off and slabs north, keeping Chimney Rock on the left, then makes a final quick ascent to an access trail to Chimney Rock, at 2.2 miles. The peak to the southeast is the 1,500-foot Cat Rock, accessible from the trailhead across from the National Park Service headquarters. Reaching it requires an ascent of 700 feet covered in less than a mile.

Back on the main trail, turn left and continue north toward Wolf Rock— a formation of Weverton quartzite named for its resemblance to the snout and mane of a wolf—reached at 2.7 miles.

Hike north from Wolf Rock, passing a trail junction at 2.8 miles; the path leads 1 mile back to the visitor center. The next 0.8 mile en route to Thurmont Vista can offer surprising solitude in this popular hiking area. Many more hikers will take the short route to Wolf and Chimney Rocks without making the circuit. And while the vistas get top billing on this hike, the huge old growth through this section is memorable.

Reach Thurmont Vista at 3.6 miles. The view to the east at the beginning of the twenty-first century is vastly different than it was at the start of the previous century. The fertile farmland of the Monocacy Valley is giving way to houses. Intense efforts are underway to preserve the valley's historic farmland.

Hiking north, pass an old cart path descending east and then reach a junction at 3.8 miles. Turn left, and descend the mountain toward the trailhead. Along the way, an interpretive trail parallels the path 100 yards west. It tells the story of the charcoal enterprise that clearcut the entire mountain in the nineteenth century. It adds little time, but some informative enrichment, to the hike.

Chimney Rock, a popular destination in Catoctin Mountain Park. Photo courtesy of National Park Service

Options: For a shorter, much easier hike, go left at the cutoff to Chimney Rock, 0.8 mile above. At the next junction, turn right to visit Wolf Rock; then hike north to Thurmont Vista as described above. You can also press on to Chimney Rock from Wolf Rock and then retrace your steps to Wolf Rock. From there, continue as described above.

Special considerations: With two outstanding vistas, add plenty of time to your itinerary for enjoying the views.

Camping: Yes, registration and a fee are required.

For more information: Catoctin Mountain Park.

16 High Knob—Catoctin Mountain, Gambrill State Park

Highlights:	A circuit along and beside the ridge of Catoctin Mountain through mature hardwood forest, offering excellent views east and west.
Location:	The hike is in Gambrill State Park, which is located 45 miles northwest of Washington, D.C.
Type of hike:	Loop; day hike.
Total distance:	5 miles.
Difficulty:	Moderate.
Elevation gain:	Minimal.
Best months:	Year-round.
Permits:	None.
Maps:	USGS Frederick, Maryland.

Finding the trailhead: From the Capital Beltway, drive north on Interstate 270 to I-70 West. In 2.5 miles, exit onto Alternate U.S. Highway 40 West. At the top of the hill, turn right onto Ridge Road, which ends at US 40. Turn right (east) on US 40. In 1 mile, turn left (north) onto Gambrill Park Road (staying right at the fork to Rock Run Area). In 1.2 miles, turn right into the trail system parking area.

Trailhead facilities: None; water is available from fountains at 0.5 mile.

Key points:
- 0.0   Trailhead
- 0.4   High Knob
- 0.8   View from outcrop
- 2.2   Gambrill Park Road crossing
- 3.3   Catoctin Trail junction
- 3.4   Yellow trail to trailhead
- 3.8   Black and green trail junction

High Knob—Catoctin Mountain, Gambrill State Park

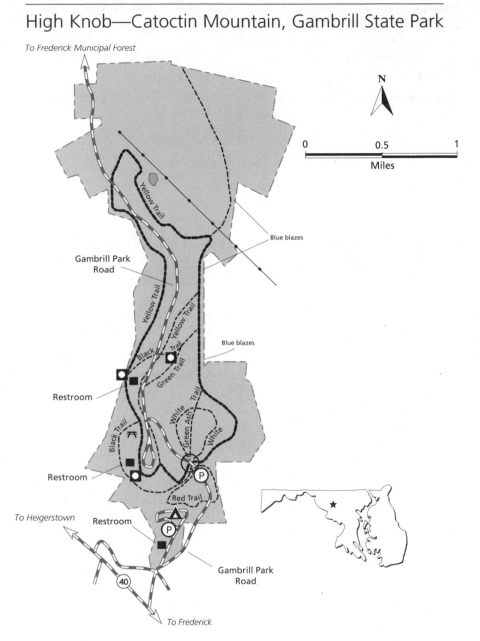

To Frederick Municipal Forest

0   0.5   1
Miles

N

Yellow Trail

Blue blazes

Gambrill Park
Road

Yellow Trail

Yellow Trail

Black Trail

Green Trail

Blue blazes

Restroom

White Trail

Green Ash Trail

White

Restroom

Black Trail

To Heigerstown

Restroom

P

Red Trail

P

Gambrill Park
Road

40

To Frederick

The hike: This hike along Catoctin Mountain offers plentiful, sweeping views north and west of South Mountain, home of the Appalachian Trail. On the hike's return on the east side of the ridge are scenes of the Monocacy River watershed. The views west are slightly marred by the distant sounds of I-70, which passes below about 3 miles to the west. But the sounds on the east side of the ridge are more likely to be those of woodpeckers and barred owls.

Begin the hike at the message board. A 5-foot relief map of the trail system gives a bird's-eye view of the hike and the southern end of Catoctin

Mountain. Crossing Gambrill Park Road, follow the trail marked with yellow, black, red, and green blazes into the woods; then go right at the fork following the yellow and green blazes, where the black trail goes straight ahead. The black trail, which will rejoin the route at 0.7 mile, offers a quieter woodland walk away from the people at High Knob but at the expense of excellent views.

Ascend steeply for 200 yards; then, in the level clearing, follow the green and yellow blazes sharply left. After another short ascent, just before a picnic pavilion, follow the yellow trail left. The green blazes continue straight ahead.

Follow the ridgeline below the "tea room," a park building open to the public and available for public functions (mentioned here because the view from the terrace is memorable). At High Knob, at 0.4 mile, pass below a limestone outcropping. It is worth a few minutes to scale to the top for the views of Sugar Loaf Mountain. Another 100 feet down the trail is an overlook with expansive views of South Mountain to the west and north. In another 200 feet is an overlook constructed of stone, perched on the ledge. Picnic tables are nearby.

Follow a descent in a tunnel of mountain laurel and white pine to the junction with the black trail, reentering from the left at 0.7 mile. Two hundred yards later, at 0.8 mile, watch for a side trail to the left that leads to an open ledge with the last sweeping view of this hike. Just beyond this point, the black trail breaks east toward the road, offering a quick return option to the trailhead by crossing the road, rejoining the yellow trail, and then turning south.

From the junction, the yellow trail follows a rocky path for a while and then again finds soft trail, for the next 1.3 miles never venturing more than a hundred yards from Gambrill Park Road. The road is not a distraction. This is a nice, casual walk under a hardwood canopy, with mountain laurel ever present.

After crossing an old cart path, cross Gambrill Park Road at 2.2 miles and enter woods on a dirt road, where locust trees are dying out and giving way to oaks and maples. At the powerline, go right and follow the utility corridor for 150 yards before ducking back into the forest cover. Over a small knob, the trail descends into a hollow with a steep rise to the right and a small pond to the left. Except in summer, when the pond is a mosquito haven, the pond is an excellent place to sit back and await deer in search of a drink. Two hundred feet beyond the pond, watch for yellow blazes breaking right, uphill. Do not go straight; if you come to the powerline, you have gone too far.

Ascend through mature oaks and hickory. The landscape uphill is open forest. The upper story is so dense that little sunlight reaches the floor in summer, the mark of a mature forest. Pass a flat seam of limestone—another great rest area—and cross a gravel road into the woods. Staying left, cross under powerlines and follow the trail into a cutout dirt road.

Just beyond, at 3.3 miles, is the junction with the blue-blazed Catoctin Trail, a 27-mile backpacking trail that begins at the same trailhead as this hike. It reaches this junction by traversing the east side of the ridge. From here, the Catoctin Trail heads north on the dirt road through Frederick City

Municipal Forest, Cunningham Falls State Park, and Catoctin Mountain National Park.

Turn right and follow the yellow- and blue-blazed Catoctin Trail south. Along here are wonderful views east through the trees of the Monocacy Valley and Braddock Heights. At 3.4 miles, the yellow trail breaks right, climbing southwest toward the trailhead. Stay left on the blue trail. For the next 0.5 mile, the blue trail descends the east ridge. To the left, the mountain gives way to a steep drop into a dark hollow; to the right is a steep rise into white pine.

At 3.8 miles, an old road enters from the right, descending down the knob. This is the black and green trail. The old road crosses the trail and disappears into the hollow, where many maps show a water source called Bootjack Spring (do not rely on it). The black and green blazes continue the descent now with the blue-blazed Catoctin Trail.

The trail bottoms out at yet another old wagon path, a remnant of the farming that once took place on the mountains here, and begins the long but gentle climb up the ridgeline. At 4.4 miles, the green trail makes a steep ascent toward the trailhead, offering a challenging shortcut. Follow the blue and black blazes and ascend on a wide path beneath birch, maple, and scattered white pine.

At the top of the climb, just as the trail levels off and finds a soft, wide dirt path, note a subtle trail to the left that forms a kind of cul-de-sac. This is a short path over a small knob to several quiet napping spots. From here, follow the level path past the junction with the red trail at 5 miles and to the trailhead.

Camping: Yes, a permit and fee are required.

For more information: Gambrill State Park.

West of the Chesapeake Bay and Susquehanna River

17 Little Bennett Loop

Highlights:	An easy loop through several forest types that includes a pleasant stroll along Stoney Brook and Sopers Branch.
Location:	The hike is in Little Bennett Regional Park, part of the Montgomery County, Maryland, system, located just east of Maryland Highway 355, about 25 miles northwest of Washington, D.C.
Type of hike:	Loop; day hike.
Total distance:	4.1 miles.
Difficulty:	Easy.
Elevation gain:	Minimal.
Best months:	Year-round.
Permits:	None.
Maps:	USGS Urbana, Maryland.

Finding the trailhead: From the Capital Beltway, drive north on Interstate 270. Exit at Maryland Highway 121 north toward Clarksburg. Go left onto MD 355, Frederick Road. Proceed to park entrance on right.

Trailhead facilities: Water and vending machines at nature center; restrooms during business hours.

Key points:
0.0	Trailhead
0.5	Stoney Brook Trail junction
1.0	Mound Builder Trail junction; start of trail to Hyattstown Mill Road
1.5	Bennett Ridge Trail junction
2.0	Woodcock Hollow Trail junction
2.7	Whitetail Trail junction
3.7	Stream crossing; nature trail junction

The hike: This splendid little hike offers Washington, D.C., and Montgomery County urbanites an almost instant retreat from the city. Although the woods here have a wild feel about them, the park area actually encompasses the former settlement of Kingsley.

As early as the eighteenth century, the Little Bennett Valley was the scene of farms and small-scale industries capitalizing on the region's abundant resources of timber, water, and vast acreage for farming. Several gristmills and sawmills, a sumac mill, and a whiskey manufacturer were established at various times along the creek. The steep and rocky slopes did not encourage

Little Bennett Loop

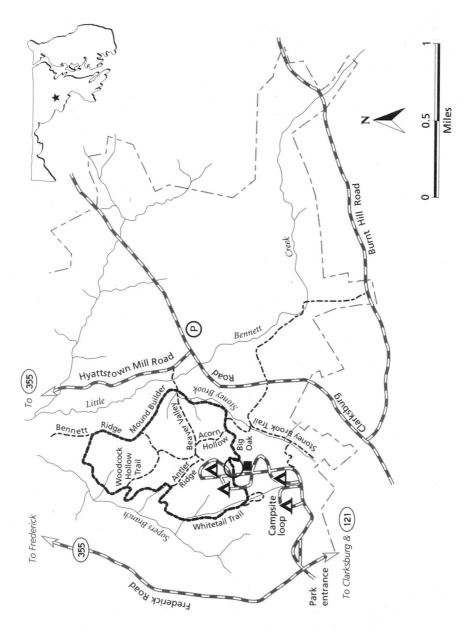

farming, but farmers gave it their best, raising tobacco first and then grain crops well into the twentieth century. A small community flourished, which was called Kingsley—named for a prominent Montgomery County family whose surname, King, now identifies several subdivisions in the region.

Start the hike on Big Oak Trail, which begins behind the nature center. In addition to the oaks along the path, there are silver maples and a pine grove. Turn right onto Acorn Hollow Trail, and descend easily into the small valley created by Stoney Brook. Reach the brook and turn left onto Stoney Brook Trail at 0.5 mile.

Walk through the wonderfully quiet hollow, interrupted only by a short rise over a small knob and a crossing of a spring babbling under cover of red cedar. At the junction with Beaver Valley Trail are the remnants of Wilson's Saw Mill, one of the many sawmills that utilized Little Bennett Creek, which is about a hundred yards east of the trail.

Reach Mound Builder Trail at 1 mile, but before turning left, continue straight for another 50 yards to enjoy a rest stop at Little Bennett Creek. From the bridge over the creek, it is a short hike to Hyattstown Mill Road and on to the Clarksburg Road Trailhead (see "Special considerations" below). Back at Mound Builder Trail, ascend through red cedar and pine. Watch for the mounds near the trail and in the woods. These are huge anthills—by themselves a worthy attraction on this hike.

Turn right onto Bennett Ridge Trail, a wide former farm road, at 1.5 miles, and walk along an open field crest until you reach Woodcock Hollow Trail at 2 miles. Turn left. Descend into the woods, through a glade dotted with sycamore and red pine; then enter a cool woods amid much older, larger sycamore and oaks. For the next 1.5 miles, walk just above Sopers

Little Bennett Creek State Park, once a thriving valley settlement, now offers suburbanites solitude.

Branch. Watch for the right descent onto Whitetail Trail, at 2.7 miles. It is a little tricky; just stay right and descend.

Cross a small stream in an open glade and pass Antler Ridge Trail at 3.1 miles. In this vicinity, you will see old farm implements and machinery still standing where they were left when the farms were sold to the county. Cross a small stream and ascend beside it. The horizontal gashes you see in the oaks, resembling huge human lips, are created by ant-loving birds. They chop the outer bark to allow the sap to run—which attracts ants and other insects—and then they swoop in for their feasts.

Reach the nature trail at 3.7 miles, staying left at the fork. Cross the stream and ascend to the nature center on a wide, accessible pathway.

Options: There are several options for short loops in the north section of the park; site maps are available at the contact station.

Special considerations: To manage automobile traffic within the park, park officials sometimes limit automobile access to the nature center parking area. In this case, you can park at the Clarksburg Road Trailhead at the junction of Hyattstown Mill Road and Clarksburg Road and start this loop at Mound Builder Trail. To reach the trailhead, reverse your driving route back to Clarksburg Road and go left. In about a mile, at the left intersection with Hyattstown Mill Road, there is trailhead parking on the right. To reach Mound Builder Trail, walk 0.25 mile west on Hyattstown Mill Road and go left at the first trail leaving the road. In 200 yards, cross over Little Bennett Creek on a footbridge and continue straight for about 50 yards to Mound Builder Trail. Turn right and follow the directions of the hike as described above; when you reach the nature center, follow the directions above from the beginning back to this spot.

Camping: Yes, a permit and a fee are required; call 301-972-9222.

For more information: Little Bennett Regional Park.

18 Schaeffer Farm Trail, Seneca Creek State Park

Highlights:	An easy loop that meanders in and out of new and mature woods and cornfields along several creeks in the Seneca Creek drainage. A good chance of seeing deer and other wildlife.
Location:	The hike is in Seneca Creek State Park in the Schaeffer Farm Trails System, just off Maryland Highway 117, 20 miles northwest of Washington, D.C.
Type of hike:	Loop; day hike.
Total distance:	3.5 miles.
Difficulty:	Easy.
Elevation gain:	Minimal.
Best months:	September–May.
Permits:	None.
Maps:	USGS Seneca, Maryland.

Finding the trailhead: From the Capital Beltway, drive north on Interstate 270 to the Maryland Highway 118 exit. Go 3 miles west and turn right onto MD 117; then almost immediately turn left on Schaeffer Road. In 2.5 miles, just as the road takes a hard right, turn left into the trail system parking area. The trailhead is at the back of the parking area.

Trailhead facilities: None.

Key points:
0.0	Trailhead
0.5	First of two footbridges; enter woods
0.7	Stream crossings
2.2	Stream crossings
3.1	Yellow trail junction

The hike: Start at the far end of the parking area, continuing past a trailhead sign for the white- and yellow-blazed trails. Enter an open field, and follow white blazes into the woods. The terrain is easy, and the trail's path is serpentine, more for esthetics than necessity. Enter a farm field and walk its perimeter. At 0.4 mile, reenter the woods along a seasonal run and begin a stretch of passing into and out of the woods.

Enter mature woods at 0.5 mile and cross two small bridges; then cross the same run (without bridges) twice more beginning at 0.7 mile. Climb a small knoll and enter another field, turning right, with the woods on your right. Circle halfway around the field, and cut through a stand of maple into yet another field. Walk along Black Rock Road for 200 yards and enter the woods beside a giant red oak surrounded by a grove of white pine and cedar, crossing an old farm road. Still in the pine, pass close to a farm house, 100 yards to the right, and then break from the road and ascend toward the

Schaeffer Farm Trail, Seneca Creek State Park

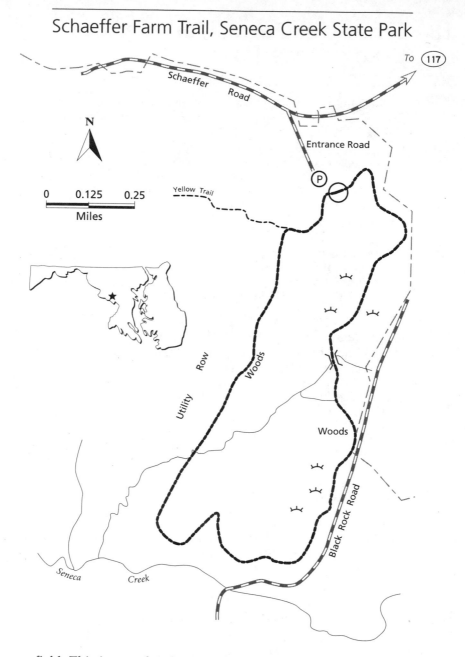

open field. This is a perfect location for spotting deer. If you sit still for ten minutes, you will almost certainly be rewarded with a sighting.

The trail bends right, and the hillside drops dramatically to the left. You can hear Seneca Creek 300 yards south and 70 feet below. The trail hugs the slope, following a tunnel of mountain laurel. At 1.3 miles, the trail moves up the ledge of a narrow hollow containing a stand of huge, mature oaks. At the top of the hollow, the trail enters the corner of a field, then ducks back into the woods at 1.7 miles. Remnant fence posts from the farm still stand.

At 2 miles, merge with a utility right of way as the trail descends, following the ground above a buried telephone line. The orange posts infringe somewhat on the scenery, but the clearing brings out berries and other edge-loving plants that attract wildlife. At the bottom of the hill, cross two small streams just above their confluence, and reenter the woods at 2.2 miles. Cross the streams again and climb steeply, with the stream on the right. For the next 0.5 mile, the trail follows mostly level ground, punctuated by gentle descents and rises over small knobs.

The yellow trail enters from the left at 3.1 miles, sharing the route with the white blazes back to the trailhead on a gentle woodland trail.

Options: There are several color-blazed trails in the park system. Contact Seneca Creek State Park for information about these trails.

Special considerations: The trails in the system were built largely by members of area mountain bicycling and equestrian organizations and are maintained cooperatively. Trail use guidelines call for cyclists to yield to hikers, but it is often easier for a hiker to step aside to allow an oncoming cyclist to pass. Be courteous. Summer months are the most popular for trail cyclists here.

Camping: None.

For more information: Seneca Creek State Park.

19 Hashawha Loop

Highlights:	A fine walk through surprisingly deep woods in a county park. There are views of Pars Ridge, the principle geologic feature of Carroll County, and passages through open meadows and cultivated fields. Watch for blue heron and other waterfowl from the boardwalk across tiny Lake Hashawha.
Location:	Hashawha Environmental Appreciation Area is located in Carroll County, Maryland, about 30 miles northwest of Baltimore and 5 miles north of Westminster.
Type of hike:	Loop; day hike.
Total distance:	4.5 miles.
Difficulty:	Easy.
Elevation gain:	Minimal.
Best months:	Year-round.
Permits:	None.
Maps:	USGS Finksburg, Maryland.

Hashawha Loop

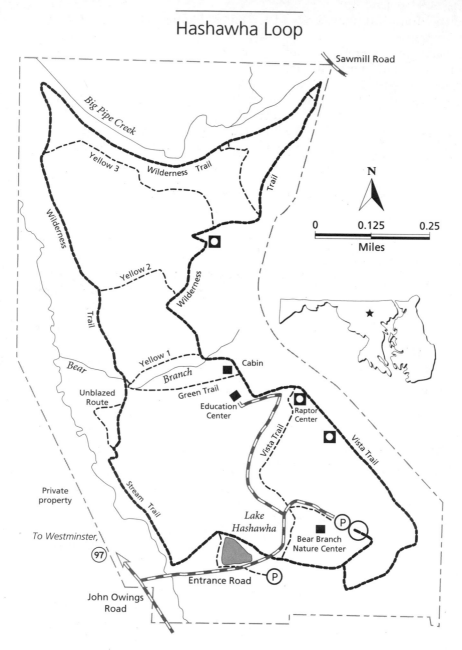

Finding the trailhead: Follow Maryland 97 north from Westminster 5 miles to John Owings Road. Turn right and go 2 miles to Hashawha Environmental Appreciation Area on the left. Proceed past the lake and up the hill to Bear Branch Nature Center. The trailhead is at the far end of the parking area.

Trailhead facilities: Water and restrooms are available at Bear Branch Nature Center. The facility, which houses wildlife exhibits and offers a wide array of programming, is open Wednesday through Saturday from 10 A.M. until 5 P.M.

Key points:
- 0.0   Trailhead
- 0.8   Raptor center
- 1.1   Wilderness Trail junction; cabin
- 1.3   Yellow Loop 1 junction
- 1.5   Yellow Loop 2 junction
- 2.1   Carriage road
- 2.6   Left ascent from Big Pipe Creek
- 3.3   Footbridge
- 3.4   Temporary split in trail
- 3.9   Bear Branch Creek
- 4.2   Park road crossing; blue trail junction

The hike: Carroll County is not known as a hiking destination. But the quiet woods, the opportunity to see a coyote ambling through a cornfield, and the extensive variety of wildflowers in the stream bottomlands all combine to make this an outing worth traveling for—especially when combined with a visit to Westminster's Main Street or other Carroll County attractions.

Following the blue blazes from the rear of the nature center parking area, descend the path to a picnic pavilion. Turn right with the blazes, and follow a wide path 250 yards to a fork in the blue trail. Go left into woods, ascending a small knob through oak and dogwood and then passing a trail leading left back to the picnic area. Ascend easily through a white pine grove, with a nice view of farmland on the right and a meadow on the left. In the distance is the scenic wooded hillside of Pars Ridge, a narrow crest running from Washington, D.C., into southern Pennsylvania and the feature that gives the region its famous rolling countryside.

At 0.8 mile, the woods open at the raptor center, which houses birds of prey that are brought here following life-threatening injuries. Take the green- and yellow-blazed trail right along the park road leading to the education center (closed to the public). Blue blazes continue intermittently, but the blue-blazed Vista Trail turns left at the raptor center.

Go right onto an old farm road. Quiet hikers will be rewarded here with views of deer and rabbit, which favor the edge where the farm fields to the right meet the woods just beyond. At 1.1 miles, the yellow-blazed Wilderness Trail skirts right into the woods. Before you turn right here, take a moment to examine the old cabin. Until the 1990s, you could actually enter the cabin to see how a not-so-removed country dweller might live in the nineteenth century. Now you will have to content yourself with an outside examination because vandals have forced a closure of the building. (For a shorter hike of about 2 miles, continue past the cabin on the green trail. Follow green blazes through new woodlands and seasonal wetland down in the bottomland of a small stream, and rejoin the hike as described below, at 3.3 miles.)

From the cabin, follow the yellow blazes leading right on a narrow path between low shrubs and wildflowers, a veritable butterfly alley in summer.

On an early August day, you may see a hundred butterflies in this 40 feet of green tunnel. Enter a pine grove, and ascend through a cool, sweet-scented canopy. If the pines here seem more plantation than wild, it is because farmers often planted pines as a fast-growing source of lumber and firewood.

Pass an unblazed trail on the right; do not follow it. Continue following the yellow blazes, and descend into a deep hollow; then ascend and emerge into an open field. The corn or other crop that may be planted here is a common feature in many Maryland parks, in which the park and agricultural uses coexist. It makes for a pleasurable hike, especially for those remembering childhood hikes through nearby farms. Turn right, and follow the line of trees for 50 yards; then enter the woods again, this time under mixed hardwoods, passing the Yellow Loop 1 junction at 1.3 miles. The loop forms a shorter, woodland loop that rejoins the main trail of this hike at about 3 miles, as described below.

Enter a field with a splendid view straight ahead of the extending Pars Ridge—the quintessential Carroll County scene. If you reach this scene late in the afternoon, pause at the woods' edge and scan the field for wildlife activity. If you are lucky, you may see a coyote ambling through the field. If you are especially lucky, it will be in pursuit of a rabbit. Continue straight across the field to a point about halfway to the trees and turn left, following a narrow, subtle rut in the tread. Your target is the edge of a row of trees extending into the field. Reaching the treeline, turn right and follow a path toward the trees; a subtle variation between two sections of the field mark your path. Descend into the trees, passing the Yellow Loop 2 marker at 1.5 miles.

Begin a long descent on a wide path, passing two yellow-blazed shortcut trails en route to the bottom. Emerge from the woods onto a gravel path in a wide meadow. Thirty yards to the right is a gated trailhead at Sawmill Road. Turn left and walk through the meadow hugging the woods to your left. Big Pipe Creek, one of the largest streams entirely within Carroll County, is 75 yards to the right beneath the birches and a few cottonwoods. Watch for deer and smaller denizens, such as gophers, scattering at the sound of you.

At 2.1 miles, just after passing a second yellow-blazed shortcut to the left, enter the woods and begin ascending on a wide carriage road. The path to the right of the trees provides stream access to Big Pipe Creek. Ascending, the hillside suddenly drops right dramatically and the creek is 50 feet below you. The next 0.5 mile is as lovely a walk as you will find anywhere in Maryland. With the ridge rising steeply to your left and the stream splashing far below, this is a place to walk slowly and savor your time.

After a gentle descent back to stream level, turn sharply left away from the creek and ascend at 2.6 miles. The trail that continues straight ahead is open to hikers but is managed for hunting in season. Check with the park office for information when hiking from September through March. Fifty yards after turning left here, be sure to stay right at the fork, following the yellow blazes.

Climb steeply for about a hundred yards and then find level ground. Over the next 0.5 mile, follow the yellow blazes past junctions with Yellow Loops 2 and 1, rambling over knobs and descending into hollows. From time to time, the trail emerges into small meadows, lush with blackberries and wildlife-viewing opportunities.

At 3.3 miles, descend to a small stream and cross on a footbridge. Continue straight in the meadow for 20 yards to reach a junction. The cabin you passed at 1.1 miles is 200 yards to the left. Turn right at this junction, following the blue blazes in and out of the woods. You have the option of taking the high trail or low trail at 3.4 miles. The high trail takes a direct route through the field, while the low trail ducks into the woods—the distance is about the same and the two rejoin as the trail enters another field in 200 yards. In this field, watch for the green blazes on a post. You will walk into the field, then turn right into its center, then left about 60 yards from the woods. If you come to the stream and a swinging rope, you have gone to far.

At 3.9 miles, reach a clearing at Bear Branch Creek. (A wooden bridge over the stream leads to an equestrian trail system.) Follow the green blazes, taking the middle left. Walk around the top of the Lake Hashawha, and follow the boardwalk across the water. Blue heron, red-winged blackbirds, and other birds are a common sight, as is the occasional snake sunning itself on the boards.

Cross the park road at 4.2 miles and turn left. Turn right onto the blue trail, and follow it about a quarter of a mile back to the trailhead.

Options: You can create a 2-mile loop by following the green trail at 1.1 miles instead of taking the yellow-blazed Wilderness Trail as described. You also can use Yellow Loop 1 or 2 for a shorter hike. The blue-blazed Vista Trail makes a 1.2-mile loop back to Bear Branch, leaving from the raptor area at 0.8 mile.

Special considerations: When the nature center is closed, no water is available.

Camping: None.

For more information: Bear Branch Nature Center.

20 Northern Central Railroad Trail

Highlights: A walk along 8 miles of the 20-mile Maryland section of the Northern Central Railroad Trail, a converted rail-trail through the rolling countryside of northern Baltimore County. Stow a bicycle at the bottom for a 16-mile hike-bike excursion.

Location: The trail, part of the Gunpowder Falls State Park system, is located in Baltimore County and stretches from the Pennsylvania line to Cockeysville, Maryland, about 5 miles north of the Baltimore Beltway. The trailhead for this hike is in Bentley Springs, 20 miles north of the Baltimore Beltway.

Type of hike: Out-and-back; day hike or overnight.

Total distance: 8 miles one-way walking (with optional return by bicycle).

Difficulty: Easy.

Elevation gain: Minimal.

Best months: Year-round.

Permits: None.

Maps: USGS New Freedom, Hereford, Cockeysville, Maryland.

Finding the trailhead: From the Baltimore Beltway (Interstate 695), travel north 17 miles on I-83 to the exit for York Road North. Go north on York Road (Maryland Highway 45) 2 miles, and turn left onto Kaufman Road. In about a mile, turn left onto Bentley Road and proceed to the parking area.

Trailhead facilities: There is a phone at Bentley Springs, as well as at White Hall and Monkton. Monkton Station has been restored as the administrative office for the state park in the region. The building also houses a museum and meeting rooms. Restrooms and water are available. Refreshments and provisions are available at the store in the Old Monkton Hotel, across from the station. There is also an outdoors store that sells hiking and biking accessories.

Key points:
- 0.0 Trailhead
- 0.5 Confluence of Beetree Run and Little Falls
- 2.7 Parkton
- 4.6 White Hall
- 6.0 Bluemount Road
- 8.0 Monkton

The hike: The trail follows the railbed of one of the oldest railroads in America, the Northern Central, completed in 1838. It operated as a milk train, taking daily early-morning runs into Baltimore. The passenger line carried Civil War wounded from Gettysburg to Baltimore, then carried the body of President Abraham Lincoln north en route to his burial in Illinois. It later become a commuter rail, with daily service to Baltimore operating until 1959.

Northern Central Railroad Trail

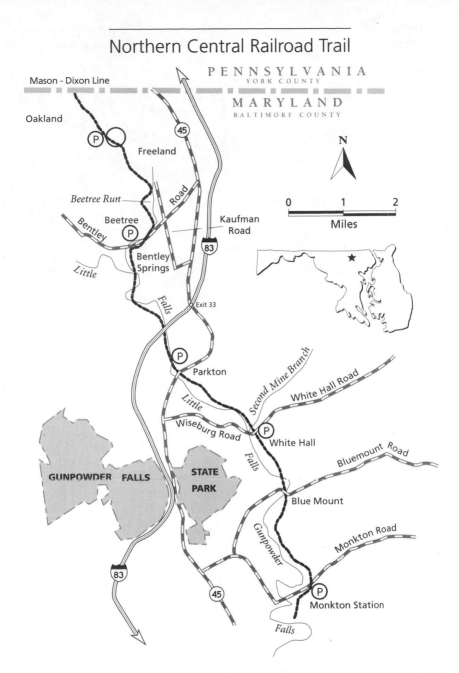

Mason - Dixon Line

PENNSYLVANIA
YORK COUNTY

MARYLAND
BALTIMORE COUNTY

Oakland

Freeland

Beetree Run

Bentley

Beetree

Kaufman
Road

Bentley
Springs

Little

Falls

Exit 33

Parkton

Little

Wiseburg Road

Second Mine Branch

White Hall Road

White Hall

Falls

Bluemount Road

GUNPOWDER FALLS STATE PARK

Blue Mount

Monkton Road

Gunpowder

Monkton Station

Falls

N

0   1   2
Miles

From the Bentley Springs Trailhead, walk south along Beetree Run. Bentley Springs is a town of old homes and farmland. It is a former resort, hosting legions of Baltimoreans trying to escape the summer heat. Little Falls joins the trail from the west, and for nearly half a mile Beetree Run and Little Falls are in view. The confluence of the two streams, at 0.5 mile, offers some of the best trout fishing around, as well as some of the more picturesque views of the surrounding countryside. After the confluence, Little Falls leaves the trail for a time.

Northern Central Railroad Trail winds its way through rural northern Baltimore County.
PHOTO BY T. MOORE, MARYLAND DNR

The trail enters Parkton at 2.7 miles. The section south of Parkton boasts some of the trail's most dramatic views of Little Falls. Then the landscape rises sharply on both sides, leaving only the stream and the trail in a narrow cut in the landscape. There is trailhead parking in Parkton.

The swiftly moving Little Falls disappears to the east, then reappears a mile later as it emerges sluggishly from a broad bend just above White Hall, at 4.6 miles. Here, Second Mine Branch drains into Little Falls, which disappears behind the tiny village. The subtle changes in the character of the stream valley and trail become more evident in this section. The valley is wider and the woods are denser than in the north. There are farms in the area, but the sense of history here is more of mills than milk. White Hall is a former paper mill town, and the look of the old as well as the new architecture ties the area more closely to the city of Baltimore than to the other villages in the area.

Just after the trail crosses Bluemount Road, at 6 miles, cross Little Falls for the final time. It disappears west and empties into Gunpowder Falls. Moving south, just above Monkton Station, the stone remains of the town of Pleasant Valley can be seen. Only a cross section of a two-story structure marks the old town from the trail. Gunpowder Falls moves behind a hill to the east, and the trail descends along a rock face into Monkton, one of a dozen historic towns along the old line.

Options: There is trailhead parking at each of the historic towns visited on the hike. You can make a shorter trip by walking as far as you like and then returning. Or, you can shuttle by leaving a car at a second location. For a truly remarkable day, plant a bicycle at the Monkton Station and make the return by bike.

Special considerations: The trail is 10 feet wide, composed of crushed limestone. At the northern section, there is plenty of solitude. As you approach Monkton, weekend bicycle traffic can be substantial. If you want the Monkton section all to yourself, travel midweek or, best of all, in winter.

Camping: None.

For more information: Gunpowder Falls State Park.

21 Gunpowder Falls North and South Loop

Highlights:	A walk through mixed hardwood and conifer woodlands along and above scenic Gunpowder Falls.
Location:	The Hereford area of the Gunpowder Falls State Park is 20 miles north of Baltimore in Baltimore County.
Type of hike:	Figure-eight loop; day hike.
Total distance:	9.6 miles.
Difficulty:	Moderate.
Elevation gain:	Minimal.
Best months:	Year-round.
Permits:	None.
Maps:	USGS Hereford, Maryland.

Finding the trailhead: From the Baltimore Beltway, travel north 12 miles on Interstate 83 to the Hereford exit. Go west on Maryland Highway 137 (Mt. Carmel Road) 1 mile, turn right (north) on Masemore Road. Trailhead parking is 2.4 miles ahead on the right, on the south side of Gunpowder Falls.

Trailhead facilities: None. There is a comfort station, open in summer, at Bunker Hill Road.

Key points:
   0.7   Mingo Forks Trail junction
   1.0   Mingo Branch crossing
   1.3   Bunker Hill Road and picnic area
   3.0   York Road
   4.0   Raven Rock Falls
   4.4   Sandy Lane Trail junction (east end)
   5.0   Panther Branch Trail junction
   6.7   Sandy Lane Trail junction (west end)
   7.2   York Road
   8.3   Bunker Hill Road
   9.6   Bridge to trailhead

The hike: You can make a day of hiking in the wooded stream valley of Gunpowder Falls and the ridges above it, or you can take one of several

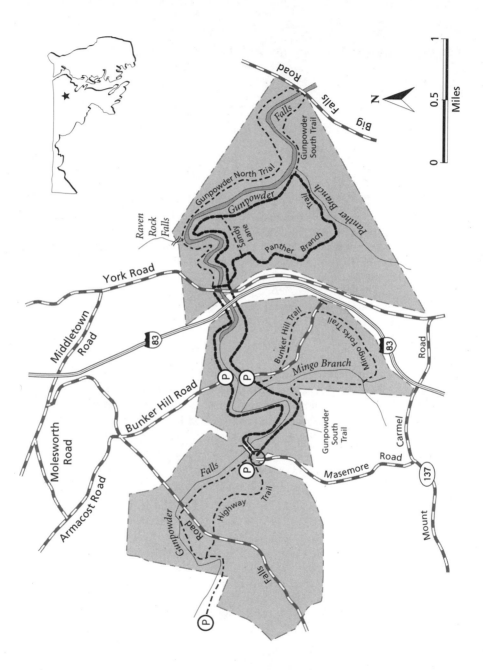

shorter loop hikes. Raven Rock Waterfall, the stone ruins along Panther Branch, and views of hemlocks clinging to the canyon above Mingo Branch are just a few of the sites along the way. You might also encounter red fox, beaver, and wild turkey.

From the trailhead, follow the white blazes over a small footbridge and walk east downstream, entering the woods. This is the only bridge over the many feeder creeks along the route, but the other crossings can be made with a few steps or a long hop over stones.

Trout stocked in Gunpowder Falls favor the bend in the river here, where beaver have created standing pools. In spring, they can also be seen in great numbers in the shallows another hundred yards downstream. The hillsides and cliffs along the river are steep enough to provide the cool temperatures and drainage favored by mountain laurel.

Stay with the white blazes as the trail breaks away from the river at about 0.5 mile and climbs through a stand of mature hemlock. Cross a seasonal stream, passable even in wet weather, and continue climbing with the stream now on the right. This is the steepest ascent of the hike, but it lasts only 250 yards and climbs only 150 feet, leveling off in a clearing at the junction with the blue blazed Mingo Forks Trail, leading south at 0.7 mile. (Mingo Forks and Bunker Hill Trails create a 3-mile loop back to this spot.)

Staying left at the fork, descend into ash and maple, with views between the trees to the north slope of Gunpowder Falls. A managed hunting area comes within 50 yards of the trail on the right. A long switchback descends steeply to the crossing, at 1 mile, of Mingo Branch, a 12-foot-wide creek offering plenty of stepping stones, except in high water when it presents a shin-deep wade.

Ascend amid white pine and black walnut to the blue-blazed Bunker Hill Trail, which leads right to Mingo Forks Trail and left to a comfort station and a picnic area. A hundred yards further, emerge from the woods to the Bunker Hill Trailhead parking and Bunker Hill Road at 1.3 miles. Fifty yards north is the old road bridge crossing. Formerly, the bridge enabled a roadway through the park. But when a flood removed it, the state chose not to rebuild it, thereby preserving the wild, remote setting. Instead of a throughway, Bunker Hill Road now serves as a quiet trailhead on both sides of the river.

Cross the road and stay left of the amphitheater below a limestone knob where finches and hummingbirds buzz beneath the pines; then rejoin the river. Stay with the white blazes, breaking from the river and climbing along a sunken road surrounded by laurel. At the top of the hill, stay to the left of a stand of white pine, taking care not to wander right at the fork with a blue-blazed trail.

For the next mile, the trail hugs the ridgeline until descending via two switchbacks to cross under Interstate 83, at 2.8 miles, and then emerging from the woods to cross York Road, at 3 miles. Just east of York Road is a junction with the blue-blazed Panther Branch Trail, which heads south, uphill. In another 100 yards, search for white blazes climbing right, taking care not to follow a false trail that continues along Gunpowder Falls. If you lose the blazes and come to an eroded section of path immediately adjacent to the river, turn back to find the white blazes, which ascend the ridgeline where it seems a cool breeze is constantly blowing.

Along the trail over the next 0.5 mile, there are a few spots to step off and enjoy the views of the canyon and, especially in winter, the hillside northwest of the river. Descending on a long switchback, the trail rejoins the river and enters a steep wooded canyon. At twilight, the trail through the canyon is a thoroughfare for white-tailed deer and other animals making their way to water. For deer as well as people, there is no easy way up the south slope. Startled animals may make a break across the river, which is deeper and swifter here, forcing an otherwise graceful creature into awkward maneuvers.

At 4 miles, pass Raven Rock Falls on the north side. A popular fishing and picnicking spot, the falls are accessible via Gunpowder North Trail, 1 mile east of York Road. But the best view of the falls is on this side of the river.

For the next mile, the trail follows river bottomland, punctuated here and there with jaunts over small knobs. In summer, the brush invades the path in places but creates an abundance of blackberries within arm's reach of the trail. Pass Sandy Lane trail at 4.4 miles. This trail offers a 0.8-mile shortcut back to York Road.

The junction with the blue-blazed Panther Branch trail is at 5 miles. Here, the white-blazed Gunpowder South Trail continues east 0.5 mile to Big Falls Road. (One option for the return hike is to continue on to Falls Road, cross the road bridge, and then head west on Gunpowder North Trail to York Road. From there, the trail follows the same route as this hike, which will arrive at York Road via the upland route.)

Follow Panther Branch Trail west (right), moving upstream through a low canyon draped by laurel on the west with black walnut and other "recovery species" on the north. The crowded stand of the fast-growing walnut and pine above the dense underbrush is evidence that this side of the stream was at one time cleared for agriculture or settlement. Perhaps because of the steep slope, the mature forest on the other side of the stream was left relatively untouched.

Ruins of earlier settlement are still evident as the trail passes the remains of a kiln and a stone foundation. At about 5.8 miles, there is a junction. The trail continuing straight ahead over a stream is a horse trail that follows Panther Branch from the other side. Stay right; the blazes may be scant for the next quarter of a mile. Keep the stream on your left, and continue uphill until Panther Branch disappears and the trail enters an open field.

Crossing the field, see the ruins of a farmhouse and buildings to the right in the distance. Then, back in the woods, go right on an old road and follow it until the blue blazes duck right onto a narrow footpath. Watch for the sign, which is easy to miss.

It is also easy to get confused at the west junction with Sandy Lane Trail, at 6.7 miles. This junction is only about a quarter of a mile west of the first (east) junction at 4.4 miles. Follow the blue blazes left; then watch for an immediate blue blaze left onto a narrow footpath, which comes to an old cart path in 25 yards. Go right on the cart path; in 20 yards another easy-to-miss left turn takes the trail back onto a narrow path, which follows a narrow ridge and descends, reaching York Road at 7.2 miles, at the same spot passed earlier on this hike at 3 miles.

Gunpowder Falls connects several state parks along its length, each with surprisingly wild hiking trails.
PHOTO BY T. MOORE, MARYLAND DNR

Cross York Road, and follow the shoulder north over the bridge 175 yards until the blue blazes of Gunpowder North Trail are visible on the trees to the left. Climb over the road barrier, and follow the blue blazes west along the north bank. The remaining 2.3 miles trace along the north bank the same territory covered in the first leg of the hike. However, on this side, the trail closely follows at river level with no elevation change—you can coast for the last 2.3 miles.

Even though you are covering what is by now familiar ground, the view and experience are quite different. There are two highlights: crossing a cascading stream just before Bunker Hill Road at 8.3 miles, and a stunning look up the hemlock-covered canyon walls at about 8.8 miles. In early evening, you may be treated to the sights of turkey roosting in the maples above the ridge and the sounds of barred owl setting out for the hunt.

Options: A 5.6-mile circuit can be made by crossing the river at York Road and heading west on Gunpowder North Trail, skipping the middle 4.2 miles. A 10.4-mile circuit is possible by taking Gunpowder South Trail to Big Falls Road and returning on Gunpowder North Trail. A 2.7-mile loop is possible by heading west from the parking area on Gunpowder South Trail for 1.7 miles and then returning via Gunpowder Highland Trail.

Special considerations: Gunpowder Falls is a stocked trout stream; licenses are required. Check at the trailhead in the fall for information on hunting season. If you stay on the trail, you will not enter hunting lands.

Camping: None.

For more information: Gunpowder Falls State Park.

22 Oregon Ridge Park Loop

Highlights:	A walk along old logging trails under mature second-growth hardwoods in Maryland's horse country, with an interlude along a secluded clear-running brook.
Location:	Oregon Ridge Park is located in Baltimore County, about 10 miles north of the Baltimore Beltway.
Type of hike:	Loop; day hike.
Total distance:	4 miles.
Difficulty:	Easy.
Elevation gain:	Minimal.
Best months:	Year-round.
Permits:	None.
Maps:	USGS Cockeysville, Maryland

Finding the trailhead: From the Baltimore Beltway (Interstate 695), travel 7 miles north on I-83 to exit 20, Shawan Road West. In 1 mile, turn left onto Beaver Dam Road; then immediately go right at the fork into the park. Continue past the beach parking area, following signs for nature center parking.

Trailhead facilities: Water and restrooms are available at the nature center, which is open until 5 P.M.

Key points:
- 0.0   Trailhead
- 0.4   Loggers Trail junction
- 0.7   Overlook; S. James Campbell Trail junction
- 1.7   Baisman Run crossing
- 2.0   Ivy Hill Pond
- 3.0   Shortcut trail junction
- 3.9   Wooden bridge to nature center

The hike: People who grow up in central Maryland usually discover at a young age the bucolic beauty of northern Baltimore County, and many are familiar with the beach at Oregon Lake. Sadly, many never discover the lush woods traversed by the park's excellent trail system. What a shame!

The bedrock beneath the trails is some of the oldest rock in Maryland. The rolling ridges are composed of metamorphic rock known as Loch Raven schist. Created 3 billion years ago by pressurized shale, the rock is easily identified by its shiny quartz, feldspar, and garnet crystals.

The ridge supplied iron ore to smelting furnaces formerly located within what are now park boundaries. Little evidence of the open pit operations remains today, at least to the casual eye.

From the parking area, locate a set of log steps at the northeast corner of the lot (you passed them as you drove in). Turn right onto the trail; then in 100 feet, turn left at the fork onto the blue-blazed Laurel Trail. Ascend a gentle grade beneath chestnut oak, accompanied by the mountain laurel

Oregon Ridge Park Loop

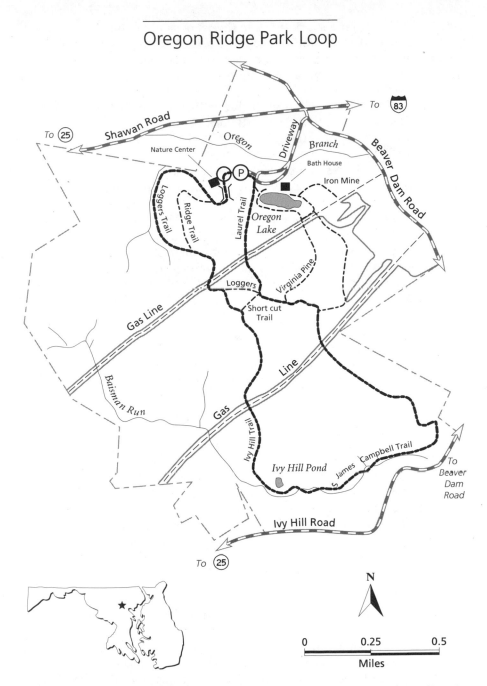

that are often found with this tree. The ridge's well-drained soils offer the perfect conditions for chestnut oak, tulip poplar, and mountain laurel, which dominate the Oregon Ridge forest.

At the top of the ridge, pass into an open meadow, maintained as a gas line right of way. It is an unnatural break in the forest cover, but it provides the opportunity for berries to flourish on the woods' edge, drawing deer and other wildlife out for a snack. Back in the woods, at 0.4 mile, turn left onto the red-blazed Loggers Trail, and follow a wide path through mature, open forest. The wide path was carved by horse teams, hauling timber from the ridge. Then pass the green-blazed Virginia Pine Trail, which breaks left (see "Options" below).

At 0.7 mile is the junction with the yellow-blazed S. James Campbell Trail, leading southeast to the right. Before turning right on this trail, continue another 100 feet and follow Loggers Trail left (do not go straight) to an overlook at a ski run.

Back on the S. James Campbell Trail, cross a second gas right of way and reenter the woods, walking below some enormous tulip poplars and red oaks. At 1.3 miles, begin a descent via switchbacks, where a brush blockade closes off an old trail. At the bottom of the ridge, the trail becomes a much narrower footpath, following Baisman Run upstream. This is a picturesque little stream through a narrow, wooded canyon—an invitation to slow down and enjoy the scenery, especially at one of the several upcoming stream crossings.

Cross the run at 1.7 miles, passing a log bench streamside. Then, over the next 0.25 mile, cross the run four more times. Coming to a T intersection, go right, staying on the yellow-blazed trail (the trail to the left leads to Ivy Hill Road). Pass beneath Ivy Hill Pond at 2 miles and begin ascending on Ivy Hill Trail, a wide logging road. Just past the pond, pass a junction with trails leading left over the run and uphill to the right. The path climbing right is a steep, wooded route reconnecting with Ivy Hill Trail about 400 yards uphill.

At the top of the hill, pass briefly into open field over another right of way at 2.4 miles. The trail junction at 3 miles creates a shortcut left to the return via Loggers Trail. Follow the white blazes for 0.25 mile to a T intersection and turn left. Passing through the right of way a final time, turn right and follow the woods' edge 160 yards before ducking left back into the woods.

The tan-blazed Ridge Trail at 3.3 miles leads right toward the nature center trailhead—a shortcut to be taken if darkness is falling quickly in the woods. But staying left on the red-blazed Loggers Trail will take you for a final stretch along the sound of water, passing near a small creek. At 3.9 miles, the tan-blazed trail rejoins Loggers Trail from the right. Just beyond, a wooden bridge to the left leads to the nature center. From there, follow the paved driveway 150 feet right to the trailhead.

Options: Several color-coded, intersecting trails make a number of shorter loops possible, some of which are pointed out here. You can create a 1-mile or 1.5-mile circuit past the Oregon Lake beach. Following the directions described above, turn left at 0.5 mile onto the green-blazed Virginia Pine Trail or, at 0.7 mile, continue on the red-blazed Loggers Trail by descending left. Both trails lead to the orange-blazed Lake Trail; turn left and follow that trail west to the nature center trailhead.

Special considerations: The trails in the park are effectively marked at major trail junctions. The mileage listed on the signs indicates the total length of the trail. For example, "S. James Campbell Trail, 1.4 miles," means that

Since the 1940s, people have ventured from Baltimore City to Hunt Valley to enjoy the view.
PHOTO BY T. MOORE, MARYLAND DNR

the trail is 1.4 miles long. It does not mean that the trail begins 1.4 miles from the sign. Also, there are several stream crossings without bridges; most are shallow enough to traipse through and all are narrow enough to rock hop across. A public beach at Oregon Lake offers a fine finish to a summer hike.

Camping: None.

For more information: Oregon Ridge Park.

23 and 24 Soldier's Delight Natural Environment Area

The 1,800-acre serpentine grasslands that make up Soldier's Delight Natural Environment Area are the largest prairie ecosystem in the eastern United States. The soil, composed of green magnesium silicate, is so dry it supports only the hardiest of grasses and shrubs. A much larger area of northern Maryland once was covered in this unusual grass-and-pine vegetation. At first glance, the rock-strewn soil and short grasses might seem an unglamorous scrub forest, but a hike through the grasslands reveals a diverse ecosystem of hundreds of plant species. However, it is not the twisting grasses that give the landscape its name. The dull green and mottled mineral that forms the underlying bedrock is termed *serpentine*.

Soldier's Delight East and West Loops

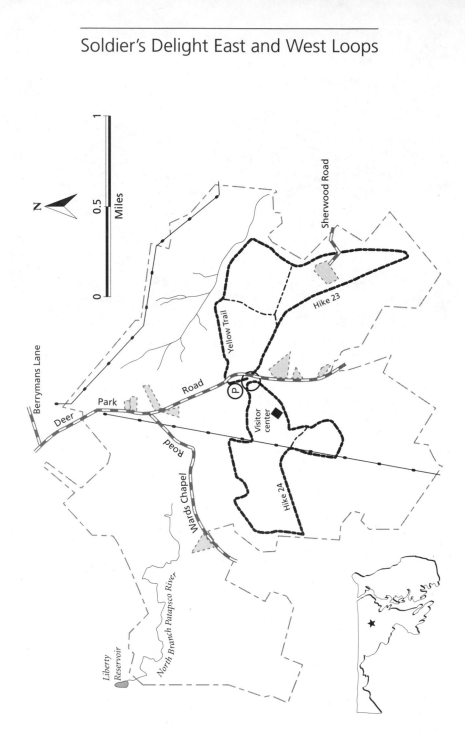

Because both hikes start from the same trailhead, information common to both hikes is provided once below, followed by information specific to each hike.

Best months: January–April; October–November.
Elevation gain: Minimal.
Permits: None.
Maps: USGS Reisterstown, Maryland.
Location: Soldier's Delight Natural Environment Area is located in Baltimore County, 10 miles northwest of the Baltimore Beltway.

Finding the trailhead: From the Baltimore Beltway (Interstate 695), drive north on I-795 to exit 7, Franklin Boulevard. Go west on Franklin Boulevard for 2 miles; then turn left on Berrymans Lane. In 0.5 mile, turn left on Deer Park Road. Trailhead parking is on the right in 2 miles.

Special considerations: On a hot, cloudless summer day, the area heats to several degrees warmer than the hardwood forests only several miles away. Although the hikes pass into and out of pine groves, offering relief from the sun, it is a lot easier to enjoy the ecology of the area in autumn, winter, or spring. There are two hikes described below, one to the east of Deer Park Road in the flatland and one white-blazed loop to the west that descends into the stream bottom.

Trailhead facilities: None. On weekdays and Saturday mornings, the visitor center, 0.25 mile past the trailhead on Deer Park Road, is open.

Camping: None.

For more information: Soldier's Delight Natural Environment Area.

23 Soldier's Delight East Loop

Highlights: A short hike through pine forest and grasslands.
Type of hike: Loop; day hike.
Total distance: 3 miles.
Difficulty: Easy.

Key points:
- 0.0 Trailhead
- 0.3 Mine site
- 0.5 Yellow trail
- 1.7 Orange trail junction
- 2.2 Red trail junction

The hike: Cross Deer Park Road and look for colored blazes to the right leading down a wide path. Follow the path into the woods, and come to the site of a former chromium mine. The surrounding area was the first chromium mine in the world; the openings at this site are the last known shafts. Continue on the path with the mine on the right.

At 0.5 mile, turn right, following the yellow blazes at a junction at which the orange blazes continue straight and the red blazes break right.

The trail makes a long, very gradual descent in and out of the woods and then breaks sharply left at about 1.3 miles. Cross Sherwood Road and reenter the woods. The orange-blazed trail joins from the left at 1.7 miles. A trail marker at 2 miles shows the way west; do not continue straight.

Follow a slow-moving stream on the right; then cross a small branch on a footbridge. Leave the stream, and continue an easy ascent. Emerge into a clearing and, at 2.2 miles, join the red-blazed trail, which cuts sharply right into a grove of oaks and pines. Cross a small stream, and emerge into open, sandy grassland. At the end of the field, the trail follows a narrow "green tunnel," with underbrush and saplings growing close to the trail.

At 2.8 miles, emerge from the woods onto Deer Park Road. Turn left, and follow the road 350 yards back to the trailhead.

Options: For a 2-mile hike just to get the flavor of grasslands, go straight on the orange trail at 0.5 mile and follow the description above from 1.7 miles.

24 Soldier's Delight West Loop

Highlights:	A walk through wild grasses and over rugged, rocky terrain.
Type of hike:	Loop; day hike.
Total distance:	3 miles.
Difficulty:	Moderate.

Key points:
- 0.0 Trailhead
- 0.5 Fork
- 0.8 Log Cabin
- 1.0 Powerline
- 1.3 Green junction
- 1.8 Stream crossing

The hike: This is an odd little hike that leaves you wondering which ecosystem you are in. There are oak–beech hardwoods, open prairie grasses, pine groves, and an almost lunar, rocky knoll at the westernmost part of the loop. The trip is somewhat marred by several hundred yards of following a utility right of way, but the landscape is so varied that your mind will not focus on the cable lines for long.

From the trailhead, follow the green trail south along Deer Park Road; then duck into a stand of trees, enjoying the shade while you can. Emerge at a dead-end in a clearing, and go right following the green blazes into an open meadow. From here, there is an expansive southwest view of the North Branch Patapsco River and the Liberty Reservoir watershed.

Pass right of the visitor center, staying on a dirt road, and come to a stone cabin. Go left before the cabin. Descend on an old cart path, with oak and remnant chestnut scattered among loblolly pines and red pines. At 0.5 mile, the green trail forks west (right) and the white trail continues straight into the woods. Remember this spot. The cabin route ahead may be difficult to find in the vegetation. If you cannot find the way, retrace your steps to here and follow the green-blazed trail to the green junction at 1.3 miles. If you are burning to see an old log cabin, you can find it more easily by reversing the route from that spot.

The trail levels off and, at the end of the field from which the green trail diverged, the woods on both sides form a dense thicket. A white blaze on a tree points left. Fifty yards past this blaze is an opening to the right that cuts through the woods and leads to an old log cabin at 0.8 mile. Continuing, come to a clearing at 1 mile, where the immense powerlines cut a swath through the landscape, offering a bit of irony in the fact that the land here is managed as a natural environment area. To its credit, the power company is participating in a management plan to restore the prairie grasses.

Turn right and ascend steeply under open skies. At the top of the hill, at 1.3 miles, the green trail enters from the right and continues along beneath the powerlines. Turn left here, following the white blazes in their descent into the woods. Stay on the trail, which may be difficult to follow at times, until you reach a fork with two trails. Here, take the hard right. You may not see blazes for a time.

At 1.8 miles, descend into a dense, cool canopy of hardwood. Cross a stream without a bridge and climb a small knoll, emerging from the woods. Were it not for the trees bordering the open area, you would swear you were on another planet. Baseball-sized rocks form the terrain, and the open rocky ground takes on ethereal shade in the late-day sun. This is the landscape that lends the name *serpentine* to the grasslands. Hug the treeline to the right, ascending. In an open meadow, watch for the trail crossing to the north of the clearing.

Continue to climb the next 0.5 mile in the open rocks. At the top of the hill, a line of oaks offers a brief respite from the sun before you emerge once again into the power right of way. Turn right, and descend to a stream in the hollow, the same stream you crossed at 1.8 miles. Turn left before crossing, and hike upstream into the woods, following the green blazes.

Cross the spring twice while continuing to ascend, steeply at times. Emerge from the woods for a steep, final ascent to the trailhead.

25 Sawmill Branch Trail, Patapsco Valley State Park Hilton Area

Highlights:	A surprisingly rugged and remote descent into a wooded stream valley to the Patapsco River.
Location:	Patapsco Valley State Park Hilton Area is a few miles outside the Baltimore Beltway near U.S. Highway 40.
Type of hike:	Loop; day hike.
Total distance:	3.2 miles.
Difficulty:	Moderate.
Elevation gain:	Minimal.
Best months:	Year-round.
Maps:	USGS Ellicott City, Maryland.
Permits:	$2 per person over age 15 on weekends, April through October.

Finding the trailhead: From the Baltimore Beltway (Interstate 695), take the U.S. Highway 40/West Frederick Road exit. Drive 2 miles and then turn left onto South Rolling Road. At the first intersection, bear left onto Hilton Avenue. Patapsco Valley State Park Hilton Area entrance is 0.8 mile ahead on the right. Once inside the park, take the first right turn and proceed to shelter 245. The trailhead is 100 yards down the access road to the camping area, leaving from behind the shelter.

Trailhead facilities: There is a spigot at the comfort station 50 yards before the parking area as well as restrooms and a playground for children.

Key points:
- 0.0 Trailhead
- 0.1 Junction with yellow/red trail
- 0.4 T intersection; view
- 0.9 Railroad bridge; Patapsco River
- 1.3 Cascades
- 1.8 Creek crossing; yellow trail junction
- 2.2 Campground access road

The hike: From the trailhead, follow the road behind the picnic pavilion 100 yards to where the red-blazed trail breaks left and descends 150 yards to a junction with the yellow and red blazes leading right. After you pass this junction and cross under powerlines in an open meadow, the real hiking begins when you reenter the woods.

The trail passes under a canopy of huge, mature red oaks, some of which are nearly 3 feet in diameter. Dogwoods cling to the rocky soil, and everywhere on the open knobs there is moss and lichen. Pass through and near picnic sites; then, just as the park drive becomes visible, break hard right following the sign for Sawmill Branch Trail and continue the casual descent toward the river.

Sawmill Branch Trail,
Patapsco Valley State Park Hilton Area

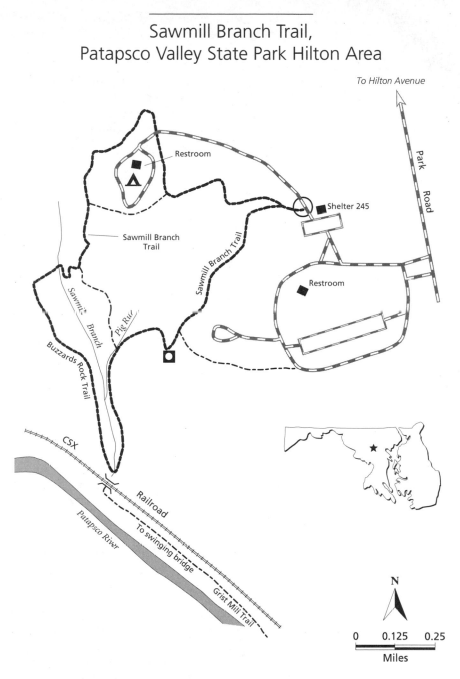

At a T intersection, at 0.4 mile, take a moment to follow a path leading left 50 yards to a ledge overlooking the shallow gorge cut by the Patapsco River—a particularly fine view in winter when the trees are leafless. Return to the T, and follow the trail's switchback into a darker, deep stream hollow, where the trail runs head on into Pig Run, a spring hatched 0.25 mile uphill and at this point tumbling beneath a vegetative cover most of the way. The trail breaks sharply left. Here, the understory drapes over the path a mere 10 to 15 feet overhead, and several downed trees left to their natural decay require minor scrambling to navigate.

Pig Run disappears just as the sound of Sawmill Branch takes over above the occasional knock-knock-knock of a pileated woodpecker or the sounds of smaller birds hobnobbing in the undergrowth. The trail meets Sawmill Branch just below its confluence with Pig Run and follows it ever downward. Beware of a false crossing of Sawmill Branch about 100 yards farther down. Sawmill Branch Trail did once cross here and make a steep ascent of the south bank, but it now crosses at the railroad bridge 150 yards farther.

The railroad bridge, at 0.9 mile, is a marvel of stone construction, creating a tunnel through which Sawmill Branch passes and Grist Mill Trail begins its southeast route along the Patapsco. Take a few minutes here to explore the Patapsco, perhaps finding a sunny spot for a picnic or a splash around on the shore. Back through the railroad tunnel, Sawmill Branch Trail crosses the creek over stones. From this point on called Buzzard's Rock Trail, it climbs upstream on the opposite side.

The trail has a much-less-traveled feel on this side, and for the next mile you will hike above and next to Sawmill Run. A series of cascades beginning at about 1.3 miles offers pools for wading and oversized granite rocks for napping, especially where the sun breaks through. The trail above the cascades may be difficult to follow because of overgrowth and downed trees. Your options are to follow a faint high-water trail for 175 yards, slabbing over a knob to rejoin the trail, or to stay with the water and make your way past the bad section—which is only about 200 feet if you follow the water.

Cross the creek stepping over rocks onto the yellow trail at 1.8 miles, and head east back toward the park. On the way, there are more outstanding red oaks and white ash, as well as a few more false trails left from recent trail relocations. Only two spots require attention to navigation. Just above the switchback after crossing Sawmill Branch, stay right with the yellow blaze at the T. Then, after crossing a campground access road at 2.2 miles, stay left on the yellow- and red-blazed trail where the red blazes break right.

The next junction is the same as the first one passed at the beginning of the hike. Turn left, and ascend out of the forest. The trail comes to the access road behind shelter 245.

Options: The park map outlines a few shorter options.

Special considerations: Throughout the hike, remnant junctions from older versions of these routes sometimes cause moments of misdirection, especially at the bottom of Sawmill Branch. Stay with the fresh blazes. On the return, a dozen downed trees over 0.5 mile cut down on traffic and add to the feeling of remoteness, but they require some hurdling. If you are hiking with children, be prepared to go slowly.

Camping: Developed campsites are available through the park office. For reservations, call Maryland's statewide reservations line for state parks and forests: 888-432-2267.

For more information: Patapsco Valley State Park.

26 Sweet Air Loop, Gunpowder Falls State Park

> **Highlights:** A wonderfully quiet hike offering a diversity of experiences: plentiful contact with Little Gunpowder Falls, a small pond in the woods, farm fields, immense tulip poplars, and small pine groves. In late July and early August, blackberries are plentiful.
>
> **Location:** This hike, in the Sweet Air Area of Gunpowder Falls State Park, hugs the Baltimore–Harford County line about 15 miles northeast of Baltimore.
>
> **Type of hike:** Loop; day hike.
>
> **Total distance:** 5.5 miles.
>
> **Difficulty:** Easy.
>
> **Elevation gain:** Minimal.
>
> **Best months:** Year-round (July and August for blackberries).
>
> **Permits:** None.
>
> **Maps:** USGS Phoenix, Maryland.

Finding the trailhead: From the Baltimore Beltway (Interstate 695), drive 7 miles north on I-83 to the Shawan Road East exit. In 1 mile, turn right onto York Road (Maryland Highway 45); then, in 0.5 mile, turn left onto Ashland Road (MD 145, which becomes Paper Mill Road). Continue straight through the intersection with MD 146, after which Paper Mill Road changes to Sweet Air Road. In 8.5 miles, turn left onto Green Road. In 1.7 miles, turn left onto Moore's Road; then, about a quarter of a mile further, turn left onto Dalton Bevard Road, which is the park access road. Proceed to the trailhead parking area.

Trailhead facilities: A small picnic shelter with one table is available; a large map of the entire area appears on the information board.

Key points:
0.0	Trailhead
0.5	Barley Pond
0.6	Little Gunpowder Trail junction
0.7	Connecting trail (red blazes)
0.8	Boundary Trail junction
1.8	Little Gunpowder Trail junction
2.0	Boundary Trail junction
2.3	Little Gunpowder Falls
3.0	Red trail; short-loop return
4.2	Boundary Trail
4.4	Open field; blueberries
5.2	Pine Loop junction

The hike: The hike begins from the small picnic shelter at the west end of the parking area. Facing the shelter, locate the white-blazed trail at the far

Sweet Air Loop, Gunpowder Falls State Park

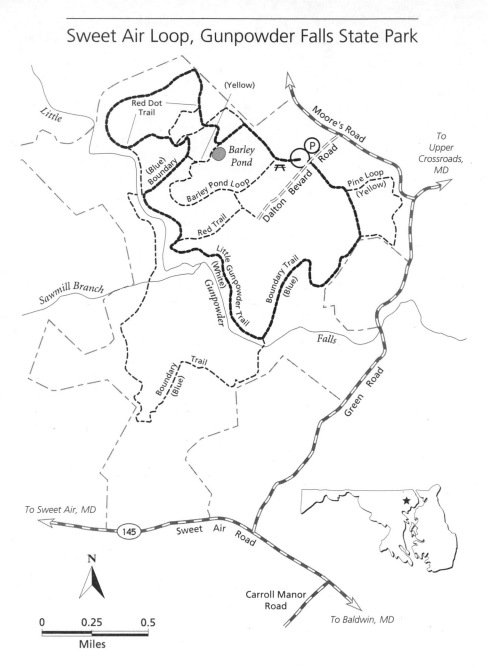

right (north end) of the clearing; a sign reads Barley Pond Loop. Enter the woods, following a wide tractor path; watch for blackberries in season.

Beyond a row of pine trees, enter a cornfield, where the yellow-blazed loop goes left. Continue straight, and walk between two sections of the field. When the corn is high, you will walk in a green tunnel scented sweetly with corn; when the corn is low or not yet planted, there is a picturesque view west.

Follow the yellow-blazed trail left as it leaves the white blazes. Enter the woods, and follow a wide path under large poplars. The understory is white with dogwoods and alive with redbud in spring. Reach Barley Pond at 0.5 mile, a quiet rest stop in a shady place. To continue, retrace your steps to where you first encountered the pond; then retreat back up the trail 75 feet from the pond and turn left onto an unmarked trail, which leads up the slope of a small hollow to the white-blazed Little Gunpowder Trail, at 0.6 mile. Turn left onto Little Gunpowder Trail; then, in about 160 yards, turn right onto a connecting red-blazed trail, at 0.7 mile.

Reach a junction with the blue-blazed Boundary Trail at 0.8 mile, and continue straight on the red trail, a quiet footpath that hugs the woods and circles an open meadow. Follow the footpath for 1 mile to a junction with Little Gunpowder Trail, at 1.8 miles. Turn left (if you want to trim a little from the hike, you can continue straight because this route will rejoin Little Gunpowder Trail about a quarter of a mile down the trail).

The Boundary Trail joins from the left at 2 miles. Follow it parallel to the white-blazed trail for 150 yards, and then break right to follow a footpath above a narrow stream valley. Ferns carpet the ground rising uphill to the right, and spring wildflowers surround the small stream. Cross a small stream just before entering a clearing, taking care to follow the established footpath so as not to add to an erosion problem caused by inappropriate travel through this section. Turn right at the clearing onto Boundary Trail, and reach Little Gunpowder Falls at 2.3 miles. Boundary Trail continues across the unbridged stream, which is fine for horses, but most hikers will find it a little deeper than they care to ford.

Turn left onto the white-blazed Little Gunpowder Trail, and follow the river downstream. The woods here are quiet and old, with tulip poplars and silver maples towering 80 to 100 feet. Anglers will find several large pools and a few small falls for plying the waters (check with park authorities for season and license requirements). At about 2.8 miles, stay left with the white trail as it ascends away from the river, leaving the equestrian trail to follow the stream.

Climb steeply, but briefly, to a ledge that moves downstream above a small hollow, and then climb gently. Pass a junction with a red-blazed connecting trail at 3 miles. (Note: You can take a shortcut back to the trailhead by going left here, then left at the next junction, then right onto the yellow-blazed Barley Pond Loop. A quarter of a mile farther, reach the white trail at the spot at which you first entered the cornfield. The trailhead is 0.2 mile to the right.)

Continuing on the white trail, follow above the river and below giant tulip poplars. Then duck deeper into the woods and cross a small stream on a wooden footbridge, before climbing a gentle rise. When you reach level ground, Little Gunpowder Falls will be 100 feet below, about 75 yards west (right). A right side trail at 3.6 miles leads 100 feet to stream access and a few nice pools.

Descend steeply to a junction with Boundary Trail at 4.2 miles. For a detour to a few very nice pools, you can go right here and follow the blue

Only ten miles northeast of the Baltimore Beltway, Little Gunpowder meanders through a countryside far removed from city bustle. PHOTO BY LISA A. GUTIERREZ

trail 175 yards. Walk upstream a short distance if you want to play in the water, or, if watering yourself in the inviting pools just downstream of the river crossing, be aware that horses also use the blue trail to cross. You can also continue over the river here by rock hopping and explore the western reaches of the park.

From the junction of the white-blazed Little Gunpowder Trail and the blue-blazed Boundary Trail, turn left (a hard left) and ascend following the blue blazes. Go right when the trail enters an open field at 4.4 miles, and watch for abundant blackberries at the woods' edge as you make your way around the field just outside the woods. Just as a house comes into view, watch for the blue blazes turning right into the woods for a brief interlude of 100 yards; then emerge again into the field uphill. Continue past the house.

Stay left after passing the house (the pathway to the right is private property; please respect it). Pass through a line of trees, and go right into another field. At the end of this clearing, enter the woods and continue straight ahead to a junction with a second yellow-blazed trail. Go left, and follow under mixed hardwoods and white and red pines. Blackberries are plentiful from here to the trailhead, and the smell of pine through here is sweet and intense.

Pass another junction with the yellow-blazed Pine Loop at 5.2 miles, and ascend a small knoll (staying to the right at a split in the trail). Emerging from the woods at the park access road, cross the road and proceed to the trailhead.

Options: A shorter, 3.7-mile variation of this hike is described above. You can also follow the Boundary Trail for a western loop that leaves this hike at 1.8 miles and rejoins it at the 4.2-mile key point shown above. This would add only about 0.5 mile but would require crossing the unbridged Little Gunpowder Falls, which averages about 12 to 18 inches deep at the crossing. A pair of old sneakers in your day pack is all you need.

Special considerations: Bring along a container of frozen cream laced with sugar for blackberries in late July and August. The cream will melt while you hike, making a great dessert. The loop described above passes close to private property in one place. Other loops within the park pass close to several houses. The trail also passes through cornfields leased to private farmers. Please respect the privacy and property of all.

Camping: None.

For more information: Gunpowder Falls State Park.

27 Wildlands Loop, Gunpowder Falls State Park

Highlights:	This loop follows the upland forests of the fall zone, crossing a few streams and visiting a pleasant waterfall, then meanders downstream along Big Gunpowder Falls as it leaves the piedmont.
Location:	This hike is located in Baltimore County, about 12 miles northeast of Baltimore.
Type of hike:	Loop; day hike.
Total distance:	5.2 miles.
Difficulty:	Moderate.
Elevation gain:	Minimal.
Best months:	Year-round.
Permits:	None.
Maps:	USGS White Marsh, Maryland.

Finding the trailhead: From the Baltimore Beltway (Interstate 695), take the Bel Air Road North exit (alternately known as Belair Road, it is U.S. Highway 1). In just under 5.5 miles, cross the bridge over Big Gunpowder Falls, and then take an immediate right into the trailhead parking area. The hike begins behind the information board.

Trailhead facilities: Information board with large map of the area.

Key points:
- 0.0   Trailhead
- 0.1   Wildlands and Stocksdale Trails junction
- 1.9   Stocksdale Trail junction

Wildlands Loop, Gunpowder Falls State Park

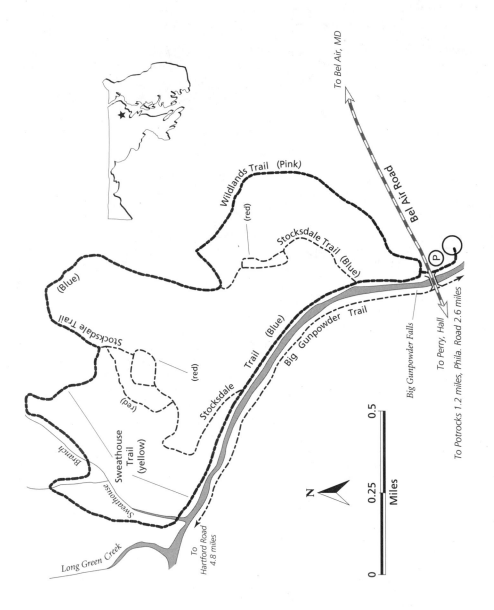

The hike: Watching Big Gunpowder Falls sliding through several narrow gorges, it is hard to believe that only 5 miles downstream the falls will spread to a delta-like, broad river more than a mile wide. From the information board, descend steps behind the board to a tunnel under the Bel Air Road (US 1) bridge. Continue past the junction with Gunpowder Falls Trail, which leads left just beyond the bridge, to a trail junction marking the beginning of the Stocksdale and Wildlands Trails. To the left, Stocksdale Trail follows the former route of the old Stocksdale Road and is the return route of this hike. Turn right into the woods, follow the pink blazes over level ground for about 100 yards, and then ascend.

As you climb, steeply at times, you will see that Big Gunpowder Falls sits at the bottom of a rather narrow ravine. This may seem rather unusual to those accustomed to thinking of the Baltimore as more closely linked to the Chesapeake Bay and the coastal plain than to the piedmont to the north of town. Here, as the falls pass through the transition known as the fall zone, the landscape is still part piedmont, and the steep grade illustrates the point. Perhaps in a few million years, the uplift that created this ravine will erode to a point at which it more closely resembles the landscape of Days Cove, an estuarine flatland only a few miles south.

At 1.9 miles, reach the end of Wildlands Trail at the junction of the blue-blazed Stocksdale Trail. To the left, Stocksdale Trail takes a shortcut to return to Big Gunpowder Falls 0.4 mile upstream from the trailhead. Go right, following the blue blazes, and continue through younger woods and fairly open meadow, remnants of the area's agricultural past. In winter, amid the brush you can still see fence posts and other reminders. The pine trees through this area are plantation planted. Some were planted by former farmers for use as firewood; the younger trees were planted by the State of Maryland at the establishment of the park as a way of protecting the falls' watershed from erosion and runoff.

Stocksdale Trail breaks left at the junction with the yellow-blazed Sweathouse Trail, at 2.7 miles —Big Gunpowder Falls is 0.9 mile downhill. The trail to the left is the actual road right of way of the old Stocksdale Road. To the right, it continues out of the park. Take the soft right, following the yellow blazes. Ascend a knoll, and begin a casual descent to Sweathouse Branch. Reach the stream, and follow the trail left for 0.5 mile of very pleasant streamside walking; the stream gurgles and, in places, tumbles toward the falls. Cross Sweathouse Branch, and then ascend upstream along a tributary of it for 0.25 mile before crossing the tributary and descending.

A side trail at 3.9 miles leads right 180 yards to a picturesque little cascade on Long Green Creek. In addition to offering a pleasant spot for soaking your feet in one of three nearby pools, the cascade is a fine illustration of the Big and Little Gunpowder Falls topography. The "falls" are casual cascades through the fall zone. Back on Sweathouse Trail, cross Sweathouse

Over a few short miles the terrain of Gunpowder Falls changes from hilly Piedmont to the meadows of the Coastal Plain. Photo by Jayson Knott

Branch again and continue east, downstream along Gunpowder Falls. If you see hikers rambling along the other side of river, they are on Big Gunpowder Trail, a 20-plus-mile footpath from the northern part of the county to Days Cove.

Rejoin the blue-blazed Stocksdale Trail at 4.4 miles. There are several places along the way in which the stream valley is more of a steep gorge that drops all the way to the stream, while on the south side of Big Gunpowder Falls there is gentle bottomland. Continue past a fork, at 4.9 miles; to the left Stocksdale Trail leads uphill on a loop that eventually leads back to this spot. Cross a small stream, and walk downstream until reaching the tunnel under Bel Air Road. Pass under the road, and return to the trailhead.

Options: For a 3-mile loop, go left onto the blue-blazed Stocksdale Trail at the 1.9-mile key point shown above, instead of going right. Then follow this blue trail 0.7 mile to the opposite end of the loop made by the Stocksdale Trail. Turn left to return to the trailhead. South of the trailhead are other loops, which are illustrated on a map at the trailhead information board.

Special considerations: The area is very popular on weekends. Early in the day and late in the afternoon, it is possible to find solitude. Also, because there are several options for hiking in the park, people tend to disperse.

Camping: None.

For more information: Gunpowder Falls State Park.

28 McKeldin Area Loop, Patapsco Valley State Park

Highlights:	Starting from the swift rapids of the South Branch, to the confluence of the North and South Branches and beyond, this hike follows the mood of the Patapsco River—sometimes lively, sometimes lazy. About two-thirds of the hike comes into very close contact with the river. The return is a woodland walk through a narrow hollow favored by white-tailed deer.
Location:	This trail is located in the McKeldin Area of Patapsco Valley State Park on the Baltimore–Howard County line, about 15 miles west of Baltimore.
Type of hike:	Loop; day hike.
Total distance:	3.5 miles.
Difficulty:	Easy.
Elevation gain:	Minimal.
Best months:	Year-round.
Permits:	None.
Maps:	USGS Ellicott City; Maryland.

McKeldin Area Loop, Patapsco Valley State Park

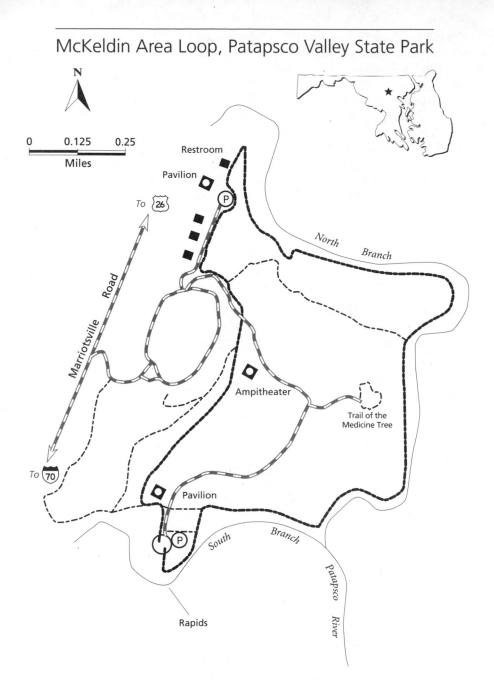

Finding the trailhead: From the Baltimore Beltway (Interstate 695), drive west on I-70 for 11 miles to the Marriotsville Road exit. Go north 2 miles to the park entrance on the right. Circle the open field, and then continue right until the park road ends at the trailhead parking. Continue the final 150 yards to the river on foot following the blacktop.

Trailhead facilities: Restrooms.

Key points:
- 0.0 Trailhead
- 0.4 Confluence of North and South Branches
- 1.3 Boulder field
- 1.5 Trail junction
- 1.7 Access road; pavilion
- 2.0 Road crossing
- 2.7 Trail to trailhead

The hike: Thanks to the topography of the area, it is possible to find solitude even when large groups are enjoying picnics in the park pavilions. The rolling landscape and cliffs provide a buffer that allows for quiet enjoyment of the stream valley.

Take some time at the outset to enjoy the cascades on the South Branch, and then walk southeast with the river on your right. A quarter of a mile downstream, the trail breaks north; a narrow path leads to a rocky point that juts into the river, making a narrow rapids. Emerge from the woods, and cross over huge boulders that seem to slide into the stream. At 0.4 mile, reach the confluence of the South and North Branches of the Patapsco River. Continue straight, now upstream, along the North Branch.

Follow the trail through a wide bottomland, which creates a broad bend. Then, as the river course comes from due north, walk beneath a steep and rocky hillside rising about a hundred feet left. For nearly the next mile, the trail follows the North Branch closely, usually through maple and scattered oak and hickory. There are some very old, immense oaks along the bottomland here, spared from farming because of the rough terrain directly

In the 1950s, Governor McKeldin led an effort to purchase Maryland stream valleys, resulting in a legacy of linear parks and trails. PHOTO COURTESY OF MARYLAND DNR

uphill. Perhaps the most interesting features along this lazy stretch of water are the occasional boulder fields, especially a sprawling one at 1.3 miles. Where the huge rocks protrude from the creek bottom, they form shady pools favored by the trout stocked here each spring.

At 1.5 miles, go left at the cutoff trail and climb, first through a long switchback and then rather steeply for a hundred yards or so. A second switchback takes the trail north again. Follow the ledge above the North Branch, moving upstream; then descend into a narrow hollow to cross a small stream, taking care not to cause further erosion. Ascend again, slowly from the hollow and then steeply for a final sprint to reach the park access road near a comfort station and picnic pavilions, at 1.7 miles.

Follow the park road 0.1 mile to a fork; go left, then left again through a parking area. Turn left onto the park road, and follow it 100 yards; cross the road and enter the woods marked by a trail sign at 2 miles. At the amphitheater just inside the woods, take the left trail at the fork. From here, the trail follows a narrow, shallow stream valley, which drops to your right. The valley is home to scores of deer, giving you ample opportunities to watch the youngest testing their gallops.

After crossing a small stream, stay right at the fork and continue along the stream valley. At 2.7 miles, just above the South Branch, go left and follow the trail 0.4 mile to the park road, emerging at the rest area. Turn right, and walk 0.4 mile along the road to return to the trailhead.

Options: There are several variations on this hike that are made possible by trails weaving through the park, at various stages of maintenance. The Trail of the Medicine Tree is a nice 0.5-mile interpretive nature trail.

Special considerations: The lush Maryland vegetation can overtake a trail in a summer. If a trail segment seems overgrown, it may be in need of a volunteer. The park is used extensively by equestrians and bicyclists. On weekdays, it is possible to find solitude in the park, but the bottomlands have undergone significant damage in recent years.

Camping: Youth groups only.

For more information: Patapsco Valley State Park.

29 Susquehanna State Park Loop

Highlights:	An easy ramble through hardwood forest with great rewards: expansive views of the Susquehanna River, old farm ruins, and, if you are lucky, bald eagles.
Location:	Susquehanna State Park is located in Harford County, Maryland, about 35 miles northeast of Baltimore.
Type of hike:	Loop; day hike.
Total distance:	4.5 miles.
Difficulty:	Easy.
Elevation gain:	Minimal.
Best months:	Year-round.
Permits:	None.
Maps:	USGS Conowingo Dam, Aberdeen, Maryland.

Finding the trailhead: From Baltimore, drive north on Interstate 95, drive north 21 miles to the Maryland Highway 155 exit west to Churchville. In 1.5 miles, turn right onto MD 161 North, then in 0.25 mile turn right onto Rock Run Road. Follow signs for historic sites for 4 miles to the trailhead at the river.

Trailhead facilities: Nature center, vending machines.

Key points:

0.0	Trailhead
0.1	Red trail junction
0.6	Views of river
1.5	Farm Road Trail junction; picnic area
2.0	Spur trail to campground
2.5	Spur trail to farm ruins
3.2	Wilkinson Road
3.6	Rock Run Road
3.7	Rock Run crossing; Rock Run Y Trail junction
4.2	Land of Promise Trail junction
4.3	Mansion

The hike: This is a fine hike for young hikers. There is plenty to see without great challenge. Plan to spend some time at the ridge overlook, enjoying the view and giving the eagles a chance to appear.

From the historic area trailhead, walk up Rock Run Road away from the river 175 yards and turn right to enter the woods following the red and blue blazes. The trail passes under hardwoods, especially poplar and chestnut oak, making an easy ascent toward the ridgeline. Beginning at about 0.6 mile and continuing for a few hundred yards are views east across the river. Find a comfortable spot and enjoy the view.

Continuing along the ridge, at 1 mile pass the Silver Spur Trail on the left and begin a slow descent through the woods. In spring, bluebells color the forest floor while dogwood and serviceberry paint the understory bright white. Pass through two narrow hollows, one of which contains a giant

The Susquehanna River is a popular weekend spot for anglers and boaters, as well as hikers and bicyclists. PHOTO COURTESY OF MARYLAND DNR

Susquehanna State Park Loop

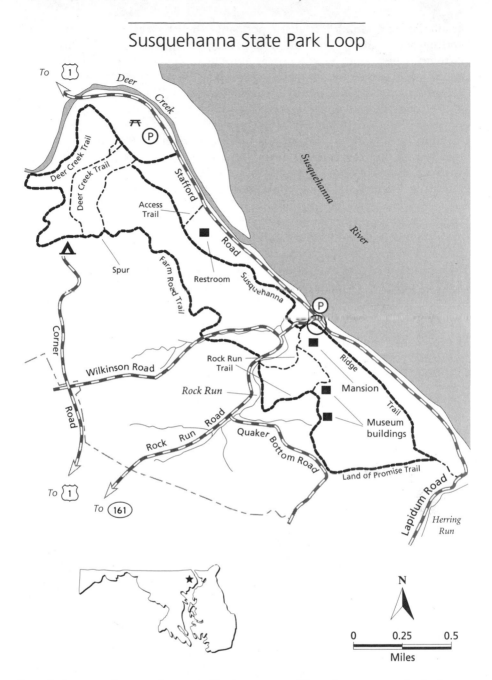

beech tree, and come to a small pine grove. The pines were planted as a lumber crop in the early nineteenth century; the remnant trees are now dying back as the hardwoods mature and block the sun from the pines.

Just beyond the pines, enter an open meadow where a post, at 1.5 miles, marks the junction with the blue-blazed Farm Road Trail. Visible from the post is a trail leading straight ahead over a small bridge; this trail leads to the picnic area. Going left at the post onto the blue trail, follow the farm road back into the woods and walk along a small brook. Walk through a narrow hollow, above which poplar and chestnut oak tower on both sides. At 2 miles, the spur trail to the right leads 0.3 mile to the campground loops.

At the top of the hill, emerge from the woods into a broad field. Following the road, the trail winds around the field under open sky. At 2.5 miles, a spur trail leads left 100 feet to old farm ruins. These ruins are worth taking the time to explore a little. If you are looking for a short hike, you can continue beyond the ruins another 75 feet to the red trail at the junction noted earlier and then turn right to return to the trailhead.

Back on Farm Road Trail, continue around the field another 250 yards, enter the woods, and slowly descend. Cross Wilkinson Road at 3.2 miles, then Rock Run Road at a point about half a mile above the trailhead, at 3.6 miles. Just beyond Rock Run Road, cross Rock Run and turn left onto the Rock Run Y Trail. For an extended hike, you can turn right onto Rock Run Y Trail, taking a left at the fork and doubling back on Land of Promise Trail.

At 4.2 miles, Rock Run Y Trail ends at Land of Promise Trail, an interpretive path that visits the historic sites along the river. Go left, passing a mansion at 4.3 miles and other historic sites, and reach trailhead parking.

Options: You can make this a short 2.5-mile hike by taking the cutoff at the farmstead ruins to return to the red trail and then heading south back to the trailhead, retracing your earlier steps.

Special considerations: The blazes in the park tend to be confusing. Old red blazes, no longer functional, still mark trees. The blue route seems to appear and disappear because blue is used both for a park trail and for Mason-Dixon Trail, a long-distance trail that passes through the park. Follow the directions provided here closely. The trail passes adjacent hunting lands. Check with the park office for details when hiking during hunting season. The hike described here starts at the historic area, but you can start at the picnic area just as easily.

Camping: Yes, at the campground; registration and a fee are required.

For more information: Susquehanna State Park.

30 Wincopin–Quarry Run Loop, Savage Park

Highlights:	A short ramble along the Middle Patuxent River to its confluence with the Little Patuxent River, then upstream, with a return via an abandoned quarry road. Most of the hike follows the streams closely.
Location:	This trail is located in Howard County, Maryland, about 20 miles north of Washington, D.C.
Type of hike:	Loop; day hike.
Total distance:	2.4 miles.
Difficulty:	Easy.
Elevation gain:	Minimal.
Best months:	Year-round.
Permits:	None.
Maps:	USGS Savage, Maryland.

Finding the trailhead: From the Capital Beltway, drive north on Interstate 95 (from the Baltimore Beltway, drive south on I-95). Exit onto Maryland Highway 32 South. In 2.5 miles, turn south on U.S. Highway 1. In 0.25 mile, turn right on Howard Street, then left on Baltimore Street. Take the third right onto Savage Road. In 1 mile, go left on Vollmerhausen Road. The trailhead is 0.25 mile on the left, just over the bridge.

Trailhead facilities: Kiosk with map of area.

Key points:
- 0.0 Trailhead
- 0.4 Quarry Run Trail second junction
- 0.5 Overlook
- 0.8 Old-growth forest
- 1.3 Bridge abutment; left turn
- 1.7 Dam ruins
- 1.9 Left ascent
- 2.1 Overlook; Wincopin Trail junction

The hike: Within minutes of setting off, you will be transported from one of the most densely populated suburbs in America to a lovely woodland along two former mill streams. Sandwiched between I-95 and US 1, Savage Park is the population epicenter of the Baltimore–Washingon corridor; however, you would never know it on this hike (except for the intrusion of highway noise in the first 0.5 mile).

From the Vollmerhausen Road Trailhead, follow the red blazes along a paved trail that turns to a dirt footpath in 100 yards. Enter the woods, and follow the trail past one left junction with the green-blazed Quarry Run Trail; then, at 0.4 mile, go left at the second junction with Quarry Run Trail.

At 0.5 mile, an overlook offers a vista over the Middle Patuxent bottomland. This is an especially nice view in winter, when the trees are leafless. Descend

Wincopin–Quarry Run Loop, Savage Park

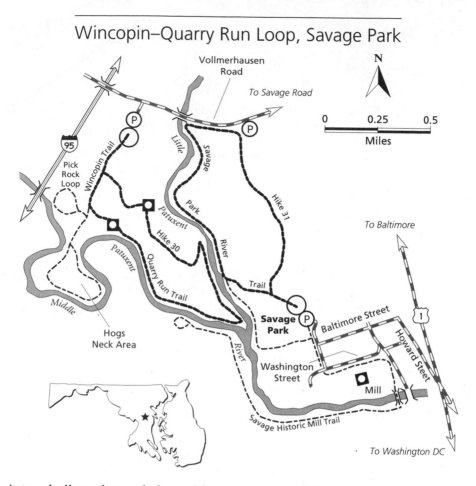

into a hollow along a ledge, with sycamore and hickory above, and over a footbridge, coming to the river's edge.

Turn left, walk downstream, and enter an area of old-growth woods of shagbark hickory and chestnut oak, at 0.8 mile. Watch for copperheads in the shallow water along the river bank. There are some great fishing spots along the trail. To avoid erosion when accessing the river, follow existing paths to the river.

At 1.3 miles, come to an old bridge abutment that offers an open view of the river and, in winter, of the confluence. Go left onto an old dirt road, still following Quarry Run Trail, and walk along the Little Patuxent, which is about 50 yards to the right and will emerge in about a hundred yards. Following the dirt road under a canopy, at 1.7 miles come to the ruins of a concrete dam abutment; a bench here offers a nice view of the river and a shady rest stop.

At 1.9 miles, the dirt road continues left and the green trail switches back abruptly left and climbs. Do not continue straight on the dirt road. A sign 200 hundred yards farther warns hikers: "No trespassing. Violators will be shot; survivors will be prosecuted."

An old dirt road once used by those planning for a dam on the Little Patuxent now serves as a woodland walking path.

Ascend steeply for 150 yards; then, as the trail finds level ground, come to a wooden overlook to the right. Just beyond, the green trail ends at a T intersection with the red-blazed Wincopin Trail, at 2.1 miles. Turn right to return to the trailhead.

Special considerations: The first 0.5 mile of the hike is within loud earshot of I-95, which intrudes upon the remote feeling of the river bottomland. Still, considering its proximity to the few million residents of the Baltimore–Washington corridor, it provides a quick escape into the woods. Nearby Savage Mill is a great spot for an after-hike lunch.

Camping: None.

For more information: Howard County Recreation and Parks.

31 Savage Park River Trail

See map on page 114

Highlights:	A quiet stream valley walk along the Little Patuxent River, with an upland return on a rail-trail.
Location:	This trail is located in Howard County, Maryland, about 20 miles north of Washington, D.C.
Type of hike:	Loop; day hike.
Total distance:	2.5 miles.
Difficulty:	Easy.
Elevation gain:	Minimal.
Best months:	Year-round.
Permits:	None.
Maps:	USGS Savage, Maryland.

Finding the trailhead: From the Capital Beltway, drive north on Interstate 95 (from the Baltimore Beltway, drive south on I-95). Exit onto Maryland Highway 32 South. In 2.5 miles, turn south on U.S. Highway 1. In 0.25 mile, go right on Howard Street and then left on Baltimore Street. Take the fifth right into Savage Park. Follow the access road to the northwest corner of the ball fields. The road ends at a parking area. The hike begins at the paved pathway into the woods.

Trailhead facilities: None.

Key points:
- 0.0   Trailhead
- 0.2   Access trail to river trail
- 1.3   Vollmerhausen Road
- 1.7   School; rail-trail
- 2.3   Asphalt access trail

The hike: Anyone living within quick access of I-95 in the Baltimore–Washington corridor can be out the door and on the trail in less than 30 minutes to enjoy a quiet stroll along the Little Patuxent River. There is not a lot to describe in this hike because it is, after all, a short jaunt through a suburban wood. Still, it is a splendid walk for a late afternoon when you have the desire for a woodland hike but not the time to get away.

The hike begins behind the ball fields, following an asphalt path to a campfire ring used by youth groups. At the ring, at 0.2 mile, a dirt footpath provides access west to the river trail. Descend through the trees, and hike upstream.

From here, it is an unremarkable but lovely hike along the narrow, shallow Little Patuxent. At about 1 mile, the trail breaks from the river, climbs a little, then descends again to the stream just before reaching Vollmerhausen Road, at 1.3 miles. Turn right and walk along a sidewalk, watching for a wide rail-trail leading right just before the parking lot of Patuxent Valley Middle School, at 1.7 miles. Follow the paved trail for about half a mile.

At 2.3 miles, rejoin the asphalt path just below the fire ring; turn left and ascend to return to the trailhead.

Options: For a short 1.5-mile walk along the Middle Patuxent River on a wide path, park at Savage Mill, a renovated collection of shops and galleries. Walk down Foundry Street 200 yards to a footbridge. Follow the trail along the river, and retrace your steps to return. Be sure to stop at the French bakery!

Special considerations: The rail-trail that provides the return loop is part of a planned path to Elkhorn Lake.

Camping: None.

For more information: Howard County Recreation and Parks.

32 Cash Lake Loop, Patuxent Research Refuge

Highlights:	A walk through pine forests and near marshy lakes in an area that is arguably the wildest place within 75 miles of Washington, D.C.
Location:	Patuxent Research Refuge is located in Prince Georges County, about 10 miles north of Washington, D.C.
Type of hike:	Loop; day hike.
Total distance:	4.7 miles.
Difficulty:	Easy.
Elevation gain:	Minimal.
Best months:	September–May.
Permits:	None.
Maps:	USGS Laurel, Maryland.

Finding the trailhead: From Washington, D.C., travel north 3.5 miles on Maryland Highway 295, the Baltimore–Washington Parkway (from Baltimore, travel south). Exit onto Powder Mill Road East. In 2 miles, turn right into the National Wildlife Visitor Center. The hike begins from the parking area in front of the center. The trailhead is adjacent to the exit road, just where the road leaves the parking area.

Trailhead facilities: The visitor center has wonderful exhibits on wildlife habitat and many other topics important to world ecology. There are restrooms, water fountains, and a gift shop featuring natural history books.

Key points:
- 0.0   Trailhead
- 0.9   Junction with Laurel Trail and then Valley Trail
- 1.5   Cash Lake Trail junction
- 2.5   Loop Trail junction
- 3.0   Goose Pond; Cash Lake Trail junction
- 3.4   Valley Trail junction

Cash Lake Loop, Patuxent Research Refuge

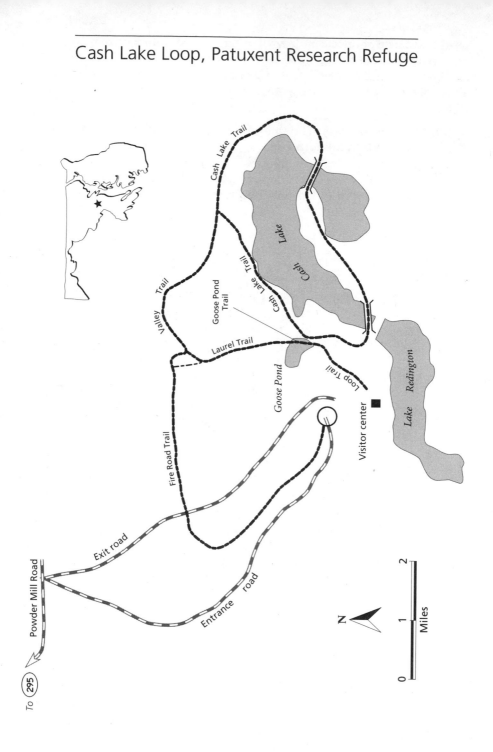

4.0   Laurel Trail junction
4.4   Goose Pond

The hike: Follow the wide path through pine and hardwoods dominated by beech and red oak. The odd-looking cuts in the forest you pass are remnants of research on the regeneration of forest species. Cross the exit road and reenter the woods; at 0.9 mile, cross the old telegraph road and reach the junction with Laurel Trail.

Just beyond, go left on the Valley Trail, traveling east. Mature oaks and beech tower above, and a woodland valley opens below. From here, it is hard to believe the Baltimore–Washington Parkway is less than 2 miles away. At 1.5 miles, turn left onto Cash Lake Trail, crossing two wooden bridges and then a fishing pier right off the trail. This is a great spot to watch the amazing variety of waterfowl and the activities of beavers building their lodges. To make the most of your viewing, consider stopping at the visitor center to purchase a booklet to help you identify the birds.

Rounding the lake to the south side, cross a bridge over an arm of the lake. This area may be closed in rainy season; obey the signs and retreat in order to prevent damage to the fragile environment. Cross another bridge, now just below the visitor center, and turn right onto the paved Loop Trail at 2.5 miles.

Enter the woods on Goose Pond Trail, traveling through a forested wetland and reaching Goose Pond at 3 miles. Plan to spend some time here. There are waterfowl coming and going and interesting demonstrations of wildlife management practices.

From the north end of Goose Pond, turn right onto Cash Lake Trail's north section, which offers outstanding views of the lake en route to a junction with Valley Trail at 3.4 miles, at the spot at which you entered the lake area earlier. Turn left to retrace your steps on Valley Trail.

Turn left onto Laurel Trail, at 4 miles. In late spring, this short trail is alive with the sounds of songbirds and the bloom of the countless mountain laurels along the trail. The trail is also known to local birders as Robbins Trail; it is dedicated to Chandler S. Robbins, a researcher whose more than 50 years of work greatly expanded the knowledge of migratory birds and the effects of habitat fragmentation on their populations.

At 4.4 miles, pass Goose Pond on your right, and continue on Goose Pond Trail to Loop Trail for a return to the visitor center.

Options: This hike is described using a loop that utilizes Valley Trail, first traveling easterly and then, after circling Cash Lake, traveling westerly to the top of Laurel Trail. This is done to include the beautiful Laurel Trail in the circuit, as well as the north section of Cash Lake Trail. A nice 3.3-mile hike can be created by returning directly to the visitor center after visiting Goose Pond.

Special considerations: Because the area is managed for wildlife research, Zero Impact Hiking is especially important. No picnicking is allowed along the trail. Bring some water, but leave the food at home. Spring rains and heavy rains sometimes make the south section of Cash Lake impassable.

When this is the case, after visiting the fishing pier, retrace your steps to continue your hike via the northern section.

Camping: None.

For more information: Patuxent Research Refuge, National Wildlife Visitor Center.

33 Jug Bay Natural Area Loop, Patuxent River Park

Highlights:	An easy walk through the marshes and woodlands along the western shore of Maryland's Patuxent River in the Jug Bay Natural Area.
Location:	Patuxent River Park is located in Prince Georges County, Maryland, about 25 miles east of Washington, D.C., and 9 miles southeast of Upper Marlboro, Maryland.
Type of hike:	Loop; day hike.
Total distance:	3 miles.
Difficulty:	Easy.
Elevation gain:	Minimal.
Best months:	Year-round.
Permits:	A special-use permit is required for all activities. The cost of an annual permit is $5 for Prince Georges and Montgomery County residents; $10 for all other residents of Maryland. Daily permits also available for $5 for Prince Georges and Montgomery County residents and $7 for everyone else.
Maps:	USGS Bristol; Upper Marlboro, Maryland.

Finding the trailhead: From Maryland Highway 4 east of Upper Marlboro, travel 2.5 miles south on MD 301. Turn left on Croom Station Road; go 1.5 miles, and turn left on Croom Road. Proceed 1.5 miles, and turn left on Croom Airport Road. The park entrance is 2 miles ahead. Turn left into the park, and go 1.5 miles to parking at the park office.

Trailhead facilities: Chemical toilets, water.

Key points:
- 0.0   Trailhead
- 0.2   Black Walnut Creek
- 0.5   Heron's Nest Observation Platform
- 0.7   Swann Point Trail junction
- 1.1   Chapman Trail junction
- 2.0   Entrance road crossing
- 2.7   Entrance road junction

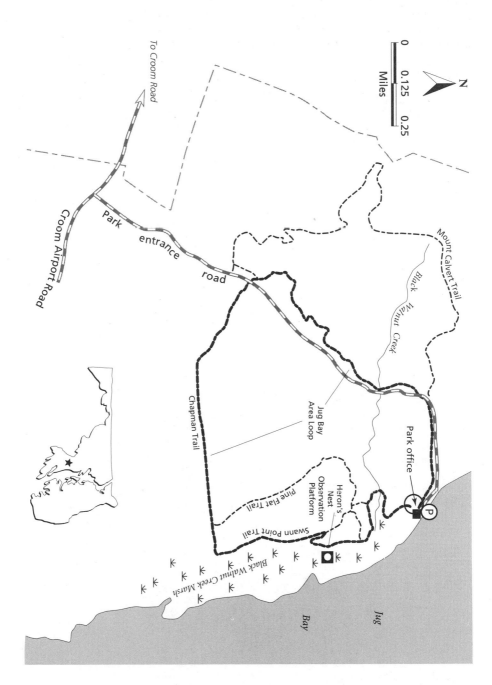

The hike: The Patuxent River Park encompasses an extended preserve system of natural lands winding through seven Maryland counties that border the 111-mile waterway. The Jug Bay Natural Area, a 2,000-acre portion of the greenway's Mid-Patuxent Region, preserves tidal marshes, vast stands of wild rice, heron and osprey nesting areas, and hardwood forests. Hiking the trails and boardwalks of Jug Bay takes you into the lively Black Walnut Creek Marsh on the edge of the Patuxent and through the thick woods on the river's western shore.

The trail begins behind the parking area, to the left of the dirt road leading to the Duvall Tool Museum. At 0.1 mile, the trail bends right, traveling behind the Tool Museum, and then bends left and crosses Black Walnut Creek at 0.2 mile. On a series of long boardwalks, walk through the marsh along the creek, past a tree house–like observation tower in an oak wood and then back into the marsh.

The boardwalk gives you a great feel for the marsh. It passes directly through the wetland over the muddy, mossy roots of trees, and by abundant ferns, the shapely leaves of arrow arum, arrowhead, and pickerelweed, and the big, broad-leaved skunk cabbage. There are also cattails and impressive stands of wild rice, whose grassy stalks can grow up to 10 feet tall. From these open areas in the marsh, listen for the rustle of muskrats in the grasses or watch for osprey fishing the river waters. And enjoy the views across the Patuxent to the forests and farms on the far shore.

The boardwalk splits at the viewshed. Turn right here, and travel along the edge of the tall, waving grasses of wild rice on the left. The trail then returns to the forest on upland soil. Stay left at the junction, and continue to a short spur on the left, at 0.5 mile, leading to the Heron's Nest Observation

The easy terrain and abundant wildlife combine to make Jug Bay a fine family hike.
PHOTO COURTESY OF MARYLAND DNR

Platform, a great place to view the marsh, the river, and several heron and osprey nesting sites. If you have the time, it is also a great place to watch for some of the other birds common on the Patuxent. At least 254 species have been sighted at the park, and the local nesters include least bitterns, blue-winged teals, Virginia rails, kestrels, hummingbirds, kingfishers, thrushes, warblers, and many more birds of water, forest, and field.

Return to the trail and continue through the forest, climbing briefly as the path bends right. As the trail levels at the junction at 0.7 mile, turn left, walk 10 yards, and then turn left again on Swann Point Trail, a wide path through the upland woods. Continue to the junction at 1.1 miles, and turn right on Chapman Trail. For the next 0.9 mile to the junction with the entrance road, Chapman Trail is a shady "forest tunnel" through stands of maple, oak, and poplar, with beds of fern blanketing the forest floor. At 1.7 miles, the path bends right—where it is marked as a horse trail—and continues to the road at 2 miles.

Cross the entrance road and turn right on the horse trail, a narrow path that winds through the woods parallel to the road. The trail joins the road for a few yards at 2.6 miles, then bends back into the woods before returning to the road at 2.7 miles, where a horse trail breaks to the left. Continue on the road back to the trailhead with views of the river through the trees on the left.

Options: There are 8 miles of trails in the Jug Bay Natural Area. From the loop trail, you can access footpaths that travel along the marsh or south to Merkle Wildlife Sanctuary. Canoeing and fishing are also popular.

Special considerations: As in all wetland areas, insects can sometimes be pesky at Jug Bay. Bring insect repellent.

Camping: Primitive tent camping for organized groups is available.

For more information: Patuxent River Park.

34 Cedarville State Forest Loop

Highlights:	An easy walk through deep, shady forest along the banks of meandering creeks.
Location:	Prince Georges County, Maryland, about 20 miles southeast of Washington, D.C.
Type of hike:	Loop; day hike.
Total distance:	5.1 miles.
Difficulty:	Easy.
Elevation gain:	Minimal.
Best months:	Year-round.
Permits:	None.
Maps:	USGS Bristol, Maryland.

Cedarville State Forest Loop

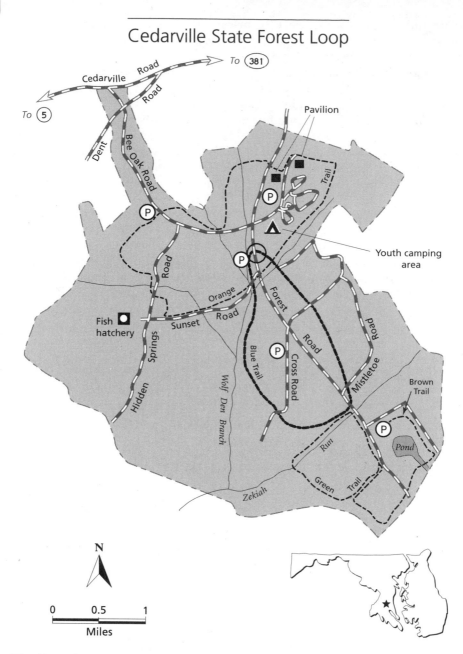

Finding the trailhead: From Interstate 495, travel 11.5 miles south on Maryland Highway 5 to Cedarville Road. Turn left, go 2.1 miles, and turn right into Cedarville State Forest on Bee Oak Road. Follow Bee Oak Road 1.7 miles to Forest Road. Turn right on Forest Road, and go 0.1 mile to the trailhead parking on the right.

Trailhead facilities: Chemical toilet.

Key points:

0.0 Trailhead
0.3 Wolf Den Branch crossing
1.7 Cross Road
2.9 Zekiah Run; Forest Road
3.3 Mistletoe Road
4.1 Cross Road
4.6 Wolf Den Branch crossing
4.9 Forest Road

The hike: On a hot summer day, there is a drowsy, languid feel to the creeks that run through Cedarville State Forest. They are known to rise up and wash out bridges, and if their steeply cut banks are any measure, they have done so often. But there is little babble to these sandy-bottomed brooks. Walking by them through stands of hardwood and meadows of lush ferns, you are more likely to hear a breeze in the trees than a wild torrent. It is a good setting for a tranquil afternoon stroll.

From the trailhead parking area, enter the woods and turn left onto the blue-blazed trail, which you will follow for the entire loop. Descend to placid Wolf Den Branch, staying left where the orange-blazed trail goes right, and follow the trail through the woods along the creek. The trail soon joins a white-blazed trail, becoming wide and gravelly, and then crosses Wolf Den Branch, at 0.3 mile.

After crossing the stream, follow the creek bank through oak and hickory groves with understories both dense and spacious. The fern-covered meadows are especially pleasing and can give the woods the lush feel of a Pacific Northwest rain forest. They may also have provided cover for moonshiners who once used the area's creeks and streams for their subtle art.

A hiker enjoys the spring blossoms in the Maryland Woods. Photo by T. Moore, Maryland DNR

Passing a big, fat-stumped oak at 1 mile, climb slightly—a rare and enjoyable occurrence in this region. At 1.2 miles bend left, splitting off from the white-blazed trail, which continues straight ahead.

Leaving the moist woods by the creek, proceed through stands of pine on a drier, sandier trail. At 1.7 miles, cross Cross Road and follow the blue blazes through an area used for target shooting. The trail bends gradually left, traveling through young oak and pine, and meets Zekiah Run, another languid watercourse. Turn left and cross Forest Road, at 2.9 miles.

Continue through the woods, crossing Mistletoe Road at 3.3 miles and Cross Road at 4.1 miles. After Cross Road, enter a beautiful stand of mature oak and poplar. Travel through the venerable trees slowly to enjoy their stature; then turn right, following blue blazes, and continue to Wolf Den Branch, at 4.6 miles. Cross the bridge over the creek. Reach Forest Road at 4.9 miles. Follow the road briefly; then cross and reenter the woods, following orange and blue blazes back to the trailhead.

Options: There are 14 miles of trails at Cedarville State Forest. For a long hike, you can include most of them in a bigger loop.

Special considerations: During hunting season, check with forest managers to see which trails are safe and open.

Camping: Youth group camping is permitted with advance registration.

For more information: Cedarville State Forest.

35 American Chestnut Land Trust Loop

Highlights:	This is a rare place of mixed hardwoods, bottomland swamp, and creeks making their way to the Chesapeake Bay. The land is privately owned and permanently protected by the American Chestnut Land Trust. There is indeed a mature chestnut tree on the grounds.
Location:	The trails are within the American Chestnut Land Trust's holdings, located in Calvert County, Maryland, about 40 miles southeast of Washington, D.C.
Type of hike:	Loop; day hike.
Total distance:	3.5 miles.
Difficulty:	Easy.
Elevation gain:	Minimal.
Best months:	September–May.
Permits:	None.
Maps:	USGS Prince Frederick, Maryland.

American Chestnut Land Trust Loop

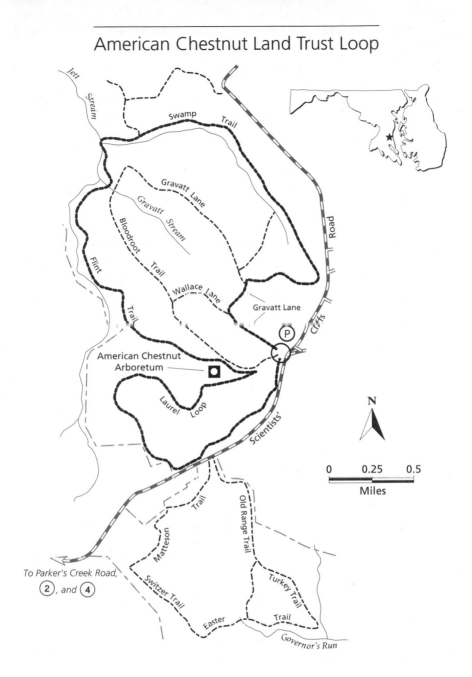

Finding the trailhead: From Baltimore, drive south on Interstate 97 to U.S. Highway 301; then go south 19 miles to Maryland Highway 4. Turn left, and drive 23 miles to Prince Frederick. From Washington, D.C., exit onto MD 4 from the Capital Beltway (I-495); go 32 miles to Prince Frederick. From the intersection with MD 231 in Prince Frederick, go 4 miles south on MD 4 (also MD 2 here). Turn left on Parkers Creek Road, cross MD 765, and turn right onto Scientists' Cliffs Road. In about a mile, the main entrance parking is on the left.

Trailhead facilities: There is a privy about a quarter of a mile into the hike. The American Chestnut Land Trust offices are across the street from the trailhead.

Key points:
- 0.0 Trailhead
- 0.5 Side path to mature American chestnut
- 0.7 Boardwalk
- 1.1 Gravatt Stream crossing
- 2.0 Laurel Loop; American Chestnut Arboretum
- 2.4 Scientists' Cliffs Road

The hike: Follow Gravatt Lane, a wide dirt farm road, 400 yards to its junction with the yellow-blazed Swamp Trail. Turn right, and follow the trail as it winds between mature hardwoods. Walk along an old farm road beneath mature hardwoods. Most of the area was cleared for agriculture, so these big trees are just entering second-growth maturity. At 0.5 mile, a path leads left to a lone, mature American chestnut. Once the tree that defined eastern North America, it was said a squirrel could hop from chestnut to chestnut from Maine to Georgia without touching the ground. Chestnut forests spared from farming or settlement were destroyed by a blight introduced from Asia in the early 1900s.

A 900-foot boardwalk, starting at about 0.7 mile, navigates you over swamp and stream crossings. Cross Gravatt Stream at 1.1 miles. Gravatt Lane climbs from here 1 mile back to the trailhead. Continue on Flint Trail, following the red blazes, to the American Chestnut Arboretum, a research area planted with hybrid American chestnuts, at 2 miles. Turn right onto Laurel Loop. In spring, the woods here are alive with mountain laurel; you would guess you were 70 miles west in the Maryland foothills. Turn left onto Scientists' Cliffs Road at 2.4 miles, and follow the road for 100 yards before getting back on the trail. Part of this trail crosses through, and at times borders, private property. Please respect this property to retain the privilege of the trail experience.

Options: There is a 1.5-mile hike along the east loop on the other side of Scientists' Cliffs Road. Parking for the loop is 0.25 mile back on Scientists' Cliffs Road. The trails, blazed in green, are well marked.

Special considerations: The landscape and hiking trails here are a real marvel of private initiative on the part of the American Chestnut Land Trust. Hikers are urged to support this nonprofit organization by sending a donation to the address shown in appendix A.

Camping: Camping is available under prearranged circumstances, such as work exchanges. Contact the office for details.

For more information: American Chestnut Land Trust.

Land between the Bays

36 Possum Hill Loop, White Clay Creek State Park

Highlights:	A short hike through the hilly fields and forests of the piedmont in northern Delaware.
Location:	White Clay Creek State Park is in northwestern New Castle County, Delaware, 3 miles north and northeast of Newark.
Type of hike:	Loop; day hike.
Total distance:	2 miles.
Difficulty:	Easy.
Elevation gain:	Moderate (trail drops and rises about 150 feet).
Best months:	Year-round.
Permits:	Parking fee: $2.50 for Delaware residents, $5 for out-of-state residents.
Maps:	USGS Newark West; Newark, East, Delaware.

Finding the trailhead: From Newark, follow Paper Mill Road 1.4 miles north to Possum Park Road (Delaware Highway 72 joins Paper Mill Road here from the right), and continue on Paper Mill Road 1.1 miles north to Smith Mill Road. Turn left and proceed 0.3 mile to the Possum Hill parking area.

Trailhead facilities: Chemical toilet.

Key points:
- 0.0   Trailhead
- 0.5   DE 72
- 1.0   View to left
- 1.5   Two stream crossings

The hike: The Possum Hill Area of White Clay Creek State Park is a small, vest-pocket preserve, which is hemmed in by roads and is not contiguous to the rest of the park. It is nevertheless a wonderful oasis of open fields, flowering hedgerows, rolling hills, and impressive stands of poplar, beech, and oak—a natural gem amid the buzz of a fast-growing, populous area.

The well-marked trail begins just a few steps from the parking area at the crest of a hill. Descend the hill on the edge of a wooded thicket with a field of unmowed grass on the right. In spring, the thicket is alive with honeybees, butterflies, and blossoms.

Marked with red blazes, the trail soon bends left, crossing a short footbridge and cutting through the thicket, then turns right and proceeds on a field edge with the hedgerow on the right. Songbirds are drawn to this edge environment, and there are plenty here singing from the branches of †

Possum Hill Loop, White Clay Creek State Park

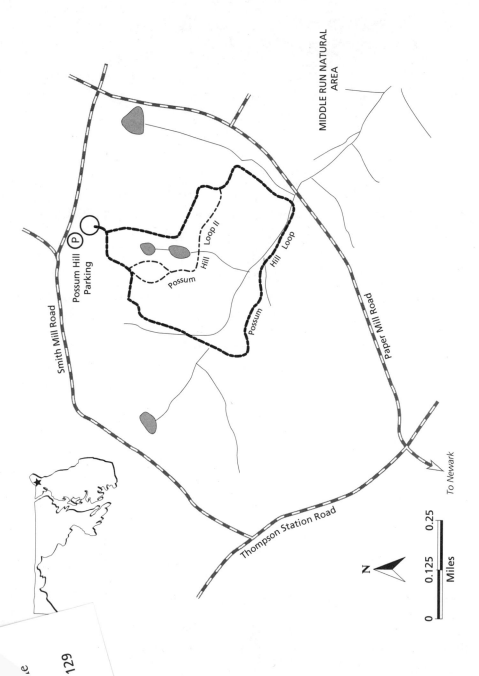

MIDDLE RUN NATURAL AREA

Possum Hill Loop II

Possum Hill Loop

Possum Hill Parking

Smith Mill Road

Paper Mill Road

To Newark

Thompson Station Road

N

0   0.125   0.25
Miles

tulip trees and the sassafras saplings. Across the open field sits an old, weathered shed, a remnant of a hillside farm.

At 0.3 mile, veer left and travel along the forest edge. The birdsong is still various and lovely here, and the tulip trees are tremendous, standing thick trunked and tall in a spacious grove with broad-leaved boughs shading the field. Continue on the edge of the woods, passing a thicket on the left and then bending right into the woods, entering the cathedral grove of poplars.

In 25 yards, follow the red blazes and turn left, where an alternate loop trail bends right (you will draw close to DE 72). Turn right at 0.5 mile. Unfortunately, cars can be seen and heard for about 0.2 mile while the trail parallels the road. But at 0.7 mile, the trail turns right, away from the road, and rises easily above a creek, quickly leaving the loud world behind.

Traveling west, as the trail drops and rises, cross a creek and rise. Although the climbs are easy, they are about as tough as you will find in Delaware, where the hilly piedmont country here on the northern border of the state rises to no more than 600 feet. As you climb the gentle ridge at 1 mile, to the left is a nice view of the creek bottom woods, looking lush and mature compared to the younger, thinner trees in the recovering forest along the trail to the right.

Emerge from the woods briefly, turn right (back into the trees), descend to two stream crossings at 1.5 miles, and then ascend. At the top of the rise, turn right into a field of tall grass and wildflowers surrounded by woods. Turn left, and travel briefly along the edge of the field, where asters, clover, and goldenrod are common, then back into the woods, where you may see a pileated woodpecker hammering away at a dead snag.

Continue on the grassy trail, passing an old barn and a post-and-rail fence on the left. Follow the path as it bends right around the bottom of a field and then turns left, ascending the hill to the trailhead.

Options: To lengthen your stay in the woods, add the park's 1-mile loop trail to your hike.

Camping: None.

For more information: White Clay Creek State Park.

37 Earth Day Trail, Middle Run Natural Area

Highlights:	A short, easy loop in a peaceful, wooded stream valley, not far from the bustling college town of Newark, Delaware.
Location:	Middle Run Natural Area is 2.5 miles north of Main Street, Newark, in northwestern New Castle County, Delaware.
Type of hike:	Loop; day hike.
Total distance:	1.4 miles.
Difficulty:	Easy.
Elevation gain:	Minimal.
Best months:	Year-round.
Permits:	None.
Maps:	USGS Newark West, Delaware.

Finding the trailhead: From Newark, travel north on Paper Mill Road 1.6 miles to Possum Park Road (Delaware Highway 72). Turn right, then immediately left onto Possum Hollow Road (Road 299). Proceed 0.4 mile to Middle Run Natural Area on the left. Follow the gravel entrance road around a big bend 0.4 mile to the parking area.

Trailhead facilities: None.

Key points:
- 0.0 Trailhead
- 0.1 Creek crossing
- 0.7 Clearing near Fox Den Road (Road 326)
- 1.3 Creek crossing

The hike: The Middle Run Natural Area is a vest-pocket park surrounded by a wave of new suburbs rolling over the hills of northwestern New Castle County. Miraculously, it preserves not only the open fields of the area's old croplands but also mature forests and stream valleys. Earth Day Trail runs along the wooded hillsides and rocky banks by a creek that winds through the preserve. Walking the path, listening to the creek spill and the birds sing, it is easy to forget that a busy university is just a couple of miles away—which makes this trail a perfect getaway for the residents and workers of this populous area.

From the parking area, enter the woods through mature oaks, tulip trees and sassafras saplings. In spring, the short umbrella leaves of mayapple carpet the forest floor by the footpath as it descends to the creek bottom. Walking downhill, you can feel the creek coming before you see it, as the air grows more cool and moist with each step.

At the creek, at 0.1 mile, turn left and then right across the bridge over the slow running stream. From here there is a nice view of the wooded hillside you just descended. In the spring and summer, with the trees leafed

Earth Day Trail, Middle Run Natural Area

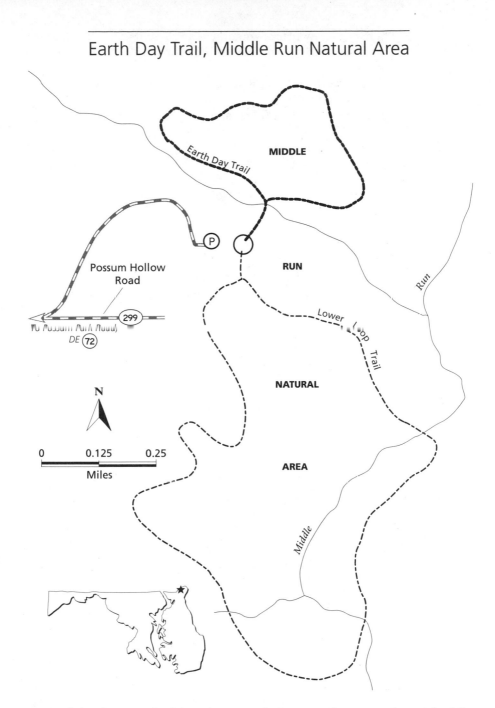

out and the ferns springing up among their roots, these woods can feel far from the suburbs.

After the bridge, the trail bends left and follows the creek. It is shady along the splashing brook, and the path winds through ferns and mayapples, over roots and rocks, and by beds of broad-leaved skunk cabbage in soggy depressions. There are many places you may want to pause and listen to the slow-moving water, especially if you have come for a lunchtime stroll on a workday.

Leave the creek and make a gentle ascent to the right on a wooded hillside that can feel magical in afternoon light. As you clear the ridge, the view through the dense forest is delightful. Just ahead is an open field. The trail cuts through a thicket and turns right, tracing the edge of the woods up to the only blemish on this otherwise pleasant walk, a pile of dumped stumps that look a bit like the remnants of a clearcut. Turn right at the far edge of the stumps, and pick up the trail as it continues on the high edge of a grassy field, at 0.7 mile. You can see Fox Den Road at the bottom of the field in the distance.

Stay along the edge of the field as it bends right along the edge of the woods. Birds are active here, flitting in and out of the trees, and woodchucks scramble for cover at your approach. Following the trail marker, turn right into the woods and descend the hillside to the streambed. With the stream on your left, follow the trail to the spur, also on the left. Cross the creek at 1.3 miles, and climb the hillside to the trailhead.

Options: There are several trails in the Middle Run Valley, including the 2.7-mile Lower Loop Trail, which traverses the open, rolling hills south of Earth Day Trail.

Special considerations: Earth Day Trail is a footpath, but some of the area's trails, including Lower Loop Trail, are open to cyclists.

Camping: None.

For more information: New Castle County Department of Parks and Recreation.

---

38 White Clay Creek Preserve Loop

Highlights:	A hike through the floodplain woodlands along White Clay Creek.
Location:	White Clay Creek State Park is in northwestern New Castle County, Delaware, about 4 miles from Newark.
Type of hike:	Loop; day hike.
Total distance:	2.1 miles.
Difficulty:	Easy.
Elevation gain:	Minimal.
Best months:	Year-round.
Permits:	Entrance fee, $2.50 for Delaware residents, $5 for out-of-state residents.
Maps:	USGS Newark West; Newark East, Delaware.

White Clay Creek Preserve Loop

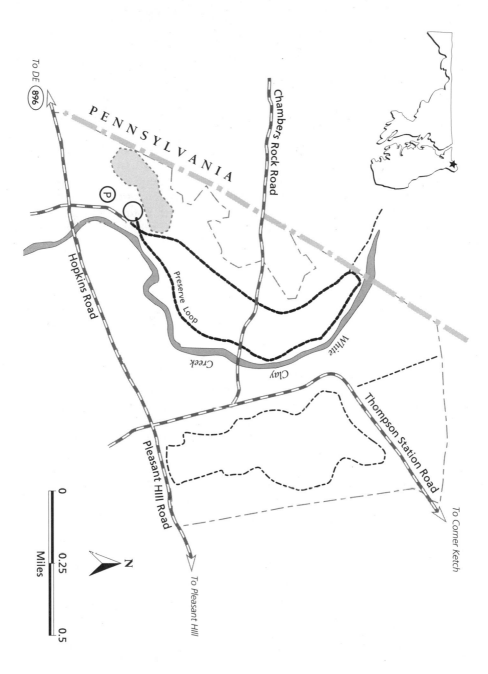

Finding the trailhead: From Newark, travel north on New London Road (Delaware Highway 896) 2.9 miles to Hopkins Road. Turn right on Hopkins Road, and proceed 1 mile to the preserve entrance on the left. Follow the dirt road 0.3 mile to the nature center parking area on the left.

Trailhead facilities: Restrooms, nature center.

Key points:
- 0.0 Trailhead
- 0.6 Chambers Rock Road
- 1.2 Pennsylvania state line
- 1.6 Chambers Rock Road

The hike: White Clay Creek Preserve Loop is the only trail in the several sections of the park that actually runs along White Clay Creek, following its banks to the Pennsylvania line, where the preserve extends across the border. The area is popular with birders, botanists, and other naturalists who like "going afield." A public journal at the nature center notes sightings of the many local birds, including red-bellied, downy, and pileated woodpeckers, osprey, kingfishers, wild turkeys, cedar waxwings, and blackburnian warblers, to name a few. There are also wild geraniums, wood violets, trillium, and trout lily in abundance, as well as mammals large and small. And recent reports say there is even a mountain lion roaming this neck of the woods!

From the parking lot, cross the dirt entrance road and enter the woods on the marked hiking trail. The path travels along the banks of the creek in the shade of maples, oaks, poplars, and sycamores, making even a midsummer walk a refreshing experience. The water is slow moving, splashing easily along, and birdsong rings from the branches of the big, old trees.

Pass by a field edge full of darting butterflies in summer, and continue along the stream's still, sunlit pools and running torrents to Chambers Rock Road, at 0.6 mile. As you approach the road in the heat of summer, the smell of hot tar mixes with the sweet and snaky smell of the creek. The trail splits as it comes to the road. Go left, cross the road, and then turn right on a grassy path, following blue blazes. Continue across the parking lot and onto a mown path that bends left along the edge of a field, under the bowing branches of sycamores and a chorus of birdsong.

Follow a woodland edge, with the field and a border of young trees on the left. To the right are bigger, more mature trees and the now-slow, still creek. Leaving the field, the path plunges into deep forest and continues along the stream. Follow the trail as it bends left where rapids shoot over the rocks beneath the stone ruins of an old bridge, and continue to the Pennsylvania state line at 1.2 miles.

At the Pennsylvania state line, the blue blazes can appear to point straight ahead. Turn left here, and proceed on a wide path marked by a white arrow on a brown post. You are now traveling on the western slope of the creek valley.

At 1.6 miles, leave the woods, cross Chambers Rock Road again, and continue on a wide path, with a wooded thicket on the right and open fields on the left. As you walk along in open country, watch for red-winged

Creative planning has helped create suburban wildlands in Delaware and Maryland.
PHOTO COURTESY OF MARYLAND DNR

blackbirds perched in the tall grasses or for the blossoms of Queen Anne's lace and goldenrod.

The trail bends left into the woods at the edge of the field, passes through a gate, and continues back to the trailhead on a dirt road that winds downhill, passing near private property. Please stay on the trail.

Options: You can continue into the Pennsylvania section of the preserve on a 3-mile trail that follows the east branch of White Clay Creek to London Tract Road.

Special considerations: Pets are permitted in some areas of the park, but they must be leashed. Check the signs at the trailhead or inquire at the contact station. Some trails are closed during the hunting season.

Camping: None.

For more information: White Clay Creek State Park.

39 Whitetail Trail, White Clay Creek State Park

Highlights:	A hike on the rolling hills of Delaware's piedmont through meadows, old fields, and impressive woodlands.
Location:	The Walter S. Carpenter Recreation Area of White Clay Creek State Park is in northwestern New Castle County, Delaware, 2.6 miles north of Newark.
Type of hike:	Loop; day hike.
Total distance:	3 miles.
Difficulty:	Easy.
Elevation gain:	Minimal.
Best months:	April–November.
Permits:	Entrance fee, $2.50 for Delaware residents, $5 for out-of-state residents.
Maps:	USGS Newark West; Newark East, Delaware.

Finding the trailhead: From Newark, travel north on New London Road (Delaware Highway 896) 2.6 miles to the entrance of White Clay Creek State Park's Walter S. Carpenter Recreation Area on the right. Turn right into the park, and proceed 0.2 mile through the fee booth to the picnic area parking.

Trailhead facilities: Restrooms, water, picnic area, telephone.

Key points:
```
0.0   Trailhead
0.7   Millstone Trail junction
1.5   U-turn
2.0   Wells Lane
```

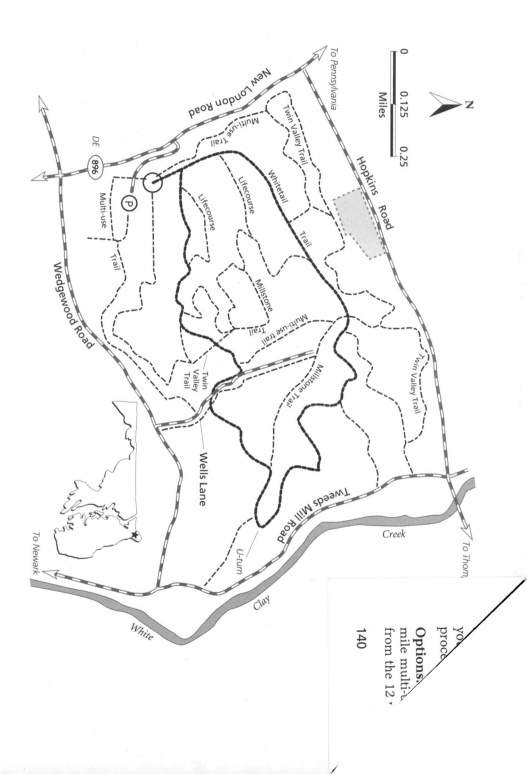

Whitetail Trail, White Clay Creek State Park

you
proce
Options.
mile multi-
from the 12

The hike: One of several sections of White Clay Creek State Park, the Walter S. Carpenter Recreation Area lies to the west of White Clay Creek's floodplain, its gently rolling hills rising up from the valley. Like the other small parcels of the preserve, the landscape is a mixture of old fields, thickets of honeysuckle, blackberries, saplings, and stream-laced woodlands with wonderful groves of beech and tulip trees. When you are finished hiking in the woods here, the preserve's shady picnic area and disc golf course make this area a great place for an all-day family outing.

From the trailhead just north of the parking area, follow Whitetail Trail, which is marked with a white arrow in a blue blaze. It is a wide grassy path passing by hedgerows and open meadows. The trail bends right at a red marker. Travel up the hill past the junction with the Life Course fitness trail, and continue along the hilltop overlooking the fields and forests rolling down to White Clay Creek.

Passing through a thicket on the hilltop, you may see a blue blaze on the left. Do not go left. Continue to follow the white arrow in the blue blaze straight across the hilltop. Just ahead is a bench beneath an apple tree with more nice views of the creek valley.

At 0.7 mile, the red-blazed Millstone Trail breaks off to the right. Proceed through a picnic area into the woods following the blue markers. The trail bends right, descends a hill, and then bends left. This begins a wonderful stretch through an impressive grove of tulip trees. As you follow the trail down to a stream crossing and on to the 1-mile marker, stop and survey the stately tulip poplars, so called for the bright, yellow-orange flowers that bloom on their high branches each spring. The tallest hardwood in North America, tulip trees grow up to 200 feet tall in the southern Appalachians. This stand does not reach that height, but it is glorious nonetheless.

The trail bends right at the mile marker and rises slightly, climbing through a young forest, and then descends, widening and winding, to a U-turn, at 1.5 miles. Follow the sharp bend to the right; then proceed 200 yards and turn left where the red- and yellow-blazed trails join the path. From here, the trail travels through mature forest again. Walking the rolling ridge above a streambed, peer into the dense canopy below and through the boughs of immense old trees.

Passing through a sycamore stand, reach Wells Lane at 2 miles. Turn right, and proceed on the road past a house on the left; then turn left onto a gravel path to the edge of a field. Pass the multi-use trail on the right, and continue around the bend to the left.

At a trail junction at 2.2 miles, with Millstone Trail on the right and Twin Valley Trail on the left, follow the blue-blazed path straight ahead. Climb through the woods to another field and turn right, following the path along the bottom edge of the field, where groundhogs lumber into the tall grass as pass. Enter the woods, following the trail as it bends to the right, and d on the wide, grassy path back to the picnic area and the trailhead.

There are several footpaths winding through the park, from a 5- trail to a 1.5-mile fitness trail. Create long or short circuits s of trails.

The Whitetail hike of White Clay Creek State Park is aptly named. PHOTO COURTESY OF MARYLAND DNR

Special considerations: Observe signs regarding pets; they are permitted in some areas of the park but must be kept on a leash.

Camping: None.

For more information: White Clay Creek State Park.

40 Hidden Pond Trail, Brandywine Creek State Park

Highlights:	A walk on the rolling, wooded slopes and the narrow floodplain of the Brandywine Valley. The hike includes a walk through Tulip Tree Woods, one of the few old-growth forests in the state.
Location:	Brandywine Creek State Park is in northern New Castle County, Delaware, 3 miles north of Wilmington.
Type of hike:	Loop; day hike.
Total distance:	2 miles.
Difficulty:	Easy.
Elevation gain:	Minimal.
Best months:	Year-round.
Permits:	Entrance fee during the summer and on weekends and holidays in the spring and fall: $2.50 for Delaware residents, $5 for others.
Maps:	USGS Wilmington North, Delaware.

Finding the trailhead: From Delaware Highway 52 in Wilmington, travel 2.4 miles on DE 100 to the intersection with Adams Dam Road (DE 92). Turn right on Adams Dam Road, and proceed 0.2 mile to the entrance of Brandywine Creek State Park on the left. Turn left after the fee booth, and go 0.5 mile to the parking area at the nature center.

Trailhead facilities: Restrooms, water, telephone, nature center.

Key points:
- 0.0 Trailhead
- 0.3 Indian Springs Trail junction
- 0.4 Old Field Trail junction
- 0.7 Brandywine Creek
- 1.0 Hidden Pond
- 1.4 Meadow
- 1.7 Tulip Tree Woods

The hike: A hike in Brandywine Creek State Park can be a revelation. Just a few miles from Delaware's largest city, the park and the elegant stone walls that define it evoke another century. In fact, the stone walls themselves are from another time, built by Italian stonemasons late in the 1800s when a member of the prominent du Pont family farmed the rolling hills. Older still is Tulip Tree Woods, a 24-acre stand of old-growth poplars, some 200 years old and up to 80 feet tall. Most venerable of all, perhaps, is Brandywine Creek, a river that has supported human settlements for more than 12,000 years. You can walk on all these hallowed grounds on an easy 2-mile hike on Brandywine Creek State Park's Hidden Pond Trail.

Hidden Pond Trail, Brandywine Creek State Park

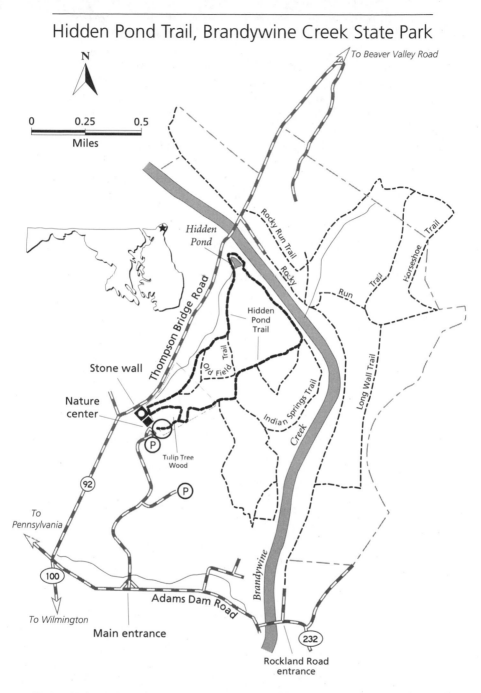

N

0   0.25   0.5
Miles

To Beaver Valley Road

Hidden Pond

Rocky Run Trail

Horseshoe Trail

Rocky Run Trail

Hidden Pond Trail

Thompson Bridge Road

Old Field Trail

Stone wall

Nature center

Indian Springs Trail

Long Wall Trail

Creek

Tulip Tree Wood

P

P

92

To Pennsylvania

100

To Wilmington

Adams Dam Road

Brandywine

Main entrance

232

Rockland Road entrance

Enter Tulip Tree Woods behind the nature center. Most stands of old-growth forest in the region are in private hands, but here you may walk among the giants. As the great botanist Donald Culross Peattie says, there is nothing overwhelming about the splendor of the tulip tree, "but rather something joyous in its springing straightness, in the candle-like blaze of its sunlit vers, [and] in the fresh green of its leaves, which...are forever turning and rustling in the slightest breeze."

The trail travels beneath the grand old trees through a spacious understory, with an open field and one of the park's stone walls visible through the trees to the right. Follow the white blazes as the trail winds through the woods, and turn right at an unmarked junction. Proceed downhill through a younger forest to the Indian Springs Trail junction at 0.3 mile. Here, Indian Springs Trail (blazed yellow) goes right. Turn left, and proceed on the grassy path to the junction, at 0.4 mile, where the red-blazed Old Field Trail continues straight ahead. Turn right.

The trail climbs through the woods, then descends through a forest thick with snags and thickets. Pass the footbridge on the right, and continue your descent to Brandywine Creek. This is a nice place for a break. In the shade of the sycamores that bend over the slow-moving creek, you can watch fish in the shallows and listen to a chorus of birdsong ringing from the surrounding woods.

At 0.7 mile, turn left at the creek and travel north along its banks. Walking the valley floor, see deep forest and rocky outcrops on the steep slope to the left and, to the right, the meadows and creek-side trees across the river. Continue straight ahead where the trail bends right, at 1 mile, and make the short circuit around Hidden Pond, which is small enough to dry into a puddle in the summer.

The loop trail rejoins the white-blazed trail, bending right and traveling upland through the woods. At 1.4 miles, the path bends right again into a meadow alive with butterflies in the spring and summer. Stay to the right along the edge of the meadow where the red-blazed trail breaks to the left, and continue straight ahead into the woods. You will soon enter the north side of Tulip Tree Woods. Continue through the forest to the edge of the park, make a U-turn at the stone wall, and then follow the footpath through the woods back to the trailhead.

Options: There are 12 miles of intertwining trails in Brandywine Creek State Park, providing great opportunities for walking many different loops.

Special considerations: Pets are permitted in some areas of the park but must be kept on a leash.

Camping: None.

For more information: Brandywine Creek State Park.

41 Rocky Run Trail, Brandywine Creek State Park

Highlights:	A hike in the deep woods on a steep hillside above Brandywine Creek.
Location:	The hike is in Brandywine Creek State Park's Thompsons Bridge Area, in Northern New Castle County, Delaware, 4 miles north of Wilmington.
Type of hike:	Loop; day hike.
Total distance:	2 miles.
Difficulty:	Moderate.
Elevation gain:	Minimal.
Best months:	Year-round.
Permits:	Entrance fee during summer and weekends in spring and fall: $2.50 for Delaware residents, $5 for out-of-state residents.
Maps:	USGS Wilmington North, Delaware.

Finding the trailhead: From Delaware Highway 52 in Wilmington, travel 2.4 miles north on DE 100 to the intersection with DE 92. Follow DE 92 (Thompsons Bridge Road) 1.4 miles to the Thompsons Bridge Area of Brandywine Creek State Park on the right.

Trailhead facilities: Chemical toilet. Restrooms and nature center are nearby, at the main section of the park.

Key points:
- 0.0   Trailhead
- 0.3   Rocky Run bridge
- 0.5   Multi-use trail
- 1.0   Horseshoe Trail junction
- 1.2   Rocky Run crossing
- 1.9   Thompsons Bridge Road

The hike: The Thompsons Bridge Area of Brandywine Creek State Park sits along the northeast side of Brandywine Creek, where a wooded ridge rises sharply from the river's narrow floodplain. Rocky Run Trail follows the grassy banks of the creek, then climbs the hillside and travels above the valley through dense forest. Just 4 miles from busy Wilmington, the trail takes you into a quiet world where the trees and birds far outnumber the people.

At the south side of the parking lot, follow the bicycle trail into the woods. The path is wide, level, and easy to walk as it travels along the creek-side meadows of the slow-moving, shallow Brandywine Creek on the right. To the left, the wooded hillside rises steeply from the side of the trail.

At 0.3 mile, cross the aptly named Rocky Run just above its confluence with the Brandywine. After crossing the bridge, turn left into the pine woods and take the trail up the hill, following green blazes. Watch closely here—navigating can be a little tricky. At the junction, there is a delta of social

Rocky Run Trail, Brandywine Creek State Park

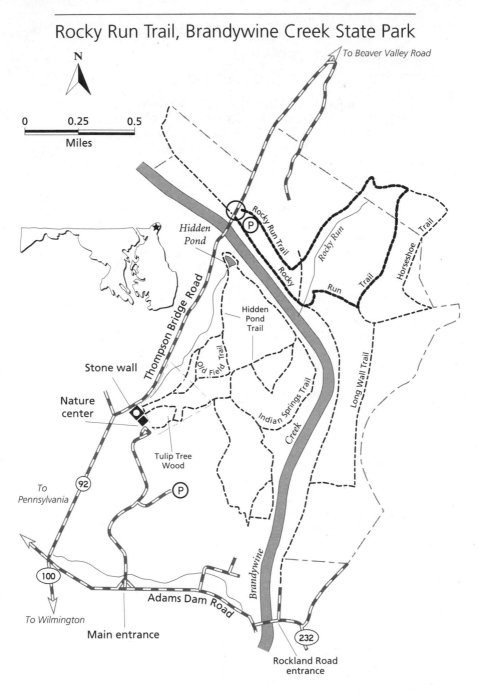

trails that cut into the woods in several directions. In addition, the green blazes blend in with the tree bark, making the blazes hard to spot. Follow the ruts and roots of the middle trail, and pick up the blazes as you enter and cross a meadow and return to the woods. To minimize environmental impacts, stay on the main trail!

A typical "green tunnel" trail of the eastern United States high above Brandywine Creek.

The gullied path meets the multi-use Horseshoe Trail at 0.5 mile. Turn left, following green blazes, and proceed on the trail as it narrows to a pleasant woodland path. Here the forest is dense and lush, and the trail passes through some wonderful stands of mature hardwoods.

At 1 mile, turn left where the path is joined once again by the orange-blazed Horseshoe Trail. Cross Rocky Run—an easy crossing, even without the help of a footbridge. Turn right, climb for 25 yards, and then turn left. The narrow, rocky trail is much like a mountain footpath here as it travels above the lush growth on the banks of Rocky Run.

Continue through a clearing, and cross a trail leading to a youth group camping area. Climb through conifers, and turn right at the crest of the hill, still following green blazes. The trail makes another short climb to the ridge above the Brandywine, then follows the ridge and descends to Thompsons Bridge Road at 1.9 miles. Turn left on the road and then left again into the trailhead parking area.

Options: If you are looking for a longer walk, add sections of Horseshoe Trail and the multi-use trail to your hike.

Special considerations: Pets are permitted but must be kept on a leash.

Camping: A youth camping area is available for official groups only.

For more information: Brandywine Creek State Park.

42 Swamp Forest Trail, Lums Pond State Park

Highlights:	A long but easy hike through the woods around Delaware's largest freshwater pond.
Location:	Lums Pond State Park is in central New Castle County, Delaware, just north of the Chesapeake and Delaware Canal.
Type of hike:	Loop; day hike.
Total distance:	7.5 miles.
Difficulty:	Easy.
Elevation gain:	Minimal.
Best months:	Year-round.
Permits:	None. Park entrance fee: $2.50 for Delaware residents, $5 for out-of-state residents.
Maps:	USGS St. Georges; *Delaware Trails Guidebook*; state park map.

Finding the trailhead: From Interstate 95 near Newark, follow Delaware Highway 896 south 5.6 miles. Turn left on Howell School Road, following Lums Pond State Park signs. Turn right into the park at 0.4 mile. Continue past the park office and fee booth to the Whale Wallow Nature Center on the left.

Trailhead facilities: Restrooms, water, picnic area.

Key points:
- 0.0 Trailhead
- 1.5 Wetlands
- 2.7 Boat ramp access road
- 4.0 Start of fishtail end of pond
- 6.0 Swimming area
- 6.5 Footbridge
- 7.0 Fitness trail junction

The hike: Delaware's largest freshwater pond, Lums Pond, was created in the early 1800s when St. Georges Creek was impounded to supply water for the locks of the new Chesapeake and Delaware Canal. Today, the pond covers 200 acres and is surrounded by oak forests, wetlands, and beaches. Swamp Forest Trail circles the entire pond, following the shoreline and occasionally drifting from the water's edge into the forest and along the edges of a wooded swamp.

From the parking area, cross the park entrance road and proceed to the far right corner of the grassy picnic area to pick up the trail. Cut through a hedgerow of trees on the right, and then turn left onto the Swamp Forest Trail. Cross the spillway and then turn left onto the footpath, which is well marked its entire length.

Follow the pond edge through a forest of red maples, poplars, and sweet gums. The presence of these trees, which tend to be adaptable colonizers of

Swamp Forest Trail, Lums Pond State Park

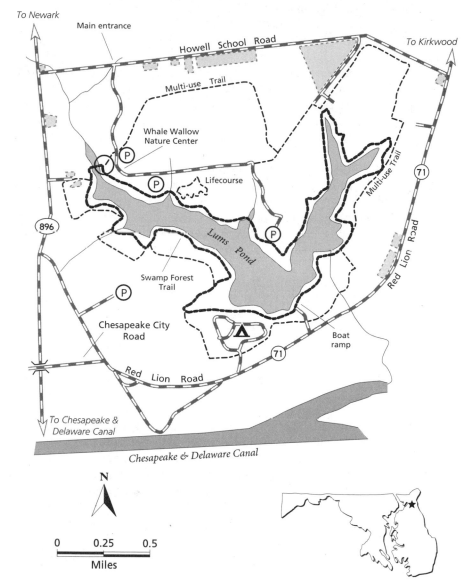

cleared land, shows that the shores of the pond were logged into the beginning of this century, probably supplying the mill powered by the dammed St. Georges Creek. There are also big, old oaks in the pondside forest, and many of the fast-growing poplars have also reached impressive proportions.

Within the first half mile, the trail also crosses wetland areas on a series of boardwalks, where you may see herons or ducks in the tall reeds. At 0.4 mile, the trail bends right, leaving the pond edge and briefly sharing a multi-use trail before turning left and continuing through the woods. At 0.6 mile, follow the trail left, where it briefly shares the multi-use path again and then returns to the edge of the pond.

Continue on the edge of the pond with views across the green rippling water to the woods on the opposite side. It is a nice stretch of easy, pleasant walking. The path travels in the shade of oaks and poplars while the sun glitters on the water. Ducks are often visible on the pond, and another vocal resident, the kingfisher, which favors wooded areas along waterways, may be seen diving for a fresh catch. Anglers here have a lot of luck reeling in bluegill, largemouth bass, catfish, crappie, and pickerel.

At 1.5 miles, after passing many gnawed stumps and fallen trees—the work of several active beaver colonies in the park—the trail breaks from the pond again, tracing a triangle around the edge of a wooded swamp and returning to the shoreline. Here, there are more nice open views across the pond, and on the trailside in early summer there is an abundance of bright orange day lilies.

Cross the boat ramp access road at 2.7 miles, and continue through the woods. For the next 3 miles, the trail follows the pond's doglegged shoreline. The views from the water's edge continue to be nice, and the trail begins to have a wilder feel as you pass the youth camping areas on the right and, at 4 miles, begin tracing a fishtail around the northeast edge of the pond. Perhaps it is the distance from the park's swimming and picnic areas that makes this stretch seem more remote than it actually is—whatever the cause, it is quiet here and feels far from the surrounding civilization.

Midway through the fishtail, from 4.6 to 5.6 miles, the well-marked trail makes several short breaks from the pond and travels along the edge of fields and thickets. At 5.6 miles, the footpath traces the wooded edge of a park recreation area, popular with disc golf players. At the south edge of this area, turn right into the clearing; then, in 25 yards, turn left, following the edge of the playing fields and passing the swimming area on the left. If you are walking on a summer day, this is a great place for a rest and a swim (the swimming area is open only when guards are on duty, during summer daylight hours).

Cut through the beach picnic area on the wide gravel path, and cross a footbridge, at 6.5 miles. The pond is picturesque here, especially to the right where it has the look of a mountain lake. The trail bends left, then follows the shoreline and continues through the boat rental pavilion. After passing the Life Course fitness trail on the right, at 7 miles, cross another footbridge, bend left at the parking area, and continue through the woods along the shore back to the trailhead.

Options: Make a day of your visit to Lums Pond—there are picnic areas, playing fields, a swimming beach, boat rentals, and a nature center.

Special considerations: Hunting is permitted in the park; check with the park office for season information.

Camping: A 68-site camping area is available; it is open April 1 through October 31.

For more information: Lums Pond State Park.

43 Blackbird State Forest Loop, Tybout Tract

Highlights:	An easy walk through natural and managed coastal-plain woodlands in the Blackbird State Forest, famous for its Delmarva Bays—the small upland ponds of mysterious origin that dot the forest's ten tracts.
Location:	Blackbird State Forest's Tybout Tract is in southwestern New Castle County, Delaware, about 15 miles north of Dover.
Type of hike:	Loop; day hike.
Total distance:	2.7 miles.
Difficulty:	Easy.
Elevation gain:	Minimal.
Best months:	February–October.
Permits:	None.
Maps:	USGS Clayton, Delaware.

Finding the trailhead: From U.S. Highway 13, 5 miles north of Smyrna, travel southwest on Blackbird Forest Road (Delaware Highway 471) 2.2 miles to the picnic area parking on the right. The trail begins across Blackbird Forest Road.

Trailhead facilities: Picnic area.

Key points:
- 0.0 Trailhead
- 0.2 Harvest demonstration area
- 0.3 Delmarva Bay (or "whale wallow")
- 0.8 Junction with trail to Sandom Branch
- 1.2 "Star Junction"
- 1.8 Access road
- 2.4 Blackbird Forest Road

The hike: Like many of Delaware's other managed woodlands, much of Blackbird State Forest has been a "forest" for less than 50 years. The trails on the Tybout Tract, for instance, pass through areas that were tilled fields until 1941, when the state acquired the land and began cultivating stands of loblolly and white pine. Along with the managed parcels, there are acres of natural hardwood forests that border the Blackbird trails. These are lovely tracts of red oak and maple, sweet gum and poplar, with the lush understory of flowering trees and shrubs common in wild coastal-plain woodlands.

The trail begins across Blackbird Forest Road from the picnic area, heading into the woods perpendicular to the road. Follow the path through young sweet gums and poplars, the colonizers of fields and clearings, to the junction at the harvest demonstration area at 0.2 mile. Here, you'll see two parcels that were cut and replanted—one in pine and spruce in 1951, the other in hardwoods in 1994—to demonstrate forest recovery. Turn left, and proceed through the young stands to the Delmarva Bay, on the right at 0.3 mile.

Blackbird State Forest Loop, Tybout Tract

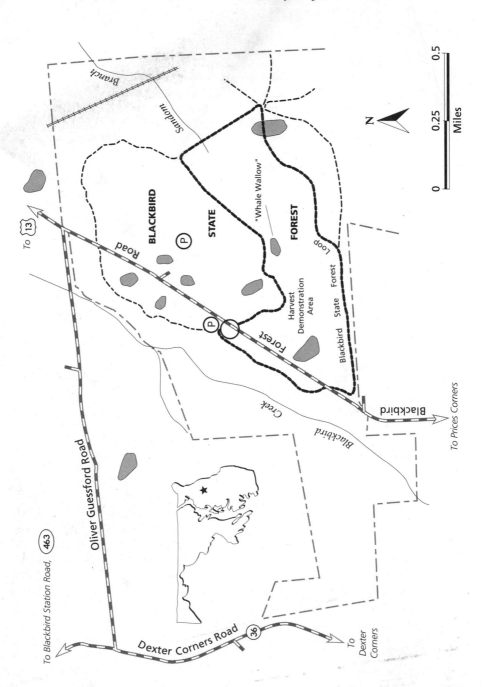

Small upland ponds that harbor a variety of rare plants, th[e]
Bays are also known as Carolina Bays, loblollies, and whale w[allows? The]
latter refers to just one of the many origin stories of these uni[que depres]
sions: legends say "wallowing" beached whales made the po[nds; others]
suggest that meteors created them. Whatever their origins, the bays are
considered a natural treasure and are protected by the Delaware Natural
Areas Preservation System.

At the junction just past the bay, turn right and proceed on a sandy dirt
road with pines on the left and hardwoods on the right. Trails will intersect,
first from the right and then from the left, before you enter a nice stand of
mixed hardwoods. At 0.8 mile, at the red marker, turn right onto the trail to
Sandom Branch, a wetland stream forded by two short bridges. Continue on
the hiking path into the fragrant, wild woods among scrambling squirrels
and lively songbirds.

At 1.2 miles, come to an unusual woodland intersection, a kind of star
with trails radiating in six directions. Simply turn right, following the red-
blazed metal post, and continue through the forest. At 1.4 miles, pass a path
entering from the right. At 1.5 miles, proceed through the junction, bearing
slightly right. Here, still in the wild forest, dogwoods and pink azaleas blossom abundantly in the spring.

The trail bends right at a junction at 1.8 miles and proceeds 100 yards
through a yellow gate to an access road. Turn right onto the crushed rock
road, and continue through shady groves of mixed hardwoods. Listen here

A fallen 200-year-old loblolly pine on a snow-covered trail. PHOTO COURTESY OF BLACKBIRD STATE FOREST

songbirds, woodpeckers hammering away at old snags, and deer bounding among the trees.

At 2.4 miles, the trail intersects Blackbird Forest Road. Turn right, cross the road, and turn left into a triangular picnic area. Cross the picnic area, and pick up the trail on the right just before the yellow gate. The blue-blazed path crosses a marsh area and then meanders through the woods to the trailhead.

Options: There are 80 miles of trails and access roads in the Blackbird State Forest. Pick up maps from the Tybout Tract office, just 0.2 mile from the trailhead, and design your own shuttle and circuit hikes.

Special considerations: Delaware State Forests are open to hunting during the fall and winter. Hiking during the state's deer hunting season is not recommended.

Camping: Yes; a permit is required.

For more information: Blackbird State Forest.

44 Bombay Hook National Wildlife Refuge Loop

Highlights:	A circuit hike on the dirt roads of a Delaware Bay wildlife refuge. Especially rewarding for those interested in watching migrating shorebirds and waterfowl, nesting bald eagles, and resident woodland mammals, such as deer, fox, woodchucks, and raccoons.
Location:	Bombay Hook National Wildlife Refuge is in eastern Kent County, Delaware, about 15 miles northeast of Dover.
Type of hike:	Loop; day hike.
Total distance:	8.3 miles.
Difficulty:	Easy.
Elevation gain:	Minimal.
Best months:	September–May.
Permits:	None.
Maps:	USGS Bombay Hook, Delaware; Refuge Auto Tour Map.

Finding the trailhead: From U.S. Highway 13 north of Dover, travel 3.8 miles east on Delaware Highway 42 to DE 9. Turn left on DE 9, proceed north 1.5 miles, and turn right on Whitehall Neck Road. Go 2.3 miles to Bombay Hook National Wildlife Area, and continue through the entrance 0.2 mile to parking at the visitor center on the left.

Trailhead facilities: Restrooms, water, nature center, gift shop.

Bombay Hook National Wildlife Refuge Loop

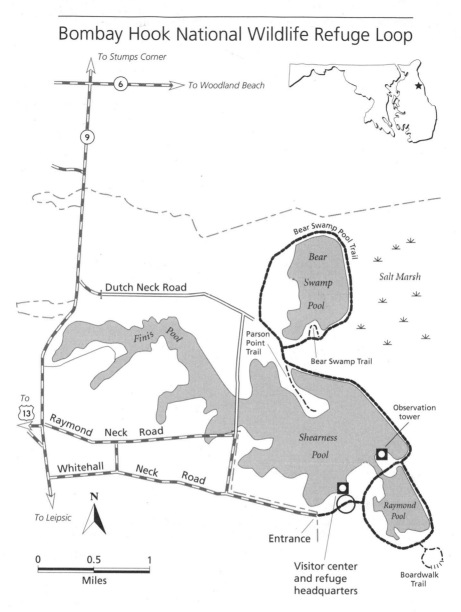

Key points:

0.0	Trailhead
0.2	Raymond Pool
1.7	Shearness Pool
3.1	Parson Point Trail junction
3.3	Split in road; Bear Swamp Pool
3.6	Bear Swamp Trail junction
5.8	Dutch Neck Road (to Allee House)
6.1	Bear Swamp Pool Loop junction
7.7	Raymond Pool
8.1	Spur to visitor center

The hike: Bombay Hook National Wildlife Refuge, on the shores of the Delaware Bay, is one of the best birding sites in the region, rivaling New Jersey's Cape May and Brigantine National Wildlife Refuge. Its extensive salt marsh—at 13,000 acres, one of the largest undisturbed tracts on the East Coast—along with its 3,000 acres of freshwater pools, wooded marshes, upland forests, and cultivated fields, provides diverse habitat for more than 260 species of nesting and migrating birds. And the birds are not alone; 34 species of mammals and a wide variety of reptiles, amphibians, and fish also make the refuge their home. The dikes, dirt roads, and short walking trails that circle and cross the refuge pass through all of the area's landscapes and provide great opportunities for watching wildlife.

Please note before embarking on a trip to Bombay Hook that you may share some of your walk with cars. The dirt roads you will travel are designed for slow-moving automobiles, most driven by avid birders cruising and stopping, cruising and stopping, with binoculars in hand. But serious birding does not really draw a crowd. Hiking here, especially on weekdays, is a lot like walking on an old country road. If that sounds appealing, you should enjoy a day of exploring Bombay Hook.

Pick up the trail—here a gravel road—in front of the visitor center, and turn left into the refuge. At 0.2 mile, turn right and begin a partial loop around Raymond Pool, one of the refuge's freshwater impoundments. Before drawing close to the edge of the pool, at 1.1 miles, you will pass through marshland grasses, meadows, open fields, and stands of sweet gum and red maple, a sampling of refuge habitats clearly favorable to the local birds: their songs and wild flights here seem to be expressions of pure delight.

Proceed around the edge of Raymond Pool with marshland stretching far into the distance on the right. On the flats near Raymond Pool, look for long-legged waders, such as black-necked stilts, ibis, and great blue heron. At 1.7 miles, go right, following signs to Shearness Pool, and continue along the edge of the vast salt marsh. This stretch is prime birding territory. During the fall, Shearness Pool is alive with some 30 species of ducks passing through the refuge. In the spring, look for migrating shorebirds—black-bellied plovers, red knots, and ruddy turnstones—resting and feeding on the mud flats of the marsh. And soaring over the whole scene are the bald eagles that nest in the edge of the woods behind Shearness Pool.

At 3 miles, the trail bends to the left away from the salt marsh, traveling through forest as it passes Parson Point Trail, a 0.5-mile spur into the woodland to the edge of Shearness Pool. If you are up to adding a mile to your hike, Parson Point Trail is a nice walk through the woods, where you may see eagles' nests, black-crowned night herons, wild turkeys, and spring wildflowers such as the jack-in-the-pulpit.

After Parson Point, the road travels briefly through woods and grassland and then splits at 3.3 miles. Go right, and begin a loop around Bear Swamp Pool. At 3.6 miles, another short spur, the 0.3-mile Bear Swamp Pool Loop, takes you to an observation tower on the edge of the pool. It is worth the detour. From the tower, which feels like a tree house set in the branches of the surrounding oaks and maples, there are great views across the mudflats

Bombay Hook is an important protected zone in the Atlantic migratory flyway. PHOTO COURTESY OF BOMBAY HOOK NATIONAL WILDLIFE REFUGE

of Bear Swamp and the salt marsh to the east. In the flats, look for the meandering, crisscrossing tracks of many creatures, from herons and egrets to the peculiar trails of tail-dragging turtles.

Back on the road, continue around Bear Swamp Pool with marsh on either side. At 4.7 miles, the road bends away from the marsh and travels through the woods. Look for deer on the flats to the left or for one of the refuge's resident foxes retreating lazily from a sunny spot in the road into the surrounding forest.

Continue through woods and cultivated fields. At 5.8 miles, at Dutch Neck Road (the road to Allee House), turn left and follow the road to the junction at 6.1 miles to complete the loop around Bear Swamp Pool. From the junction, retrace the road past Parson Point and Shearness Pool to the loop around Raymond Pool, at 7.7 miles. Go straight at the junction with the Raymond Pool Loop. Pass the Shearness Observation Tower on the right and then turn right, at 8.1 miles, and return to the trailhead at the visitor center.

Options: There are short but interesting detours on Parson Point Trail, Bear Swamp Pool Trail, and Boardwalk Trail. You also can create an 11.6-mile round trip by including other roads and trails; see the auto tour map at the visitor center.

Special considerations: The wildlife is abundant on the refuge all year. In summer, bring insect repellent. Pets must be kept on a leash.

Camping: None.

For more information: Refuge Manager, Bombay Hook National Wildlife Refuge.

45 Norman G. Wilder
Wildlife Area Loop

Highlights:	A long, easy walk on dirt fire roads through mature forests and upland swamps in an area managed for wildlife.
Location:	The Norman G. Wilder Wildlife Area is in Kent County, Delaware, about 10 miles southwest of Dover.
Type of hike:	Loop; day hike.
Total distance:	8.2 miles.
Difficulty:	Easy.
Elevation gain:	Minimal.
Best months:	February–August.
Permits:	None.
Maps:	USGS Marydel; Wyoming, Delaware.

Finding the trailhead: From Dover, travel 8.5 miles south on U.S. Highway 13 to Road 32. Turn right onto Road 32, and proceed 0.7 mile to the intersection of Road 108 and Road 240. Go straight on Road 108 (here called Evans Road) 1.1 miles to the stop sign. Turn right, continuing on Road 108 (now called Firetower Road), and go 0.5 mile to the Norman G. Wilder Wildlife Area headquarters on the right.

Trailhead facilities: None.

Key points:
- 0.0   Trailhead
- 0.5   Road 246 (Berrytown Road)
- 1.8   Cow Marsh Ditch
- 3.3   Junction of Roads 250 and 108 (Five Foot Prong Lane and Firetower Road)
- 3.7   Road 249 (C&R Center Road)
- 5.1   Road 248 (Beagle Club Road)
- 7.0   Road 108 (Firetower Road)

The hike: Named for a notable Delaware conservationist and wildlife biologist, Norman G. Wilder Wildlife Area is a preserve managed primarily for hunting. The trails are well-maintained fire roads, closed to vehicles, which pass through fields, forests, and swamps that are protected to provide habitat for game. During the hunting seasons from September through January, a trip here would be ill advised. But throughout the rest of the year, the lengthy trail and the flat, wooded terrain make this a good hike for those who like to walk far and fast.

The trail begins on the dirt road to the left of the office, with the fire tower visible above the trees to the left. Walk between a thicket on the left and a wooded hedgerow on the right where young red maples, sweet gums, and willows shade the path. Pass fields and meadows on the left, and then enter the woods. The trail here is wide, soft, and shady and the forest young

Norman G. Wilder Wildlife Area Loop

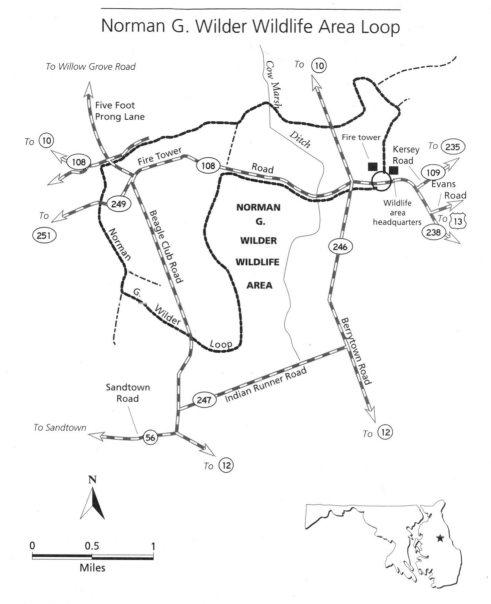

but lush, with holly and bayberry tangling beneath a canopy of loblolly pine, sweet gum, and tulip poplar.

Stay to the left as the trail passes two spurs and a wildlife clearing on the right. Continue through the woods as the fire road makes a horseshoe bend and crosses Road 246, at 1.5 miles. Barricades block automobile access to the fire road on both sides—duck under the gates or step around them.

Past the road, the trail is sandy and the trees beside the lane provide little shade. A hat, sunglasses, and some extra water will help get you through this sunny stretch. And it is worth it. Soon, the trail passes through an impressive stand of mature oaks, some as tall as 100 feet. Also look for honeysuckle and wild azalea.

At 1.8 miles, after passing a clearing on the right, cross Cow Marsh Ditch, which is aptly named. It is a drainage channel that looks every bit like a ditch. The water is a dark, muddy shade of brown that appears rather toxic but is actually colored by the organic content of the soil.

Leaving Cow Marsh Ditch behind, continue on the sunny trail past a side trail on the left, at 2.1 miles, and on to the junction of Roads 250 and 108, at 3.3 miles. Cross Road 250, which enters the intersection from the right, and then cross Road 108. Turn right, and follow Road 108 for about 150 yards on a rutted horse trail; then turn left into the woods on a narrow, shady footpath.

Go straight into the woods, passing a fire road on the right. The trail winds through a holly grove and crosses Road 249, at 3.7 miles. Again a sandy fire road, the trail continues through the woods. At 4.3 miles, a spur shoots off the trail to the left. Soon after, follow the narrow hiking trail that cuts off the road to the left. Be careful here—the trail is not marked and it is easy to miss. If you come to an area of wide-open croplands, you have gone too far.

Once on the shady foot trail, pass through a young pine forest and then cross Road 248, at 5.1 miles. Passing a field on the left, the fire road then makes a long bend to the left and continues through the woods. This is a nice stretch. The trail does not cross a road for nearly 2 miles, and it passes through shady groves of old oaks with honeysuckle and wild azalea winding through the understory.

At 7 miles, the fire road meets Road 108. Turn right, and continue along the roadside. The shoulder is not wide, but the band of grass between the road and the woods gives you enough room to walk safely. If you are with a group, walk in single file. Although roadside walking can be annoying, here it is actually quite pleasant. There is little traffic, and the roadway is bordered by the forest on the left and open fields on the right, where birds are plentiful. Ahead, the fire tower appears on the horizon, where the road passes the trailhead.

Options: There are 16 miles of fire-road trails in the wildlife area. It would be hard to create a longer loop, but you could add some spurs to your walk or plan a shuttle hike.

Special considerations: Use insect repellent during summer.

Camping: Yes, with permission from the wildlife area headquarters.

For more information: Delaware Division of Fish and Wildlife.

46 Killens Pond Loop, Killens Pond State Park

Highlights: A walk around an eighteenth-century millpond through diverse wetland and upland forests.
Location: Killens Pond State Park is in Kent County, Delaware, 13 miles south of Dover.
Type of hike: Loop; day hike.
Total distance: 3.2 miles.
Difficulty: Easy.
Elevation gain: Minimal.
Best months: Year-round.
Permits: None. Fee during summer season and on weekends and holidays in May, September, and October.
Maps: USGS Harrington, Delaware.

Finding the trailhead: From U.S. Highway 113, travel west on Delaware Highway 12 through Frederica and continue 5 miles to Chimney Hill Road. Turn left on Chimney Hill Road and go 1.2 miles to Killens Pond Road. Turn right and, in 0.1 mile, turn left into the park. Continue 0.7 mile on the park entrance road to the parking lot.

Trailhead facilities: Restrooms, water, picnic areas, telephone.

Key points:
- 0.0 Trailhead
- 0.1 Killens Pond Loop junction
- 0.5 Spur to pond view
- 0.9 Murderkill River bridge
- 1.7 Killens Pond Campground
- 2.5 Road 384; boat launch
- 3.1 Killens Pond Loop junction

The hike: Set in the farm country of central Delaware, Killens Pond State Park straddles the boundary between southern and northern forests. Here you will see the loblolly pine and American holly forests typical of the wet, sandy plain to the south as well as stands of mature hardwoods common in the rolling hills to the north. In places on the Killens Pond Loop, the trail itself seems to be the boundary between the two habitats, with the tall pines and dense undergrowth of coastal lowlands on one side and groves of giant poplars and oaks on the other—both, in rather different ways, quite beautiful. Add several nice views of the pond, and you have all the ingredients for an interesting, scenic, and refreshing walk.

The well-marked loop begins beneath the log gateway of Pondside Nature Trail. The pine duff path enters the woods and, at 0.1 mile, meets the trail's return loop. Go right, and continue along with the pond to the left. For the next 0.5 mile, the trail passes through the pine and hardwood forests mingling at the edges of the path. Here, flowering dogwoods and several

Killens Pond Loop, Killens Pond State Park

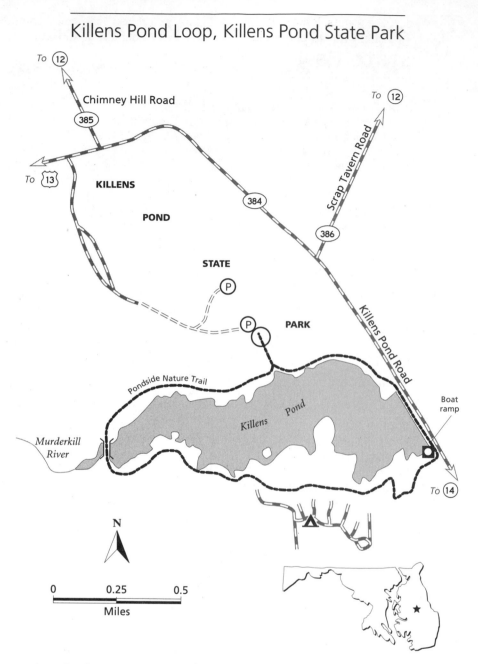

species of oaks migrate between the sweetbay, ferns, and climbing vines of the marsh and the upland stands of poplar. There may not be a better place to experience the diversity of Delaware's woodlands.

At 0.5 mile, at a fork in the trail, you may go left 50 yards for a view of the 66-acre pond. It is worth the detour. In the spring, the pinxter flower, sometimes called pink azalea, blooms abundantly here. And, from the edge of the pond you can gaze over the still water, listen to birdsong, and watch for ducks and cormorants. Back at the fork, bear to the left and continue through a lovely grove of tall, stately poplars. The trunk of one giant, just to the left of the trail, takes two people to reach around!

At 0.8 mile, the trail bends left around the edge of the pond and then intersects a sandy road. Turn left and, at 0.9 mile, cross a bridge over the narrow Murderkill River. Before it was made a millpond in the late 1700s, the Killens Pond area was the floodplain of the Murderkill and the site of several Native American settlements and hunting camps. The river's peculiar name, legend has it, commemorates the massacre of a group of Dutch traders by the local tribe. And the name *Murderkil* is not redundant; the Dutch *kil* is a stream, creek, or channel. From the bridge, the view of the pond and the surrounding marsh forest is quite nice.

Turn left after the bridge. The trail bends along the pond through holly and up a rise to a bench and a view, at 1.1 miles. From a little clearing surrounded by oak and poplar, dogwood and pink azalea, the view and the setting here invite a rest.

Bear left at the fork, following trail markers down the rise and close to the pond. Watch the snags for sunning turtles and perching ducks, and note the dead bald cypress, well drilled by woodpeckers. Continue in the lowlands over boardwalks and then up a slight rise at 1.5 miles to another nice view of the pond.

At 1.7 miles, the trail enters Killens Pond Campground, with the cabins on the right. Continue straight, across an unpaved access road, and head back into the woods on a slope above the marsh. The trail runs through the woodlands behind the campground and, at 2.1 miles, turns right. To the left is a short spur to the pond.

Proceed, winding through hardwoods, to the boat launch at Road 384, at 2.5 miles. Turn left and walk the shoulder over the spillway at the edge of the pond; then turn left through the opening in the post-and-rail fence, at 2.6 miles. Follow the pond edge, on the left, past a canoe rental area and enter the woods on a wide, sandy trail in the shade of loblolly pines. To the right, a short nature trail loops through a stand recovering from a severe winter storm in 1994. From the path, you can see the many trees and limbs downed by five bitter days of ice and wind.

Continue to the fork, at 2.8 miles, and bear to the left following the Pondside Nature Trail sign. After 50 yards, another spur breaks left from the trail to the edge of the pond. Proceed to the right through mixed pines and hardwoods to the entrance spur at 3.1 miles. Turn right, and return to trailhead.

Options: Bring a fishing rod, or rent a canoe and try the Murderkill River Canoe Trail.

Special considerations: Bring insect repellent in summer.

Camping: Primitive and improved sites, in addition to cabins, are available.

For more information: Killens Pond State Park.

47 Prime Hook National Wildlife Refuge Loop

Highlights:	A short walk through coastal forest and wetlands on the western shore of Delaware Bay. A great hike for birders.
Location:	Prime Hook National Wildlife Refuge is in Sussex County, Delaware, 22 miles southeast of Dover and 13 miles northwest of Rehoboth Beach.
Type of hike:	Loop with out-and-back spur; day hike.
Total distance:	1.6 miles.
Difficulty:	Easy.
Elevation gain:	None.
Best months:	October–April.
Maps:	USGS Lewes, Milton, Delaware.

Finding the trailhead: From Delaware Seashore resorts, travel north on Delaware Highway 1, 1.5 miles north of the Broadkill River to DE 16. Go right on DE 16 and, after 1.2 miles, turn left on Road 236 (Turkle Pond Road) into Prime Hook National Wildlife Refuge. Trailhead parking is 1.5 miles ahead at the visitor center.

Trailhead facilities: Visitor center, restrooms, picnic tables.

Key points:
0.0	Trailhead
0.1	Jonathan J. Morris Homestead
0.2	Marsh boardwalk
0.3	Upland forest
0.5	Dike Trail
1.0	Dike Trail turnaround
1.6	Boardwalk trail on return

The hike: Prime Hook National Wildlife Refuge—8,817 acres of fresh and tidal marsh, upland forest, and croplands on the shores of the Delaware Bay—is home to a wonderful array of birds, mammals, and reptiles and is an important stopover for migrating waterfowl. On an easy 1.5-mile stroll on the Refuge Loop, you can see fine examples of each of the coastal habitats as well as of the area's abundant wildlife.

The Refuge Loop begins on Boardwalk Trail, across the parking lot from the visitor center. For the first quarter of a mile, the trail is like a garden path: a wide, grass walkway bordered on both sides by multiflora roses teeming with songbirds, rabbits, and groundhogs.

A short detour to the left, at 0.1 mile, leads to the site of the Jonathan J. Morris Homestead, thought to have been established around 1750. Fruit trees, the bright white stones of the family cemetery, and grassy cropland are all that remain, but in this peaceful setting it is easy to imagine life on the Morris farm.

Prime Hook National Wildlife Refuge Loop

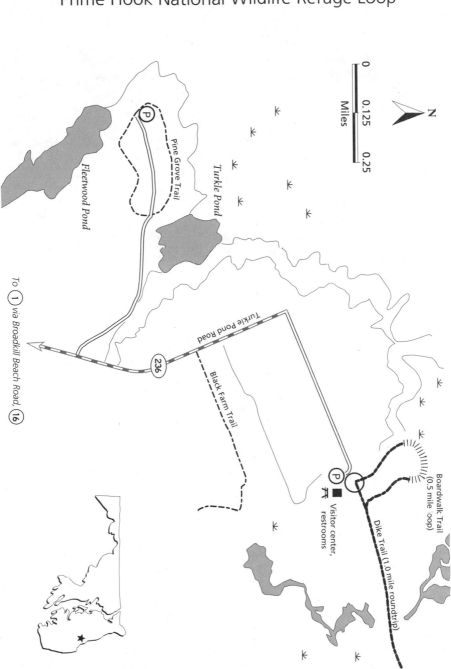

Prime Hook is home to an array of birds and is an important stopover for migrating waterfowl.
PHOTO BY MELISSA NIMMERRICHTER

Continue on the trail under sweet gum trees to the marsh boardwalk, at 0.2 mile, and proceed into wetlands about 50 yards. Where the boardwalk turns right, pause to observe the teeming life of a marsh community. Close to the boardwalk you may see turtles and green frogs sunning or ducks and muskrats swimming by in the shallow water. In the marsh grass, red-winged blackbirds roost and hunting hawks glide just above. And across the vast wetlands, there are forested islands bright with color in the spring and fall.

Proceed on the boardwalk another 50 yards, turn right, and wind through a forest of young maples and sweet gums, groves of holly and an occasional stately pine. The woods here rustle with warblers and thrashers hopping in the brush, blue jays flitting in the branches, and woodpeckers hammering away at rotten trunks.

At the forest edge, the trail enters a field. Turn left on the sandy path, and proceed to the Dike Trail junction, at 0.5 mile. Dike Trail runs a straight 0.5 mile along the edge of another great expanse of marsh. With the woods to the left and the marsh to the right, the birding is excellent. While walking the path, you may see such residents as great blue herons, egrets, hawks, and vultures as well as ducks and shorebirds. And, in the fall, the legions of migrating geese are an annual Atlantic-shore spectacle.

At 1 mile, the trail dead-ends in the marsh. Turn around here and return to the trailhead, perhaps focusing your attention on the woodland birds and wildlife, now on your right.

Options: Pine Grove Trail, a 0.8-mile loop, and Black Farm Trail, a 1.2-mile walk, are two more easy hikes in the Prime Hook wildlands.

Special considerations: Mosquitoes in the late spring and summer make the Refuge Loop a true October-to-April trail. In any season, bring binoculars for birding.

Camping: None.

For more information: Refuge Manager, Prime Hook National Wildlife Refuge.

48 Redden State Forest Loop

Highlights:	An easy walk through a tract of Delaware's largest state forest in the heart of loblolly pine country. A good hike for exploring the natural and cultural history of a relatively new wild and managed forest.
Location:	Redden State Forest is in central Sussex County, 3.5 miles north of Georgetown and about 35 miles south of Dover.
Type of hike:	Loop; day hike.
Total distance:	5 miles.
Difficulty:	Easy.
Elevation gain:	Minimal.
Best months:	Year-round.
Permits:	None.
Maps:	USGS Georgetown, Delaware.

Finding the trailhead: Travel 3.5 miles north from Georgetown on U.S. Highway 113 to Road 565. Traveling east on Road 565, go 0.4 mile and turn right at the entrance to the Headquarters Tract of Redden State Forest. Proceed 0.2 mile to parking at the office.

Trailhead facilities: None.

Key points:
0.0	Trailhead
0.4	Redden Lodge
1.5	State forest harvest area
2.0	Bootlegger ruins
2.3	Wildlife plot
3.5	State forest harvest area
4.7	Forest fire site

The hike: Early in the 1900s, Redden State Forest was not a forest at all. Until the 1930s, the 1,767 acres of woodlands here were primarily open fields and meadows separated by hedgerows—a quail hunting retreat for the executives of the Pennsylvania Railroad Company. All the forest growth, both natural and managed, has occurred since then. A walk through the

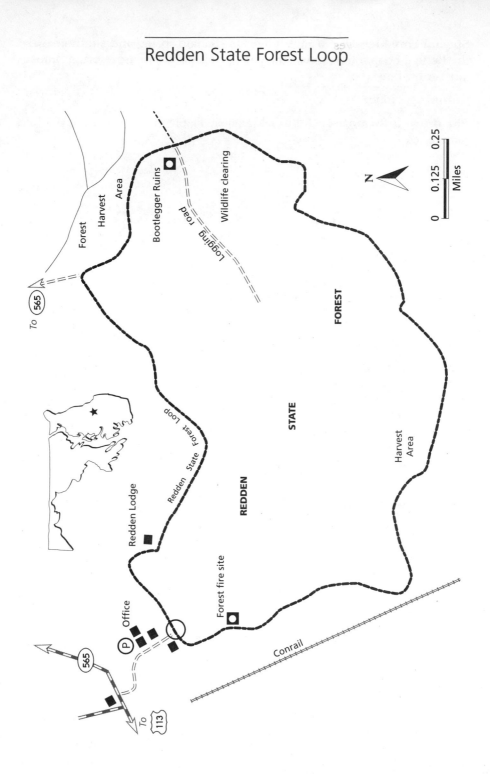

Redden State Forest Loop

Forest Harvest Area

To 565

Bootlegger Ruins

Logging road

Wildlife clearing

N

0   0.125   0.25

Miles

FOREST

STATE

REDDEN

Redden State Forest Loop

Redden Lodge

Forest fire site

Harvest Area

Office

P

565

To 113

Conrail

forest's natural groves of mixed hardwoods and its planted and harvested stands of loblolly pine reveals the young woodland's many layers of human and natural history.

From the parking lot, walk past the state forest office and turn left onto an unpaved access road, following the sign for the Redden Lodge. An educational trail, perpendicular to the road, also begins here. This 0.1-mile path is a good introduction to the area's ecology.

Proceed on the wide, unimproved road through a natural stand of loblolly pine and mixed hardwoods. This is an area of the forest left to develop in its natural state. The canopy of pines, maples, and oaks and the understory of holly and maple and sweet gum saplings are typical of a young forest on the coastal plain.

At 0.4 mile, the trail loops around the Redden Lodge, built in the early 1900s to house the Pennsylvania Railroad's hunting retreats. The lodge was placed on the National Register of Historic Places in 1980 and was renovated in 1995. It is wheelchair accessible and available for meetings, celebrations, and educational programs.

Continue on the wide, sandy trail through pine forest. Although there are some Virginia and yellow pines, the predominant tree throughout the forest is the loblolly pine, a southern species that occurs from east Texas to central Delaware. The tree—used for lumber, plywood, and paper—is the most valuable timber species in Delaware. It is also wonderfully fragrant, musical in the wind, and a provider of a shady home for many woodland creatures.

As you will see at 1.5 miles, clearcutting is the typical method of harvesting loblolly pines. This type of harvest yields a high financial return and, according to forestry officials, mimics natural fire by exposing loblolly seedlings to the direct sunlight they require to mature. However, the method also alters the forest landscape and remains controversial.

Turn right where the trail meets the clearcut, and continue on. The harvest area will be on your left and the uncut forest on the right. As unsettling as the harvest may be, it does provide an edge habitat for birds and animals. As you walk along between woodlands and clearing, you may see hawks and songbirds or a fox retreating into the forest.

The trail soon bends to the right, turning into a refreshing woodland. In season, dogwoods blossom here beneath the tall pines. At 2 miles, the path passes the mossy foundations of two small houses, believed to be the homes of bootleggers early in the century. Whether they supplied the hunting lodge with spirits is purely speculative.

Just past the bootlegger ruins, an old logging road intersects the trail on the right. Continue straight ahead to the "wildlife plot" on the right, at 2.3 miles. The plot is a narrow strip of pasture between the trail and the woods that provides a grazing area for wildlife. At the end of the pasture, stay to the left and turn right where the trail changes from slightly primitive to the harder surface of the access road. Turn left at a short stone post with a yellow blaze.

Continue through pine forest to another harvest area, at 3.5 miles. At 4 miles, the trail bends to the right near the state forest border and, at 4.7

miles, enters an area burned by a fire in April 1995. The fire was caused by a spark from a train on the nearby railroad and burned 209 acres of forest. You will see the charred bark of burned trees and a new generation of loblolly pines taking root in the clearing. The trail turns right at the edge of the clearing and returns to the office and parking area.

Options: Walk the 1-mile educational trail to start or finish the state forest loop.

Special considerations: State forest lands are open to hunting during the fall and winter seasons. The trail is unmarked but easy to follow.

Camping: Primitive camping is available with a permit. No fee is required.

For more information: Redden State Forest.

49 Cape Henlopen State Park Loop

Highlights:	A circuit hike through the diverse landscapes of Cape Henlopen, including marine forest, sand dunes, salt marsh, ocean beach, and bay shore.
Location:	Cape Henlopen is in Sussex County, Delaware, along the Atlantic coast, 1 mile east of Lewes and about 135 miles from Washington, D.C.
Type of hike:	Loop; day hike.
Total distance:	6.6 miles.
Difficulty:	Easy.
Elevation gain:	Minimal.
Best months:	Year-round.
Permits:	None. Entrance fees are collected daily during the summer and on weekends and holidays in spring and fall.
Maps:	USGS Cape Henlopen, Delaware.

Finding the trailhead: From Delaware Highway 1, travel east on DE 9 following signs to the Cape May–Lewes Ferry. Go 5.6 miles and turn right on Cape Henlopen Drive. Proceed 1.3 miles past the ferry terminal on the left to the park's fee booth. Trailhead parking is 100 yards ahead on the left at the Seaside Nature Center.

Trailhead facilities: Restrooms, water.

Key points:
0.0	Trailhead
0.5	Cape Henlopen Drive
1.0	Great Dune Overlook Spur
1.3	Observation tower; Dune Overlook Trail System
1.4	Dune Overlook Trail
1.7	Walking Dune Spur junction

Cape Henlopen State Park Loop

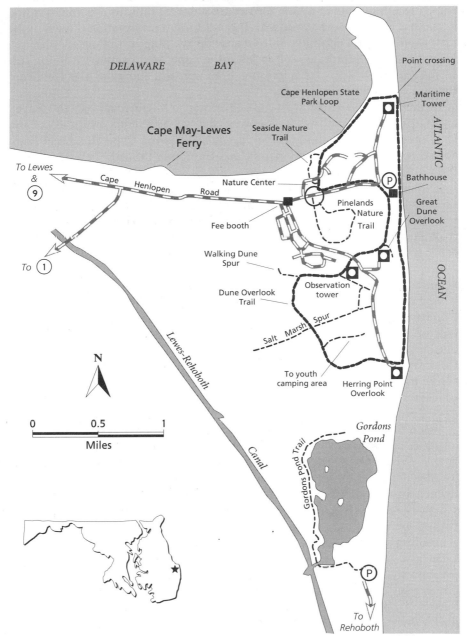

DELAWARE BAY

Cape May-Lewes Ferry

Cape Henlopen State Park Loop

Seaside Nature Trail

Point crossing

Maritime Tower

ATLANTIC

To Lewes & ⑨

Cape Henlopen Road

Nature Center

Fee booth

Pinelands Nature Trail

⒫ Bathhouse

Great Dune Overlook

To ①

Walking Dune Spur

Dune Overlook Trail

Observation tower

OCEAN

Salt Marsh Spur

Lewes-Rehoboth

N

To youth camping area

Herring Point Overlook

0   0.5   1

Miles

Canal

Gordons Pond Trail

Gordons Pond

⒫

To Rehoboth

2.2   Salt Marsh Spur junction
3.3   Herring Point Overlook
4.8   Swimming area; bathhouse
5.5   Point Crossing
5.8   Delaware Bay
6.4   Seaside Nature Trail

The hike: There are few state parks that can match the diversity of Cape Henlopen. On a half-day hike on the park's trails and shorelines, you can wander in the shade of a pine forest; see bitterns, rails, and herons wading in a salt marsh; explore World War II bunkers and observation towers in the sand dunes; spot breaching dolphins while walking in the ocean surf; see migrating hawks and shorebirds from the cape; and examine a living fossil—the ancient, armored horseshoe crab—on the shores of the Delaware Bay.

From the Seaside Nature Center parking area, turn left on the paved hiking-biking path and walk east, with the "parade field" on the right and fragrant pines and beach grass on the left. Cross the Cape Henlopen Point access road and, at 0.5 mile, cross Cape Henlopen Drive before bending to the right into the dunes.

Traveling south, you will hear the surf pounding the shore and see rolling sand dunes held in place by beach grass, heather, and bayberry, all salt-tolerant plants. Pine trees grow in the slopes of the dunes, too, but even they look like shrubs here, "pruned" by the salty winds. Surprisingly, flowering trees also take root in the sandy soil: beach plum, common along the Delaware coast, and a few sturdy, out-of-place dogwoods bloom each spring despite the harsh sea air.

At 1 mile, the trail bends right at the Great Dune Overlook Spur. You may want to take a quick side trip 50 yards to the left, to the overlook, where you will find nice views of the ocean beach. You will also see an old artillery bunker, one of several dug into the dunes of Cape Henlopen to defend the Delaware River during World War II. In fact, much of the state park was an active military base during the war and, as you proceed west (right) on the trail, you will walk through a row of old barracks and pass an observation tower, at 1.3 miles.

Just a few yards to the right of the trail, the 75-foot concrete observation tower is open to the public. Climb the spiral staircase to the observation decks—where GIs scanned for German subs patrolling the North Atlantic—for another great look over the dunes to the roaring surf. At the base of the tower, continue the loop hike following the Dune Overlook Trail System, which bends to the left into scrubby pines. At 1.4 miles, the trail meets Dune Overlook Trail, marked with yellow blazes. Bear right onto an old, crumbling access road, which runs behind the park campground. Traveling west, away from the coast, notice the forest growing more diverse as the soil becomes less sandy and the air less laden with salt. Here, oak, maple, sweet gum, and honeysuckle mix with the durable pitch pines.

At 1.7 miles, follow the yellow blaze left at the Walking Dune Spur junction. Continue through the mixed forest on a crushed clamshell path into a salt marsh. For the next half a mile, the trail cuts through tall marsh grass and along the edge of still pools. In spring, the frogs and red-winged blackbirds are lively and loud, and year-round the air is soaked with the pungent aroma of the tide-soaked mudflats. At 2.2 miles, at the Salt Marsh Spur junction, you may want to turn right and travel 0.25 mile west, deeper into the marsh, to a good spot to watch for herons, bitterns, rails, and hawks.

Continue straight on the Dune Overlook Trail for nice, open views of the wetlands and the surrounding woods.

The trail reenters the pine forest, becoming quite sandy as it bends towards the coast, at 2.7 miles. On a warm day in spring or summer, you may see a beautifully marked eastern hognose snake sunning on an open section of the trail. At 3.3 miles, where a yellow blaze directs you left down a paved access road, cross the road and proceed to the dune crossing on the left, just before the Herring Point Overlook. From the point, have a look down the shore to Gordon's Pond and Rehoboth and then take off your boots or sport sandals before descending the dunes to the beach.

The beach at Cape Henlopen is broad and flat in most places—great for walking. The park, however, does allow SUVs on certain areas of the beach for surf fishing; if walking around a few vehicles parked close to the shore or ducking beneath fisherman's lines will ruin your walk, save this hike for the cooler months.

While you walk north on the beach, the dunes rise on the left to the dramatic bluff of the Great Dune and the ocean rolls in at your feet. For the next 2 miles, you may want to stride with the rhythm of the waves or wander slowly along looking for washed-up blue crabs, razor clams, or iridescent mussel shells. At any pace, watch for sandpipers in the surf, black scoters flying swiftly over the waves and, in the summer, families of dolphins breaching and diving less than 100 yards offshore.

Continuing up the beach, at 4.8 miles pass the park swimming area and the bathhouse, where you will find restrooms and snacks during the summer season. Also in the dunes is the eastern terminus of the American Discovery Trail, a 6,000-mile cross-country path that runs to Point Reyes, California. At the trailhead, there is also a hawk-watch platform. Each spring, volunteers gather here to count migrating hawks, osprey, eagles, and other raptors following the Atlantic coastline.

At 5.5 miles, turn left off the beach and take the Point Crossing, just north of the Maritime Tower, over the dunes to the Delaware Bay. From October to March, you may want to continue 1.4 miles around Cape Henlopen Point to the bay. But from April to October, the point is closed to protect the breeding grounds of the endangered piping plover, a shorebird that nests in shell-lined depressions in the sand close to the dunes. Once common, the birds were hunted to near extinction for their feathers early in the century and are now threatened by coastal development and recreation. Each year, about a half-dozen plovers fledge on the Cape beaches.

From the dune crossing, cross the point parking lot and descend the dunes to the bay shore, at 5.8 miles. Turn left, and follow the shoreline southwest. You will almost surely see spiny, helmet-shaped horseshoe crabs lining the beach. The Delaware Bay region is one of the few places in the world where horseshoe crabs flourish. Each spring, during the high tides of the new and full moons, the crabs spawn on the bay beaches, laying millions of tiny eggs, a ritual they have performed without much change for 250 million years. With equal precision, migrating shorebirds land on the beaches and devour the eggs, building strength for the long flight to their Arctic breeding grounds.

Amazingly, enough crabs and birds survive the arduous spring to repeat the rite each year.

Continue along the bay shore to Seaside Nature Trail, at 6.4 miles. Turn left onto the interpretive trail, and follow it 0.2 mile to the trailhead at Seaside Nature Center.

Options: On the loop hike, you can take the 0.2-mile Salt Marsh Spur or the 0.2-mile Walking Dune Spur to further explore Cape Henlopen's habitats. In fall and winter, add the Cape Point Spur to the hike. Also try Pinelands Nature Trail, a 1.6-mile hike through the Cape's maritime forest.

Special considerations: Wear sport sandals or a lightweight shoe you do not mind stuffing into your pack while you walk the beach. Remember, there may be SUVs on the beach. In summer, bring insect repellent for the salt marsh sections of the trail and sunscreen and sunglasses for the beach sections.

Camping: Yes; a fee is required.

For more information: Cape Henlopen State Park.

---

50 Delaware Seashore State Park

Highlights:	A hike in the surf along Delaware's Atlantic shore.
Location:	Delaware Seashore State Park is in Sussex County, Delaware, about 140 miles from Washington, D.C., and 50 miles southeast of Dover, Delaware.
Type of hike:	Shuttle or out-and-back; day hike.
Total distance:	5 miles one way.
Difficulty:	Easy.
Elevation gain:	Minimal.
Best months:	Year-round.
Permits:	None. Fee collected daily during the summer and on weekends and holidays in the spring and fall.

Finding the trailhead: Traveling south on Delaware Highway 1, 0.5 mile south of Dewey Beach, turn left into Delaware Seashore State Park at Tower Road. Proceed through the fee booth into the parking area. (For a shuttle hike, park your shuttle car 5 miles south on DE 1, in the lot at Indian River Inlet Southeast Day Area.)

Trailhead facilities: Restrooms, bathhouses, and snack bars at Tower Road and Indian River in season; portable toilets at Indian River year-round.

Key points:
    0.0   Trailhead
    0.9   Key Box Road

Delaware Seashore State Park

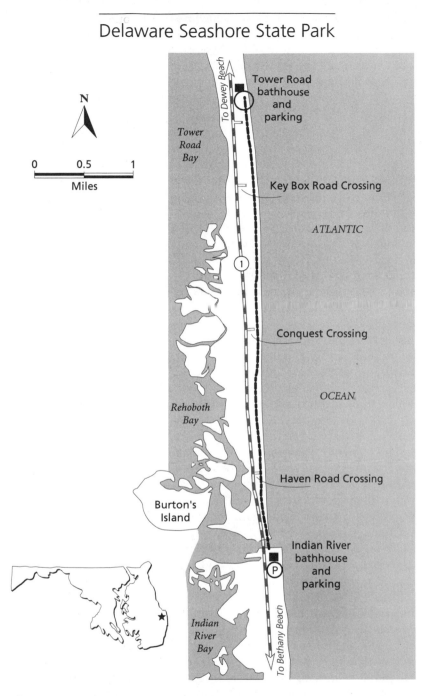

The hike: A walk on the beach in Delaware Seashore State Park presents a lot of unusual options for a hike. You can leave your boots behind and walk barefoot; choose the distance of the hike by parking your shuttle car in one of three places along the shore; and during the summer, end your stroll with a swim in the ocean, a shower, and some soft ice cream. That is not to say you should limit your beach hikes to the summer—the beach is powerful and fascinating in all seasons, and on a day in the winter, spring, or fall you may have the shore to yourself.

Before beginning the hike select a lot for parking your shuttle car. The walk from Tower Road to the Indian River Inlet Bathhouse is 5 miles.

From the south parking area at Tower Road, walk over the dunes through one of the marked crossings. Pause at the crest, and get a feel for the narrow barrier island you will be walking on. From here to just north of Bethany Beach, the Delaware coastline is in most places no more than a quarter of a mile wide. The slim beach is backed by the bulwark of the dunes, held in place in the sea winds by beach grass and islands of stubby pines. The dunes, in turn, give way to salt marsh, and the marsh to the shallow waters of Rehoboth Bay. On your sandy perch above the waves, you can peer across the coastal landscape and quite easily imagine how storms have joined the ocean to the bay.

Descend the dunes to the beach and head south (right). Because there is no beach "trail," you are free to walk knee deep in the surf, along the water's edge, or in the soft sand. Wherever you choose to hike, there is a lot to see. Collectors will find a colorful array of periwinkles and whelks, razor clams and mussels, beach glass and twisted driftwood. Depending on the season, birders can spot long-legged sanderlings stabbing in the sand for a meal, terns diving headfirst for fish, or scoters in swift flight across the water. Others may look to the sea for the fins of porpoise swimming offshore. Whatever draws your eye, the rhythm of the surf, the spacious sky, and the undeveloped beachfront make this is a great place to walk.

As you stroll down the beach listening to the wind and surf, you are likely to come across people fishing at the crossings of Key Box Road (0.9 mile), Conquest Road (2.1 miles), Conquest Crossing (2.5 miles), and Haven Road (4.2 miles). Surf-fishing vehicles are permitted on the beach, and some people park fairly close to the water and secure their poles in tubes pressed into the sand or attached to their front bumpers. You may have to duck under a few lines or walk in soft sand around the vehicles. Or, you may want to stop and watch someone reel in a big bluefish—it is quite a sight.

At the Indian River Inlet at 4.8 miles, turn right at the jetty and cross the dunes through the fenced walkway, to the steps up to the Indian River Bridge. Climb the stairs, turn left, and cross the bridge. From the bridge, one of the highest public places on the Delaware shore, you will have great views out over the Atlantic, of the beach you just walked, and of fishing boats cruising through the inlet on their way to and from the bustling Indian River Marina. You may also see daredevil terns soaring back and forth under the bridge, putting on a show in the teeth of the wind.

Continue over the bridge and down the stairs to the Indian River parking area. If your walk has been a summer stroll, head back over the dunes, take an ocean dip, and finish your day on the beach with a cool drink or a soft-serve cone from the snack bar.

Options: Park at any of the road crossings mentioned in this hike and wander a bit.

Special considerations: Bring sunglasses and sunscreen for a no-shade day.

Camping: Yes, across DE 1 from the Indian River parking area, from mid-March to mid-November. A fee is required.

For more information: Delaware Seashore State Park.

51 Nanticoke Wildlife Area Loop

Highlights:	An easy stroll through mixed hardwood and pine forest along the edges of fields and hedgerows. A nice blend of rural and woodland landscape.
Location:	The Robert L. Graham Nanticoke Wildlife Area is in the southwest corner of Sussex County, Delaware, about 45 miles south of Dover and 5 miles west of Laurel.
Type of hike:	Loop; day hike.
Total distance:	2.5 miles.
Difficulty:	Easy.
Elevation gain:	Minimal.
Best months:	Year-round, except during deer hunting season.
Permits:	None.
Maps:	USGS Sharptown, Delaware.

Finding the trailhead: From Delaware Highway 13, travel west on DE 24 through Laurel and continue 1.2 miles to Road 494 (Old Sharptown Road). Turn right on Road 494 and, at 2.2 miles, bear left, staying on Road 494. Travel another 1.6 miles to the Nanticoke Wildlife Area entrance sign, and turn right on the access road. Proceed 0.2 mile to the parking area for deer stands 1 and 2, on the right.

Trailhead facilities: None.

Key points:
- 0.0   Trailhead
- 0.1   Adams family graveyard
- 0.8   Wild area boundary
- 1.5   Horse trail junction
- 1.6   Deer stand 12 trail junction
- 2.2   Access road

Nanticoke Wildlife Area Loop

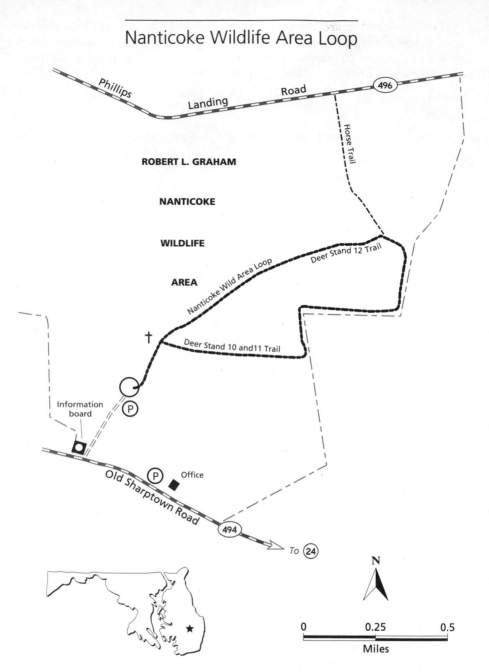

The hike: The Nanticoke Wildlife Area is primarily managed as a hunting area, and the trails are mostly travel routes to deer stands tucked into the wooded corners of small clearings. Hiking here during the deer hunting season, therefore, is not advised, but during the rest of the year walking the area's paths is thoroughly enjoyable. Passing through dense forest and along the edges of cultivated fields, the trails provide an opportunity to stroll in both bright, open spaces and shady groves.

From the parking area, continue up the access road on foot beneath the branches of big oaks. On the left, at 0.1 mile, is a nineteenth-century graveyard—the burial plot for the Adams family, presumably a clan of Sussex County farmers. The old white stones, some listing and propped up, sit among wildflowers beneath a cedar tree bearing birth dates as early as 1806 and inscriptions such as that on the stone of Hyram M. Collins, who died in 1852, "in full hope of immortality."

Just past the graveyard, follow the access road right and then turn right again onto the trail leading to deer stands 10 and 11. There is a barrier here that defines a small parking area for hunters. Proceed on the trail with the forest on the left and a wooded hedgerow backed by a small field on the right. For the next 0.6 mile, you will walk along the edge of a typical coastal-plain forest of loblolly pines mixed with red maples, oaks, and sweet gums. Although this woodland community may be commonplace in Sussex County and the southern coastal region, it is hardly without charm. The tall loblollies are wonderfully fragrant and musical in the wind, the oaks stand strong and majestic, and the sweet gums, with their star-shaped leaves, medicinal sap, and prickly fruit, are distinctive and beautiful.

On the right, the trail passes wood-bordered fields lined with wildflowers in the spring. These open areas are prime habitat for birds and other wildlife who favor browsing in the fields and perching on its edges. It is no accident that most of the hunting stands sit just inside the woods on the margins of clearings; at dusk, you are likely to see deer gather here. Areas such as these are also good places to watch and listen to birds.

At the end of the field, the trail crosses a concrete barrier at the wildlife area boundary, at 0.8 mile. Turn left here, and follow the trail along the edge of a large cornfield on the right. Keeping to the field edge, the trail turns right, bends left at 1.3 miles, and soon breaks into the woods to an intersection with a marked horse path, at 1.5 miles. Turn left on the horse path, continue 100 yards, and then go left again on the trail to deer stand 12, where a gate blocks the path to stands 13 and 14.

The sun-dappled path winds through the woods and then passes a small clearing where you will see deer stand 12 in the back left corner. Beyond the clearing, the path is soft and grassy and passes through nice stands of oak and pine with spacious groves of holly growing beneath their sheltering branches. At 2.2 miles, the trail crosses a barrier and joins the sandy access road leading back to the trailhead.

Options: If you like walking on rural roads, you could extend your circuit hike, continuing past stands 13 and 14 to Road 496, traveling west (left) on 496, and then south (left) on the unpaved access road for stands 15 and 16 back to the trailhead.

Special considerations: Do not hike during deer hunting season.

Camping: No.

For more information: Nanticoke Wildlife Area.

52 Fenwick Island State Park

Highlights:	A walk on the ocean and bay shore of a barrier island on Delaware's Atlantic coast.
Location:	Fenwick Island State Park is located in the southeast corner of Sussex County, Delaware, 1.5 miles north of Ocean City, Maryland.
Type of hike:	Out-and-back with spur; day hike.
Total distance:	5.3 miles.
Difficulty:	Easy.
Elevation gain:	Minimal.
Best months:	Year-round.
Permits:	None. Fee collected during summer and on weekends and holidays in spring and fall.
Maps:	USGS Bethany Beach, Assawoman Bay, Delaware.

Finding the trailhead: From Delaware Highway 1, turn into Fenwick Island State Park parking area 1.5 miles north of Ocean City, Maryland, and 6 miles south of Bethany Beach, Delaware.

Trailhead facilities: Bathhouse, restrooms, and snack bar in season; portable toilets year-round.

Key points:
- 0.0 Trailhead
- 2.4 Observation tower
- 2.9 York Beach crossing
- 3.1 Assawoman Bay Recreation Area
- 3.3 York Beach crossing
- 5.3 Fenwick Island bathhouse

The hike: Sandwiched between the bustling resorts of Bethany Beach, Delaware, and Ocean City, Maryland, Fenwick Island State Park offers an alternative to a day on a crowded beach. Although the beaches on the southern tip of the island are backed by neighborhoods of new vacation homes, much of Fenwick Island is undeveloped. This is largely because the island is not much more than a sliver of sand between the Atlantic Ocean and Little Assawoman Bay. Wind and surf so easily alter its shoreline and dunes that only the brave or foolish try to build here, leaving the coasts of ocean and bay in the state park relatively wild.

From the parking area, cross the dunes on the bathhouse boardwalk. Looking west, you will see an extremely narrow island. Descend the steps to the beach and turn left, heading north. For just over a mile, there are private homes in the dunes, a few precipitously crowding the shore. But at 1.1 miles, the beach, from ocean to highway, is undeveloped public land. Here, you can often leave the crowds behind and settle into the world of the Atlantic shore. On Fenwick Island, that is a world of dynamic change.

In places, you may see the shoreline sharply cut by storm waves or the dunes sculpted by constant winds—the sand is shifting everywhere. The

Fenwick Island State Park

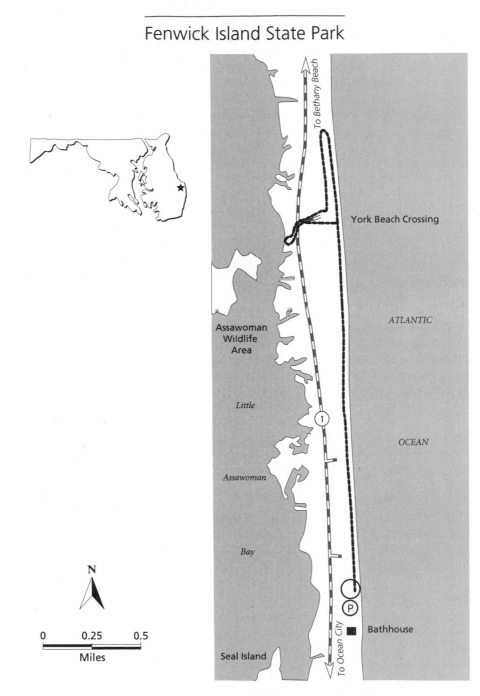

sandpipers and the noisy sanderlings take it all in stride, riding the winds and running like pacers in the retreating surf. If you dig in their moist hunting grounds, you may come up with a handful of mole crabs, the Sisyphus of the shore. Peterson's *A Field Guide to the Atlantic Seashore* says these little egg-shaped crabs, often called sand crabs, "live in the turmoil of broken waves on sandy beaches, moving up and down the beach with the tide, constantly burrowing and being exhumed." Change indeed.

At 2.4 miles, an observation tower stands in the dunes to the left. Built in the early 1940s, the concrete tower, one of many lining the Delaware and New Jersey coasts, was used to watch for German submarines during World War II. Most of the structures, which look like monumental sandcastle towers, are still standing. One, at Cape Henlopen, is open to the public. Turn around here and return down the beach, heading south half a mile to the York Beach crossing, at 2.9 miles. Turn right, and cross the dunes through the fenced passage. At DE 1, turn left and walk 0.1 mile to the Assawoman Bay Recreation Area, on the right. Crossing to the bay gives you a good feel for the slimness of Fenwick Island and provides a scenic spot to watch birds.

The Assawoman Bay Recreation Area, at 3.1 miles, is a little pocket of land along the wild bayshore. From the slim, sandy beach, you can gaze across the calm inland bay to the green forests of the Assawoman Wildlife Area. Herons, osprey, and cormorants nest in the surrounding marshes and can frequently be seen fishing the bay waters. With some luck, you may see a bald eagle soar from a perch on a snag or hear in the tangled pines an owl hooting as the sun goes down. A shady picnic area here is a nice place to rest, but in the summer the insects can be pesky.

Return to the ocean shore via the York Beach crossing at 3.3. miles, and turn right, heading south down the beach to the Fenwick bathhouse. Your footprints will almost surely be washed away.

Options: You may skip the loop to Assawoman Bay and limit your hike to the beach, beginning your return to the bathhouse wherever you please.

Special considerations: Sunscreen and sunglasses, and insect repellent for the trip to the bay, will make the walk more comfortable. Take care crossing DE 1, especially during the busy summer season.

Camping: None at Fenwick Island; camping permitted at other nearby state parks.

For more information: Fenwick Island State Park.

53 Seahawk Nature Trail, Holts Landing State Park

Highlights: On the shore of one of Delaware's inland bays, a walk along the edges of marsh, pond, forest, meadow, and bay shore.

Location: Holts Landing State Park is in Sussex County, Delaware, on Indian River Bay, about 6 miles northwest of Bethany Beach.

Type of hike: Loop; day hike.

Total distance: 1.7 miles.

Difficulty: Easy.

Elevation gain: Minimal.

Best months: Year-round.

Permits: None. Fee collected during summer and on weekends and holidays in spring and fall.

Maps: USGS Bethany Beach, Delaware.

Finding the trailhead: From Delaware Highway 1 in Bethany Beach, travel west 3.5 miles on DE 26 to White's Neck Road (Road 347). Turn right on to White's Neck Road, go 2 miles, and turn right on Road 346. Go 0.4 mile to the Holts Landing State Park entrance, and continue 0.7 mile to trailhead parking at the ball field.

Trailhead facilities: Restrooms, picnic pavilion, shady picnic areas.

Key points:
- 0.0   Trailhead
- 0.1   View of Indian River Bay
- 0.3   Fork
- 0.7   Woodland pond loop junction
- 1.2   Woodland pond loop junction
- 1.4   Clearing

The hike: Seahawk Nature Trail does not cover a lot of ground, but the lands it does cross are quite diverse. From sandy beach to wildflower meadow, from salt marsh to freshwater ponds and poplar groves, the path winds through many worlds. Short, easy, and interesting, this is a great trail for introducing children to the outdoors.

From the parking lot, cross the ball field toward the bay and the log gateway marked Seahawk Nature Trail. The path begins by crossing a grassy flat and a short bridge, and then follows the shoreline of Indian River Bay. Proceed on a narrow, wild beach with beach grass and marsh on the left and the shallow inland bay on the right, the first of the many "edges" you will encounter. Just 0.1 mile into the hike, you have already reached a nice view of the bay, its far shore to the north, and Burton's Island to the east.

Continue along the beach, and follow the trail left at the osprey nest platform and into a broad meadow busy with bees, butterflies, and wildflowers in the

Seahawk Nature Trail, Holts Landing State Park

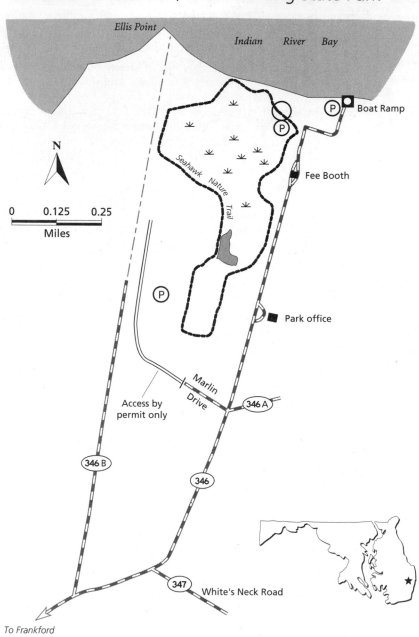

spring. At 0.3 mile, the trail splits to the right, crossing the meadow to a stand of loblolly pines and then following the forest edge.

The trail then cuts left, back across the meadow, and soon follows yet another margin, this between a forest of pines, oaks, and dogwoods on the right and a pond and marsh on the left. As with all edges, this one is teeming with life. Songbirds dart in and out of the woods, a squawking blue heron sails above the trees and perches on a pine branch over the pond, and egrets wade carefully in the dark, shallow water while jabbing for minnows and frogs. Along a row of phragmites, the invasive and pervasive marsh reed, the trail bends right into the woods, at 0.5 mile, and continues through skinny pines, maples, and sweet gum.

A pond on the left, at 0.7 mile, is partially hidden by a hedgerow of pine and oak. At the end of the pond, the trail begins a 0.5-mile rectangular "loop"—or box—through the woods that will lead back to this spot. Follow the well-marked trail to the right, proceed about 50 yards, and then go left, traveling through a young stand of poplars growing in the shade of oaks and pines. The trail intermittently crosses primitive camping clearings, turns left at 1 mile, turns quickly left again, and then returns to the beginning of the box at the pond shore, at 1.2 miles.

Follow the trail to the right, and proceed between two ponds dotted with birdhouses mounted on posts. The houses provide nesting sites for wood ducks and other cavity nesters, birds that typically nest in now-rare climax forests. The metal collars on the posts protect the ducks' eggs from raccoons and snakes. In the light of day, it is unlikely that you will those predators lurking around the ponds, but the sunning turtles will wait a long time before they slide off their logs into the dark green water.

The trail bends around the pond on the left and then breaks into the woods to the right, emerging in a clearing near the fee booth at 1.4 miles. The path bends left at the edge of the clearing, cuts back into the trees, and winds through the forest to the trailhead.

Camping: Youth camping only.

For more information: Holts Landing State Park.

54 Burton's Island Loop

Highlights:	An easy, interpretive hike on boardwalks, sand, and soft upland soil through salt marsh and coastal forest. With good facilities near the trailhead and interesting options, a walk on the nature trail at Burton's Island makes a great family outing.
Location:	Burton's Island is just north of Indian River Inlet in Delaware Seashore State Park, 50 miles southeast of Dover and 7.5 miles south of Rehoboth Beach.
Type of hike:	Loop; day hike.
Total distance:	1.5 miles.
Difficulty:	Easy.
Elevation gain:	Minimal.
Best months:	October–May.
Permits:	None.
Maps:	USGS Bethany Beach, Delaware.

Finding the trailhead: From Rehoboth Beach, travel 7.5 miles south on Delaware Highway 1, and exit to the right into Delaware Seashore State Park Marina, just north of Indian River Inlet Bridge. Turn right at the park office, and proceed on Inlet Road 0.5 mile past the marina and public boat storage area to trailhead parking.

Trailhead facilities: On the access road, about 150 yards before the trailhead, there are restrooms, a snack bar, picnic tables, telephones, and an observation deck.

Key points:
- 0.0 Trailhead
- 0.2 Return loop junction
- 0.3 Boardwalk; Rehoboth Bay salt marsh
- 0.4 Cedar, pine, and holly grove
- 0.5 Salt marsh detour
- 0.8 Indian River Bay beach
- 1.3 Loop junction

The hike: Burton's Island is the largest island in an archipelago of small islands that separates Rehoboth Bay from Indian River Bay, just behind the barrier beach of the Delaware Seashore State Park. This easy 1.5-mile walk around the island affords great views of inland bays and close-up observations of the creatures of the salt marsh and upland forest. From boardwalks over tidal creeks, you will see wading shorebirds, muskrat tracks, and skittering fiddler crabs as well as osprey, great blue herons, and egrets gliding over the wetland grasses. A shady picnic table on the Indian River Bay shoreline is a perfect place for lunch. Bring the kids!

From the trailhead, cross the causeway to Burton's Island and proceed on hard and soft sand through short cedars and marsh grass. To the right, out across the marsh, look for osprey on a nesting platform. Nearly extinct

Burton's Island Loop

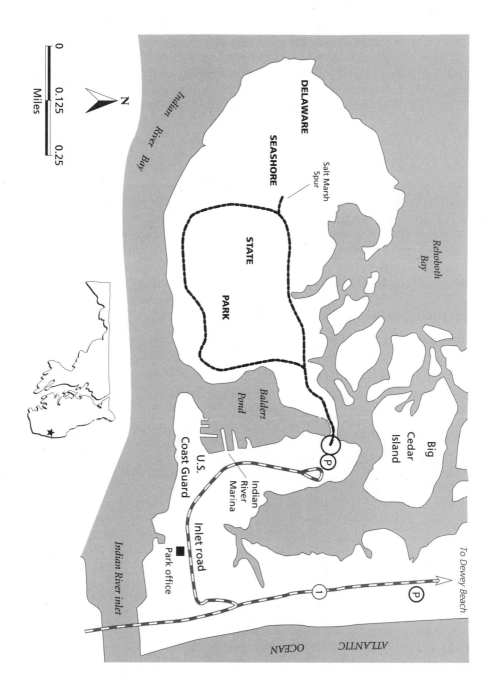

30 years ago, osprey—or fish hawks—have made a strong comeback and may now be seen nesting and fishing all along the Delaware coast.

At 0.2 mile, the return loop intersects from the left. Continue right to a boardwalk, at 0.3 mile, one of several that cross the tidal marshlands. At low tide, look for muskrat tracks or watch a retreating fiddler crab disappear into a hole in the mud, waving his oversized claw. This is also a good place to gaze across the marshland flats, where sandpipers, herons, and egrets feed in the spawning grounds of crab, bluefish, and flounder.

After the boardwalk, the trail enters a shady grove of cedar, pine, and holly, at 0.4 mile. Here the path changes from sandy to a soft upland soil that supports a more varied community of trees, vines, and shrubs. At 0.5 mile, the trail bends left at a short spur. A 10-yard detour takes you into the marsh for wide-open views and, if you wish, a few steps in the salty marsh grass. This is another great spot for heron watching.

Back on the trail, wind through woods and wetlands to a sandy rise at 0.8 mile. Here, a picnic table sits in the shade overlooking a narrow beach on the Indian River Bay. Refreshing breezes and a lovely view of the inland bay make this an ideal spot to rest, eat, or daydream.

The trail continues along the beach for 30 yards before entering the woods and then crossing a boardwalk with the marina to the right. At 1.3 miles, the trail completes the island loop. Turn right, and proceed on the sandy trail back to the causeway and the trailhead.

Options: Swim in the Atlantic or walk along the shore at a guarded swimming beach on the south side of Indian River Inlet. Walk the docks of the active marina, just south of the trailhead.

Special considerations: Bring binoculars for birding and insect repellent during summer.

Camping: Yes; a fee is required.

For more information: Delaware Seashore State Park.

55 Ocean City Boardwalk

Highlights:	A whimsical evening stroll on the carnivalesque Ocean City Boardwalk and along the beaches of the seaside resort.
Location:	Ocean City is in Worcester County, Maryland, on the Atlantic Ocean, 150 miles southeast of Washington, D.C.
Type of hike:	Out-and-back; night hike.
Total distance:	6 miles.
Difficulty:	Easy.
Elevation gain:	Minimal.
Best months:	Year-round.
Permits:	None.
Maps:	USGS Ocean City, Maryland.

Finding the trailhead: From the U.S. Highway 50 entrance to Ocean City, turn right on Philadelphia Avenue, go eight blocks south, and bear left to the public parking at Ocean City Inlet (25 cents per 15 minutes).

Trailhead facilities: Public restrooms, telephones, food, and water line the boardwalk.

Key points:
0.0   Trailhead
0.5   Fishing Pier, Playland, Sportland, Dolle's Salt Water Taffy
1.5   Beach patrol

The hike: Take a step onto the Ocean City Boardwalk and you enter another world. The smell is an unmistakable and inimitable mix of fresh sea air, caramel corn, hot-pressed T-shirt decals, funnel cakes, cotton candy, and French fries with vinegar. Then there is the neon—the bright spinning Playland Ferris wheel and the iconic swirls of Dolle's Salt Water Taffy glowing green. And games. Kids in the glare and racket of Sportland, pumping quarters into Froggers and Asteroids, skee-ball and the Gypsy Palm Reader. A haunted house. More food. It is not your typical hike, but a midsummer stroll on the boardwalk sure is a lot of fun.

The south end of the boardwalk is the perfect place to start. From there you can peer out over Ocean City Inlet lit by the glare of the resort, which is, after all, what this place is all about. Here also is the Ocean City Lifesaving Museum and a signal of what is to come—life-size models of the biggest fish caught off the coast, all baring their formidable teeth. Among them are an 11-foot mako shark, a 1,210-pound tiger shark, and a giant blue marlin, leaping from the deep blue sea.

Walk on; you have only begun. On the left, watch the Tilt-a-Whirl and the Matterhorn squeeze screams from even the most tightlipped tourists. And at Wicomico Street at 0.5 mile, where things really kick into gear, take

Ocean City Boardwalk

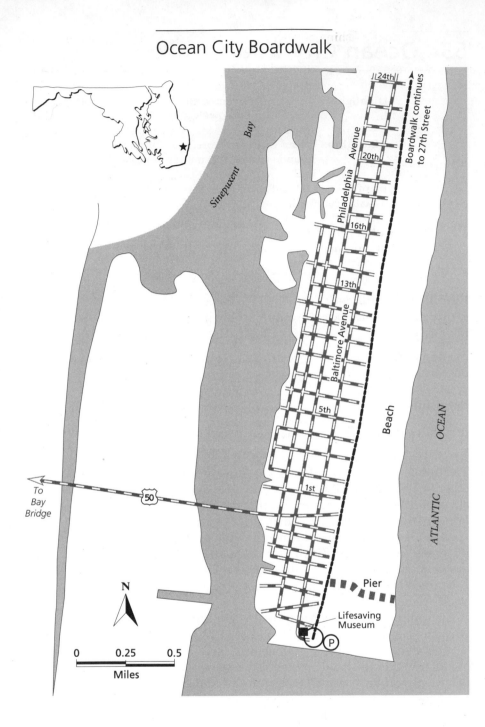

a detour onto the fishing pier with its collection of carnival rides, soft-serve ice cream, and pizza.

After the pier, the beach sand is just a step away off the boards—but so are portrait painters, and body painters, and body piercers, too. And skate shops and surf shops and Belgian waffles with piles of fruit and ice cream and every other bit of fun this linear circus has to offer.

The ocean is always there, pounding away and inviting you to take its hand. Do like the people staying in the beachside hotels do, sitting in their wide-open balconies like the stars on Hollywood Squares—be courted by the waves. And when you have had your fill of the carnival atmosphere that is the boardwalk, go to the sea. Walk back to your car on the beach, and enjoy the spectacle from a distance while you cool your heels in the surf.

Special considerations: The boardwalk is a great place for a winter walk. In the winter it is a quiet place, where the only sounds are the surf and the seagulls and where solitude reigns.

Camping: None.

For more information: Ocean City Convention and Visitors Bureau.

56 Assateague Island Loop

Highlights:	A backpacking trip along the Atlantic shore of an undeveloped barrier island.
Location:	Assateague Island is an Atlantic barrier island, just south of Ocean City, Maryland, and about 170 miles southeast of Washington, D.C.
Type of hike:	Loop; three-night backpacking trip.
Total distance:	25 miles.
Difficulty:	Moderate.
Elevation gain:	None.
Best months:	October–April.
Permits:	Backcountry camping permit, $5; park entrance fee, $5.
Maps:	USGS Ocean City, Tingles Island, Whittington Point, Maryland.

Finding the trailhead: From Ocean City, Maryland, travel 1.3 miles west on U.S. Highway 50 to Maryland Highway 611. Turn left on MD 611, drive south 6 miles, and turn left, continuing on MD 611 and following signs for Assateague Island National Seashore. Pass Barrier Island Visitor Center, proceed 1.3 miles, and turn right into the national park. The camping registration office is 2.5 miles ahead on the left, just after the park fee booth.

Trailhead facilities: Outdoor showers, restrooms, telephone, water, emergency phones on the back trail.

Assateague Island Loop

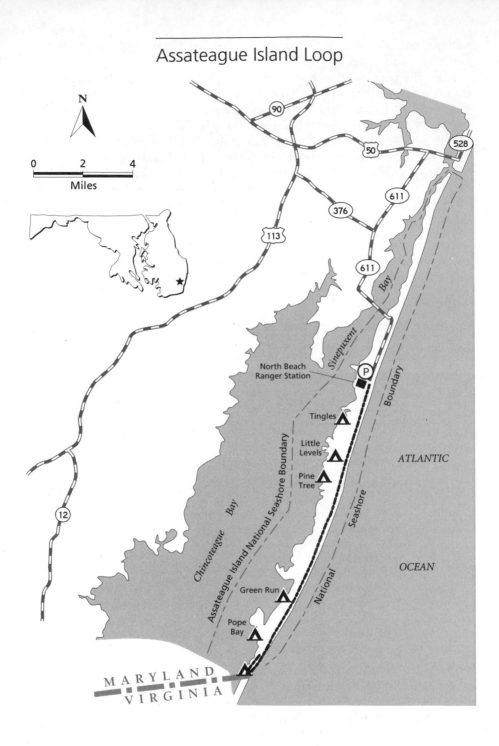

Key points:

   0.0   Trailhead
   4.0   Little Levels campsite
 12.5   State Line campsite
 20.0   Pine Tree Campsite

The hike: Assateague Island is one of a string of sand spits and barrier islands that define the Atlantic coast of the Delmarva Peninsula. But unlike the rest of the shoreline in Maryland and Delaware, Assateague is a protected national seashore and almost all of its 37-mile length is undeveloped. Walking the island beaches and camping with the surf pounding nearby provide a wonderful opportunity to experience the wild Atlantic shore. And Assateague is much more than wind and waves and shifting sand. Behind the dunes are pine forests and marshes, and the entire island is alive with wild horses and foxes, dolphins and blue crabs, horned owls and pelicans, and a host of other creatures of ocean and bay.

Like most backpacking trips, an overnight hike on Assateague requires some planning. In fact, backpacking on the beach has its own particular requirements. There is no fresh water on Assateague, for example, so you must carry all you plan to use. And because the island is managed to preserve its wildlife and natural character, there are a few rules to follow. Here is what you need to know to enjoy your trip.

The Assateague hike we suggest is a 12.5-mile walk south on the beach and a 12.5-mile return trip on the path behind the dunes. But there are lots of options. There are two ocean-side campsites and four bayside sites (there is no backcountry camping elsewhere), so you can choose the length of hike that suits you. The important thing is to choose in advance. The park requires that you register at the North Beach Ranger Station before you hike. The fee is $5, and you must tell the rangers the number of people in your party, the length of your stay, and where you plan to camp each night. (There is parking set aside for backcountry hikers in the lot near the registration office.)

There are also registration deadlines. Advance registrations are not accepted—permits are available up to 24 hours before your departure—but you must register by noon if you plan to hike to the far campsites at State Line or Pope Bay, and by 5 P.M. (3 P.M. during Standard Time) if you are going to stay at the other sites. The rangers are competent and courteous, and registration is a breeze if you are prepared.

After registering, cross the dunes on the boardwalk, turn right, and head south down the beach. The first day of this four-day, three-night trip is a 4-mile walk to Little Levels campsite, the first site south of the ranger station. On a typical backpacking trip, a 4-mile walk would make for a pretty short afternoon stroll, but it is a good distance for starting a beach hike. It will give you a chance to get a feel for carrying a pack in soft sand and time to explore after you have set up your first campsite, which you will find in the dunes to your right at 4 miles. (On the ocean side, signs with a hiker icon will point out campsites. On the bay side, look for the canoe icon.)

Be aware that the ocean-side sites like Little Levels have no protection from the wind or sun. But that is part of a beach-hiking adventure. Use sand anchors to keep your tent in place, rig a flysheet for shade, and enjoy a night of listening to the waves. It is a chance to live every kid's dream of not having to leave the beach at the end of a long summer day. (All campsites on the island have chemical toilets nearby.)

Day two is an 8.5-mile walk to the border of Maryland and Virginia, where Assateague Island National Seashore becomes Chincoteague National Wildlife Refuge. Continuing south from Little Levels, a full day of walking and exploring the wild Atlantic shore lies ahead. On the beach, you will see the myriad shells, husks, and bones of washed-up sea life as well as Assateague's diverse community of shorebirds—from the common willet to the endangered piping plover—running in the wet sand just ahead of the surf. Offshore, look for the peculiarly graceful brown pelican gliding by or flocks of swift terns diving into the swells for fish. And, of course, watch for the famous wild ponies, which you may encounter grazing on beach grass as you make your way south to the State Line campsite at 12.5 miles. The State Line camp, like Little Levels, is a simple, modest site in the dunes west of the shoreline.

Day three of the hike provides good opportunities for exploring the bayside of Assateague. From State Line, facing the ocean, go left and follow the path

Historians differ on the origin of the ponies on Assateague Island, but everyone agrees they are a prime attraction.

through the dunes, heading north. Here you will find a world quite different from the wide, flat beach and pounding surf of the ocean side. Behind
the cover of the dunes, there are pine forests and salt marshes, wildflowers
and woodland birds and tangles of highbush blueberry. More surprising to
many are the healthy populations of mammals in the bayside woods and
thickets, including deer, muskrats, raccoons, and even red foxes, who den in
Assateague's shifting dunes.

Traveling on the dune path, you will pass Pope Bay camp at 13.5 miles
and Green Run camp at 15.5 miles. Pine Tree camp, at 20 miles your destination for your last night out, is a 7.5-mile walk from State Line. Pine Tree,
a forested bay-shore camp, offers a picnic table, fire ring, and much more
protection from the wind and sun than the ocean-side sites have.

Day four is a 5-mile hike back to the ranger station. You may continue
hiking the bayside path or cross the dunes, turn left, and head north in the
Atlantic surf.

Options: As mentioned, you may stay at any of the designated campsites
and hike along the ocean or on the back trail.

Special considerations: In addition to selecting your campsite in advance,
you should also remember to bring along beach-hiking gear. On Assateague,
you will need the following:

- Containers for all the water you will use—at least 2 quarts per person
  per day (fresh water is available at the trailhead only)
- Sunscreen
- A hat and sunglasses for shade
- A poncho for sudden squalls
- Insect repellent (in summer)
- Mosquito netting (in summer)
- Swimsuit
- Rigging for a "shade sheet"

Also consider your tolerance for mosquitoes—they can be fierce in the summer. Pets are prohibited in the backcountry. As every ranger will tell you, the
wild ponies bite and kick. If you swim, watch the currents and do not swim
alone! Walking on sand can be challenging. Go easy, and do not fight the sand.

Camping: At designated sites only.

For more information: Assateague Island National Seashore.

57 Paul Leifer Nature Trail, Furnace Town Historic Site

Highlights:	A short, easy walk through bald cypress swamps and upland forests in the Nature Conservancy's beautiful, 3,000-acre Nassawango Creek Preserve.
Location:	Furnace Town Historic Site is in Worcester County, Maryland, 135 miles southeast of Washington, D.C., and 15 miles southeast of Salisbury, Maryland.
Type of hike:	Loop; day hike.
Total distance:	1 mile.
Difficulty:	Easy.
Elevation gain:	Minimal.
Best months:	Year-round.
Permits:	None; $3 entrance fee.
Maps:	USGS Snow Hill, Maryland.

Finding the trailhead: From the Salisbury, Maryland bypass, travel 13.5 miles southeast on Maryland Highway 12 and turn right on Old Furnace Town Road. Proceed 1 mile to Furnace Town Village parking on the left. The trail begins in the historic village at the old Nassawango Iron Furnace.

Trailhead facilities: Restrooms, telephone, and a nature shop at the visitor center.

Key points:
    0.0   Trailhead
    0.2   Preserve boundary
    0.3   Swamp boardwalks
    0.4   Upland forest
    0.6   Canal towpath

The hike: Before European settlement, much of the farm country of the Delmarva Peninsula was a vast forest. Along the creeks of southeastern Maryland, the woodlands were lush groves of giant bald cypress, Atlantic white cedar, and loblolly pine. There were orchids and lady's slippers, butterflies and salamanders, hawks and warblers, otters and snakes. While much of the original forest has been cleared, a sliver much like the original survives on Nassawango Creek. Here, on the Paul Leifer Nature Trail in a Nature Conservancy preserve, you can walk among the old groves and see an especially rich community of wild creatures. Bring the kids. The trail is short and easy, and the forest is wonderfully diverse, active, and mysterious, making this a great introduction to the outdoors.

The short loop trail begins near the old brick furnace, used by settlers between 1828 and 1850 to make pig iron from bog iron ore dug from Nassawango Creek, oyster shells from the bay, and charcoal from the surrounding woodlands. From a tended lawn at the base of the furnace, the path enters a forest that survived the heavy logging. Amazingly, in just a

Paul Leifer Nature Trail, Furnace Town Historic Site

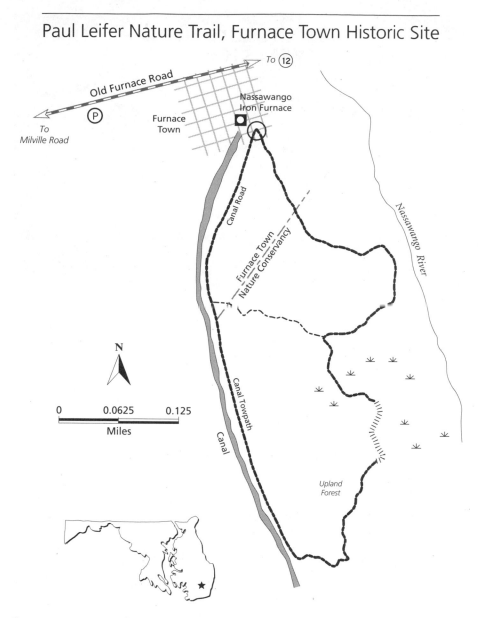

few steps, you truly are in the woods. The loblolly pines are giants, the birdsong is sweet, and the forest floor is dense with groves and tangles. Beneath the old, thick-trunked pines are maples and oaks, sweet gums and sassafras. Holly, highbush blueberry, and sweet pepper bush make a lush understory. And springing up at trailside are jack-in-the-pulpits, cranefly orchids, and the luscious flower of the pink lady's slipper orchid.

At the preserve boundary, at 0.2 mile, the trail bends and winds through holly groves, soon crossing a series of boardwalks through a bald cypress swamp. An aquatic tree, the bald cypress sends many of its roots up for air rather than down into the soaked, oxygen-poor soil. From the boardwalks,

Nassawango Iron Furnace Town Historic Site and the adjacent Nature Conservancy preserve connect natural and human history. PHOTO COURTESY OF FURNACE TOWN FOUNDATION, INC.

at 0.3 mile, look to the left where the knobby roots—or "knees"—rise up out of the shallows. Along with swamps in southern Delaware, the Nassawango swamps are home to the northernmost stands of bald cypress in North America.

After the boardwalks, the trail leaves the wetlands and enters the drier upland forest, at 0.4 mile. Here, the path is covered in holly leaves and spiny sweet gum balls, and the woods are thick with ferns and Muscatine grapevines. The birds are lively, and there are deep shade and dappled sunlight. Proceed through the woods to Furnace Town Canal, and turn right onto the canal towpath, at 0.6 mile.

Dug in 1825, the mile-long canal carried barges from the creek to the furnace loaded with oyster and clam shells for smelting or with pig iron on its way up the Chesapeake to the port of Baltimore. Following the canal towpath with the forest on your right, look to the left for an interpretive sign pointing out an iron seep. Here iron-rich water sinks into the sandy streambed, forming the "bog iron" that drove the Furnace Town boom in the mid-1800s. Walking the towpath back to the furnace beneath the tall loblolly pines, be thankful that Nassawango Creek's iron was too impure to compete in the marketplace, ending a local industry that may very well have left little of the forest we enjoy today.

Special considerations: Bring insect repellent in summer; check for ticks after your hike.

Camping: None.

For more information: Furnace Town Foundation.

58 Pocomoke State Forest Hiking Trail, Milburn Landing

Highlights: An easy loop hike through the woodlands and along the swamps of the Pocomoke State Forest on Maryland's Eastern Shore.

Location: Pocomoke State Forest and Park is in Worcester County, Maryland, about 140 miles southeast of Washington, D.C., and 22 miles southeast of Salisbury, Maryland.

Type of hike: Loop; day hike.

Total distance: 4.5 miles.

Difficulty: Easy.

Elevation gain: Minimal.

Best months: October–April.

Permits: None.

Maps: USGS Snow Hill, Maryland.

Finding the trailhead: Travel 16 miles south on Maryland Highway 12 from the Salisbury bypass, and turn right on Nassawango Road (also called River Road). Proceed 5 miles to Camp Road, a dirt road on the right just after the Nassawango Country Club. Turn right on Camp Road, and go 0.6 mile to trailhead parking on the left.

Trailhead facilities: None.

Key points:
    0.0   Trailhead
    0.3   Camp Road junction
    0.9   Nassawango Road
    1.2   Pocomoke River wetlands
    2.8   Overgrown cemetery
    3.2   Nassawango Road
    3.7   Forest boundary
    3.9   Forest Trail turnoff
    4.2   Camp Road Junction

The hike: The Pocomoke River runs through southeastern Maryland from southern Delaware down to the northern border of Virginia. Before emptying into the Chesapeake Bay at Pocomoke Sound, the river drains the fertile farmlands west of Ocean City and the deep, shady woods of southern Worcester County. In the Pocomoke River State Forest, you can experience the river's wilder side as you walk among the pine, poplar, magnolia, and mountain laurel that flourish on its banks.

From the parking lot, turn right on Camp Road and proceed 0.3 mile to the trailhead on the right. Cross a shallow gully, and walk into the woods following white blazes. The forest along the dirt road and the footpath is a classic example of the diverse mix of trees in Maryland's coastal-plain woodlands.

Pocomoke State Forest Hiking Trail, Milburn Landing

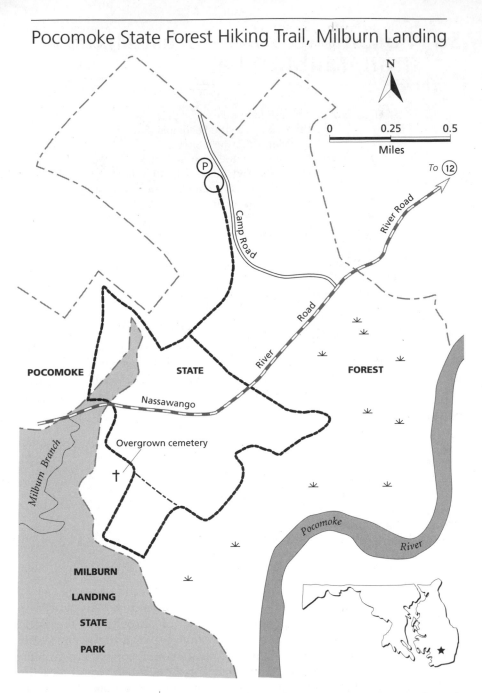

There are loblolly pines, common in the South, growing with hardwoods, common in the piedmont to the north. There are sweet gum, sassafras, and oak as well as a lush evergreen understory of holly and sweetbay magnolia. In the spring, the blossoming mountain laurel are particularly showy.

Walking the footpath, you are soon traveling through holly groves in the shade of the oaks and pines. At 0.6 mile, the trail bends left and can be a bit wet for a stretch. With the branches of young sweet gums and oaks offering shade, you may have to step over ruts in the trail that often hold enough water to harbor bugs, frogs, and tadpoles in the spring. But the path levels and grows grassy before long, and soon the going is easy again.

At 0.9 mile, the trail crosses Nassawango Road. Duck under the gates on either side, and proceed on the white-blazed footpath with young, skinny pines on the left and a mixed forest on the right. Pass a bench, where the pines begin to give way to hardwoods, and follow the trail as it bends left through mountain laurel and descends slightly into a grove of big tulip trees on the edge of the Pocomoke River wetlands, at 1.2 miles.

Turn right, and travel along the edge of the forested wetlands. This is a very nice stretch. The tulip trees are tall and stately, and where they dominate, the ground is carpeted in ferns. In some places, loblolly pines mix in and at others the groves of holly and laurel are dense. At 1.7 miles, the trail bends left, descending slightly to cross a streambed on an old, mossy culvert, and then ascends, bending right, into a more spacious wood where you can see far down the trail and into the trees.

At 2.1 miles, the trail dips into a grassy meadow and forks. Turn left, following white blazes (if you go straight here, the trail does rejoin the loop, but it misses a nice stretch of forest and an old graveyard hidden in the woods), and proceed through another lovely grove of tulip trees and fern meadows. At 2.4 miles, the trail turns right, and then, shortly, right again at a log bench in a small clearing. Proceed into the woods, staying right and following white blazes.

On the left, at 2.8 miles, is an old, overgrown cemetery, where the mostly illegible gravestones collect moss or lay toppled against trees. For all its eeriness, the graveyard is a surprisingly lively place. There are white-tailed deer about, birds flitting in the sapling branches, and a busy hive of bees buzzing around a long crack in the trunk of an old loblolly pine.

Just after the cemetery, the trail travels through tall grasses, turns left into the woods, and then turns right, heading back to Nassawango Road. The trail is grassy here and infested with ticks. You may want to stop and pick them off as you go.

At 3.2 miles, cross Nassawango Road, turn left, and pick up the trail on the right, where it continues through the woods to the forest boundary, at 3.7 miles. At the boundary are a bench and a field visible through a thicket. The trail turns sharply right here, following white blazes and continuing through the forest. At 3.9 miles, the trail bends to the right and then splits sharply left. Although this section of the trail is narrow, it is well marked. Follow it through the woods to the beginning of the loop trail, turn left, and proceed to Camp Road, at 4.2 miles. Turn left on Camp Road, and return to the parking area.

Special considerations: Where the trail is grassy, the ticks are plentiful.

Camping: Yes, at nearby Milburn Landing State Park.

For more information: Pocomoke River State Forest.

59 Milburn Cypress Nature Trail, Milburn Landing State Park

Highlights:	A short but enchanting walk through one of the northernmost stands of bald cypress. You may not drive all the way from Baltimore or Washington, D.C., for this quick stroll, but it just might be worth it. This hike is ideal for a short detour en route to the beach.
Location:	Pocomoke River State Park is in Worcester County, Maryland, about 145 miles southeast of Washington, D.C.
Type of hike:	Loop; day hike.
Total distance:	1 mile.
Difficulty:	Easy.
Elevation gain:	Minimal.
Best months:	September–May.
Permits:	None.
Maps:	USGS Pocomoke City, Maryland.

Finding the trailhead: From Salisbury, Maryland, travel south on Maryland Highway 12 for about 13 miles from the Salisbury Bypass. Turn right onto Nassawango Road, and go 6 miles; turn left into Milburn Landing State Park. Turn right onto the boat launch access road, following signs to the launch. The trailhead is at the opposite end of the parking area from the river. Look for a big sign.

Trailhead facilities: Comfort station.

Key points:
- 0.2   Hollies; loblolly pines
- 0.3   Park road
- 0.4   Cypress swamp
- 0.7   Park road

The hike: This hike is very short and is out of the way for most hikers, except for local residents and visitors to the family campground. Although your leg muscles will forget the walk before you have left the park, the magic of the swampland is, without exaggeration, unforgettable.

From the nature trail sign, enter pine forest and bear right at the fork. Giant loblolly pines grow straight to a towering height of 80 feet, forming the upper story above some of the tallest holly trees you will ever see.

Cross the park road at 0.3 mile and, 175 yards farther, reach the cypress swamp. The bald cypress grow in shallow, brackish swamps. To keep from drowning, the root systems develop knobby, knee-like outcrops that protrude from the water. These "bald" knees are the tree's breathing mechanism.

The trail is easy to follow; it would be difficult to get lost. Just plan to take longer to walk a mile than you have before, because you will continually stop in wonder. Follow the signs and blazes. Cross the park road again

Milburn Cypress Nature Trail, Milburn Landing State Park

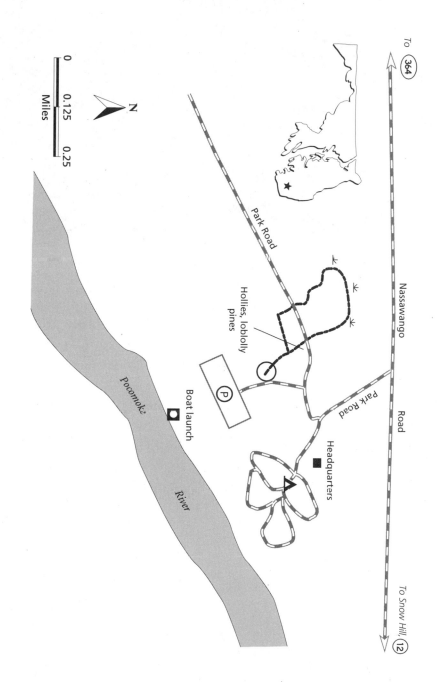

The lazy, wide Pocomoke supports diverse wildlife and a range of human activities.
PHOTO BY JAYSON KNOTT

at 0.7 mile, passing beneath the white pines and more loblolly. At the fork, turn right to reach the parking lot.

Special considerations: The environment here is extremely fragile; stay on the trail.

Camping: Developed campsites and small cabins are available; registration and a fee are required.

For more information: Pocomoke River State Forest.

60 Blackwater National Wildlife Refuge Loop

Highlights:	An easy walk on a paved "wildlife drive" through the Blackwater National Wildlife Refuge, a Chesapeake wetland area on the Blackwater River. An important nesting and feeding area on the Atlantic Flyway, the refuge is a great Eastern Shore birding site.
Location:	Blackwater National Wildlife Refuge is in Dorchester County, Maryland, 105 miles southeast of Washington, D.C.
Type of hike:	Loop; day hike.
Total distance:	4.4 miles.
Difficulty:	Easy.
Elevation gain:	Minimal.
Best months:	Year-round.
Permits:	None; $3 entrance fee.
Maps:	USGS Blackwater River, Maryland.

Finding the trailhead: From the Maryland Highway 50/301 split, 9.5 miles east of the Chesapeake Bay Bridge, take MD 50 east through Cambridge, Maryland, and turn right on MD 16 East. Travel 7.2 miles, and turn left on MD 335. Go south 3.5 miles, and turn left into the Blackwater National Wildlife Refuge on Key Wallace Drive. Proceed 2.5 miles, and turn right onto Wildlife Drive. Travel 1 mile to the parking area at Woods Trail.

Trailhead facilities: None.

Key points:
- 0.0   Trailhead
- 0.3   Dike
- 0.6   Blackwater River marsh
- 0.9   Osprey nest site
- 1.4   Key Wallace Drive fork
- 1.6   Key Wallace Drive
- 3.0   Egypt Road
- 3.3   Wildlife Drive entrance
- 3.7   Marsh Edge Trail fork

The hike: The Blackwater River is one of more than fifty rivers that drain into the Chesapeake Bay, the largest estuary in North America. Along its banks are acres of Eastern Shore marsh and pine forests—a dynamic wetland ecosystem that includes nursery waters for fish, feeding grounds for migrating geese and resident muskrats, nesting sites for osprey and peregrine falcons, and woodland habitat for songbirds and the endangered Delmarva fox squirrel. On a walk on Wildlife Drive in the Blackwater National Wildlife Refuge, you may see all these creatures and more. Ornithologists have identified 287 species of birds on the refuge grounds, including

Blackwater National Wildlife Refuge Loop

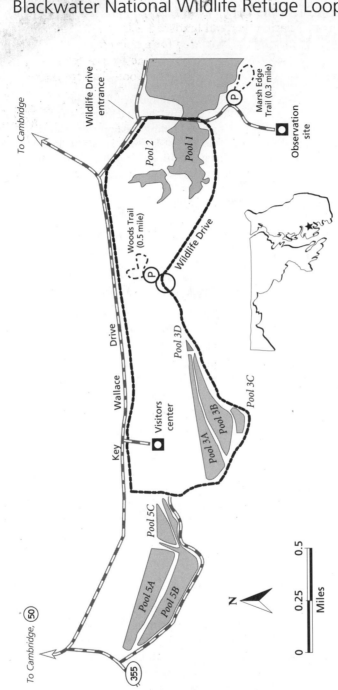

To Cambridge

Wildlife Drive entrance

Marsh Edge Trail (0.3 mile)

P

Observation site

Pool 2

Pool 1

Woods Trail (0.5 mile)

P

Wildlife Drive

Wallace

Key

Drive

Visitors center

Pool 3D

Pool 3A

Pool 3B

Pool 3C

Pool 5C

Pool 5A

Pool 5B

To Cambridge, 50

355

To Cambridge, 50

N

0   0.25   0.5

Miles

one of the largest populations of nesting bald eagles on the Atlantic Coast. Take a brisk hike on the easy, paved trail, or spend the day bird watching and exploring the varied wetland landscapes on short side trips.

The hike begins at the parking area for a short nature trail, Woods Trail, 1 mile along Wildlife Drive. If you have time to explore, you may want to start the day with a walk on the 0.5-mile Woods Trail for a close-up look at the area's woodlands.

The road leaves the woodland area and, at 0.3 mile, crosses a dike that separates the brackish Blackwater River and marsh, on the left, from freshwater impoundments on the right. The impoundment water levels are closely controlled—they are drained in summer for planting food crops for resident birds and flooded in the fall to provide resting sites for migrating waterfowl. Much wetland wildlife moves comfortably back and forth from the salty, tidal river to the freshwater wetland. Great blue herons, for example, will eat crabs and mussels as readily as they will gulp down a frog.

At 0.6 mile, the view across the Blackwater marshlands is unobstructed. On the far side of the river are wooded islands, and along the near shore, depending on the season, you may see terns, Canada geese, egrets, cormorants, and several species of ducks, sandpipers, and gulls. Close by, red-winged blackbirds sing from their perches in the marsh grass.

Continue around a wide bend and, at 0.9 mile, look left to the osprey nest on a platform just 25 yards offshore. All the platforms in the refuge—built to replace the tall trees osprey naturally nest in—are occupied by nesting pairs, which is a good sign for the endangered "fish hawk." During the spring and summer, this platform allows a particularly close look at activity in the nest. You may even see the osprey hunting or returning to the nest, talons deep in a big, silvery fish.

At 1.2 miles, the road bends right and follows the edge of a wood, a typical wetland stand of loblolly pine mixed with oaks, red maple, and sweet gum. Just ahead, at 1.4 miles, come to the Key Wallace Drive fork. (Here, you may take a 0.3-mile detour to a good site for spotting bald eagles.) Continue straight to Key Wallace Drive junction at 1.6 miles.

Turn right on Key Wallace Drive. Continue down the arrow-straight road with woods on the left and croplands on the right. Although you are on a public road, this is still a good place to look for wildlife. You may see white-tailed or sika deer browsing on the edge of the fields, groundhogs running for cover, or a red-tailed hawk soaring above. Listen for woodpeckers and warblers in the forest.

Egypt Road intersects from the left at 3 miles, where Key Wallace Road bends right. Proceed to the Wildlife Drive entrance at 3.3 miles, and turn right. Cross the Little Blackwater River on a dike. At 3.7 miles, you can go left 0.2 mile for a short side trip on Marsh Edge Trail, a 0.3-mile loop. Or you can hike 0.3 mile to an observation site on the Blackwater River, another good bird-watching spot.

Go straight at the Marsh Edge Trail fork, and follow Wildlife Drive sharply right back to the trailhead through a stand of loblolly pines, holly, and mixed hardwoods. The forest here is home to the endangered Delmarva fox squirrel,

Nearly 300 bird species have been identified on Blackwater National Wildlife Refuge grounds.
PHOTO BY MELISSA NIMMERRICHTER

which once ranged from southeastern Pennsylvania to Virginia but now resides in only four counties on the Eastern Shore.

Options: Woods Trail, Marsh Edge Trail, and the Observation Site are all connected to Wildlife Drive.

Special considerations: Bring insect repellent in summer.

Trailhead facilities: None.

Camping: None.

For more information: Blackwater National Wildlife Refuge.

61 Eastern Neck National Wildlife Refuge Loop

Highlights:	An easy walk through a quintessential Eastern Shore landscape on a Chesapeake Bay island.
Location:	Eastern Neck National Wildlife Refuge is in Kent County, Maryland, about 85 miles northeast of Washington, D.C.
Type of hike:	Loop; day hike.
Total distance:	4.6 miles with side trip.
Difficulty:	Easy.
Elevation gain:	Minimal.
Best months:	Year-round.
Permits:	None.
Maps:	USGS Landford Creek; refuge map.

Finding the trailhead: From the Maryland Highway 50/301 split east of the Chesapeake Bay Bridge, follow MD 301 north 8.7 miles to MD 213. Travel on MD 213 north for 18.7 miles; turn left onto MD 213 West, and proceed 0.5 mile to MD 20. Go south on MD 20 for 12 miles to Rock Hall. Turn left on MD 445, following signs for the refuge. Go 6 miles on MD 445 to the refuge border, and continue 1.4 miles to the Wildlife Trail parking area on the left.

Trailhead facilities: Restrooms at Boardwalk Trail.

Key points:
- 0.0   Trailhead
- 0.3   Spur to observation blind
- 1.6   Tubby Cove Boardwalk Trail junction
- 2.2   Boxes Point Trail junction
- 3.4   Refuge road

Eastern Neck National Wildlife Refuge Loop

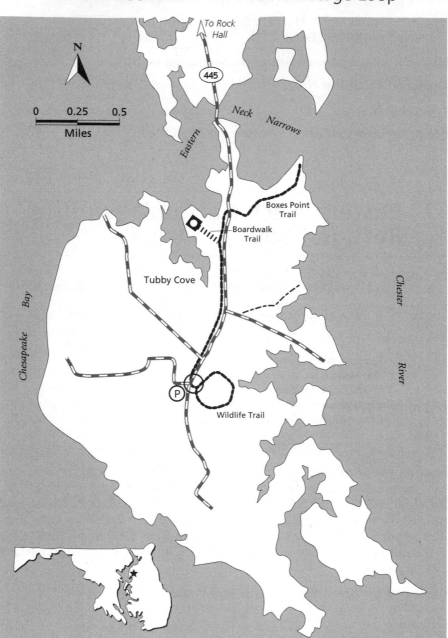

The hike: When people talk lovingly of the charms of the Eastern Shore, the land and life of Eastern Neck National Wildlife Refuge is what they have in mind. A 2,285-acre island on the northeastern shore of the Chesapeake Bay, Eastern Neck National Wildlife Refuge preserves tidal marsh, mixed pine and hardwood forests, river and bay shorelines, and open fields. Traveling through all these habitats, the trails on the island provide a great opportunity to see the landscapes that define the region and the many birds, mammals, and aquatic creatures that make these places home.

The hike on Eastern Neck is less of a loop than it is a series of forays into the different landscapes linked by the refuge road. It begins with the Wildlife Trail's short loop, travels the roadside for just over a mile and then takes two spurs on the north side of the island—one into the marsh and the other through the woods to the Chester River—before returning down the roadside to the trailhead.

From the parking area, enter the woods on the 0.5-mile Wildlife Trail. In just a few steps, you are in a lush and lively forest. There are splendid groves of mature trees, dense tangles of saplings and vines, and many areas where the forest floor is carpeted with ferns. The birds, of course, are abundant, from singing warblers and wrens to menacing vultures perched on the thick, high limbs of the trees. At 0.3 mile, a short spur to the right takes you to an observation blind on the edge of a narrow marsh. From here, look along the slow, meandering stream for great blue and green-backed herons, or muskrats nibbling on the marsh grass.

The Wildlife Trail then loops back to the parking area. Turn left and proceed to the refuge road, with an open field bordered by forest on the right. Turn right and travel up the roadside. For the next mile, the road will pass through field and forest, thicket and marsh. Used by refuge visitors only, the road is not busy, nor does it remove you from the natural world. Along its length, there are great views out over the open marsh and lots of opportunities for watching woodpeckers, hawks, and songbirds in the woods and fields, and ducks, geese, and wading shorebirds on the marsh. In fall and spring, refuge staff have counted more than 40,000 waterfowl traveling through the preserve.

At 1.6 miles, take Tubby Cove Boardwalk Trail out into the marsh. It travels 0.25 mile to an observation tower on a narrow, wooded spit. As you cross the marsh, there are great views of the bay and many good chances to see osprey fishing the waters along the shore. Male osprey feed their mates during courtship and their young while they grow, so they must catch as many as six fish a day. From the boardwalk, you can see them at work, plunging to the water to snatch a fish near the surface. The osprey will then turn the fish headfirst for a more aerodynamic flight and carry it home to the nest.

After finishing Tubby Cove Boardwalk Trail, turn left up the refuge road and proceed to Boxes Point Trail, just ahead on the right, at 2.2 miles. Boxes Point Trail travels 0.6 mile (one way) to the Chester River. It is a wide, grassy path that passes through field and forest and then cuts through an area managed for the endangered Delmarva fox squirrel. Here, controlled burns have cleared the understory and left a widely spaced, cathedral-like stand of trees, a habitat the squirrel favors. The trail then passes a small pond frequented by herons and meets the shoreline at Boxes Point, a good spot to view the Chester River and the far forested shore.

Retrace your steps on Boxes Point Trail. Back at the refuge road, 3.4 miles into the hike (including the detour to the Chester River), turn left and follow the road back to the trailhead.

Options: Duck Inn Trail, off a side road midway up the refuge drive, is another one-way trail on the island you may want to try. It is a 0.5 mile spur through marshlands.

Special considerations: The insects can be pesky throughout summer. Bring insect repellent or consider hiking here in autumn or early spring, when the bugs are thin and the birds are plentiful.

Camping: None.

For more information: Eastern Neck National Wildlife Refuge.

62 Trap Pond State Park Loop

Highlights:	An easy circuit hike on three park trails in a forest of stately conifers and hardwoods. Circle a pond and bald cypress swamp, the northernmost stand of bald cypress trees in the United States.
Location:	Trap Pond State Park is in southwestern Sussex County, about 55 miles south of Dover and 5 miles east of Laurel, off Delaware Highway 24.
Type of hike:	Loop; day hike.
Total distance:	4.8 miles.
Difficulty:	Easy.
Elevation gain:	Minimal.
Best months:	Year-round.
Permits:	None.
Maps:	USGS Trap Pond; state park map.

Finding the trailhead: From Delaware Seashore resorts, take Delaware Highway 1 North to DE 24 and travel west 29.5 miles to Road 449. Turn left on Road 449, and drive 1.2 miles to the main entrance of Trap Pond State Park. Turn left into the park, pass the entrance station, and continue 0.25 mile to the end of the bathhouse parking lot. The Trap Pond Loop begins along the shore of the pond beneath the log gateway marking the Island Trail Trailhead.

Trailhead facilities: Restrooms, bathhouse, telephone, picnic pavilion, nature center.

Trap Pond State Park Loop

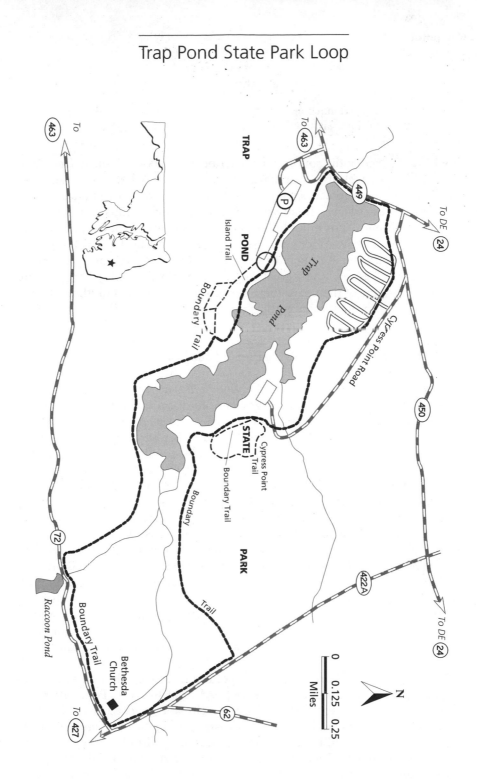

Key points:
- 0.0   Trailhead
- 1.5   Road 72; Raccoon Pond
- 2.0   Bethesda Church
- 2.3   Road 422A
- 2.6   Boundary Trail junction
- 3.3   Cypress Point Trail junction
- 4.5   Road 449

The hike: Tucked in the southwest corner of rural Sussex County, Trap Pond State Park is a jewel of a state park. Amid broad, flat fields of wheat and soybeans, the park protects a wonderful 2,109-acre parcel of wetlands, forest, and bald cypress swamp. In an afternoon on the park's trails, you can stroll through towering stands of loblolly pine and shady groves of oak, holly, dogwood, and sweet bay. Among the trees and swamps, bird life is abundant; walk quietly and you are likely to see kingfishers, ducks, great blue herons, osprey, hawks, kestrels, and a great variety of songbirds. And, where the trail hugs the shoreline of the pond, there are great views of the tall, thin-trunked bald cypress with their knobby roots bulging out of the shallows.

The loop begins on Island Trail, a single-track hiking path that runs parallel to the wide, sandy Boundary Trail to the right and the Trap Pond shoreline to the left. The trailhead is marked by a log gateway; the trail, by directional markers.

This is a perfect place to enter the woods. For about a quarter of a mile, the trail meanders through a lovely example of southern Delaware's lowland forest, with its canopy of tall pines, oaks, and sweet gums and its ornamental, garden-like understory of holly and sweet bay. The pine duff path runs along the shoreline and then bends deeper into the forest beneath abundant dogwoods, flowering white in spring and bearing red leaves and berries in the autumn. A bridge crosses a sliver of bald cypress swamp, and then the trail rejoins the shoreline for open views of the pond. Along the water's edge, look for great blue herons, loons, and canvasback ducks, or peer up above the treeline for soaring osprey or black vultures.

Island Trail turns sharply right just before a group camping area and crosses Boundary Trail, at 0.4 mile. At the crossing, turn left onto Boundary Trail. Bear right at the campground fork, and follow the wide, sandy path into a shady grove of tall, stately pines. A quarter of a mile farther, the trail bends left, drawing close to the pond and, rather suddenly, into a stand of mixed hardwoods. Look to the left through the trees and you will get a closer look at a majestic bald cypress stand and rows of turtles sunning on fallen logs.

The trail then bends away from the pond into a much thinner—and sunnier—pine grove; at 1.5 miles, it meets Road 72 at Raccoon Pond. Turn left on Road 72, passing Raccoon Pond on the right, and proceed around a bend past an old corn crib and down the arrow-straight roadway toward Bethesda Church, which you will reach at 2 miles. This half-mile stretch of road could be much worse. There is little traffic on this rural route. To the right is a wide-open soybean field and to the left a planted stand of pine, which makes up for its regimented look with the soothing music of the wind in its branches. But in the middle of the day, it can get rather bright and hot here, so bring a hat, sunglasses, and a little extra water to help you stay cool.

Bethesda Church, at 2 miles, is worth half a mile on the road. Built in 1878, the weathered clapboard church sits abandoned in a clearing, surrounded by nineteenth-century gravestones. The church's tall windows are shuttered, wildflowers shoot up through the brick walkway, and the headstones bear wonderful carvings and interesting epitaphs. This is a great place to pause for a rest and a quick look around.

Just past Bethesda Church, cross Thompson Branch and turn left on Road 62. The road is straight for 0.25 mile, bends to the right, and then turns sharply left onto Road 422A, at 2.3 miles. Proceed on the roadway, past several homesteads on the left and a wheat field on the right, to the Boundary Trail marker, at 2.6 miles. Turn left into the woods.

Back in the forest, you will appreciate the strong pine scent, the soft duff underfoot, and the shade of the big tulip trees as you walk the straight path to Cypress Point Trail, at 3.3 miles. Cypress Point Trail is another marked nature trail, a short loop that parallels Boundary Trail and then circles back into the woods. It is a little hard to find because it is marked for hikers traveling in the opposite direction. The first marker you see, on the left, is for a 50-yard path to the swamp. Take a look if you like. Then proceed on Boundary Trail another 200 yards. There, you will see a marker on the right. *Go left here.* You will quickly see the backside of a Cypress Point Trail marker (number 10) on the left.

Follow Cypress Point Trail along the edge of the pond for about a quarter of a mile. It passes a boardwalk that extends into a bald cypress swamp, rejoins Boundary Trail for 50 yards, and then cuts back to the water's edge and a lovely spot for viewing the expanse of a bald cypress stand. This is the northernmost grove of this aquatic tree in the United States. Once an extensive bald cypress swamp, the area was logged and the swamp dammed to power a sawmill in the late 1700s. It was not until the 1930s that the federal government purchased 1,000 acres around the pond and the forest began to recover. In this spot, to the left of a bench beneath a big pine, you can touch the soft, copper-colored bark of a giant bald cypress and feel the sturdiness that drew the attention of so many loggers.

Cross a footbridge through a grove of sweet bay, and travel 250 yards to a youth group campground. Cut right across the campground parking lot to the entrance, follow the hard sandy road 200 yards, and then turn left into the woods on Boundary Trail. Follow the trail 0.25 mile to the public campground. Enter the campground, go 50 paces, and proceed through a post-and-rail walkway and across a bridge over a swampy branch. Turn left sharply, walk to the pond, and follow the trail along the water's edge to the boat ramp at the far side of the campground. At the stop sign, at 4.5 miles, turn left onto Road 449.

Follow Road 449 across the Trap Pond dam, which was rebuilt in the 1930s by the Civilian Conservation Corps. Look left for a great open view of the pond and the surrounding forest. Cross the spillway and turn left toward the park office and the beginning of the Trap Pond Loop.

Special considerations: Entrance fees are required during summer and on weekends and holidays in May, September, and October. Wear a cap, and thoroughly check your scalp and skin for ticks after your hike. During summer, bring a cap and sunglasses for the road portion of the loop, and bring a swimsuit for a post-hike swim.

Camping: There are 152 campsites on the pond's northern shore as well as two primitive areas for youth groups.

For more information: Trap Pond State Park.

Appendix A: Resources

MARYLAND

American Chestnut Land Trust
Box 204
Port Republic, MD 20676
410-586-1570

Antietam National Battlefield
P.O. Box 158
Sharpsburg, MD 21782-0158
301-432-5124

Assateague Island National Seashore
7206 National Seashore Lane
Berlin, MD 21811
410-641-3030

Bear Branch Nature Center
300 John Owings Road
Westminster, MD 21158
410-848-2517

Blackwater National Wildlife Refuge
2145 Key Wallace Drive
Cambridge, MD 21613
410-228-2677

C&O National Historical Park
P.O. Box 4
Sharpsburg, MD 21782
301-739-4200

Catoctin Mountain Park
6602 Foxville Road
Thurmont, MD 21788-1598
301-663-9330

Cedarville State Forest
11704 Fenno Road
Upper Marlboro, MD 20772
301-888-1410

Cunningham Falls State Park
14039 Catoctin Hollow Road
Thurmont, MD 21788
301-271-7574

Deep Creek Lake Recreation Area
898 State Park Road
Swanton, MD 21561
301-387-4111

Eastern Neck National Wildlife Refuge
1730 Eastern Neck Road
Rock Hall, MD 21661
410-639-7056

Fort Frederick State Park
11100 Fort Frederick Road
Big Pool, MD 21711
301-842-2155

Furnace Town Foundation
Box 207
Snow Hill, MD 21863
410-632-2032

Gambrill State Park
c/o Greenbriar State Park
21843 National Pike
Boonsboro, MD 21713
301-791-4767

Green Ridge State Forest
28700 Headquarters Drive NE
Flintstone, MD 21530
301-478-3124

Gunpowder Falls State Park
2813 Jerusalem Road
Kingsville, MD 21087
410-592-2897

Herrington Manor State Park
222 Herrington Lane
Oakland, MD 21550
301-334-9180

Howard County Recreation and Parks
7120 Oakland Mills Road
Columbia, MD 21046-1677
410-313-4700

Little Bennett Regional Park
23705 Frederick Road
Clarksburg, MD 20871
301-972-6581

New Germany State Park
349 Headquarters Lane
Grantsville, MD 21536
301-895-5453

Ocean City Convention and Visitors Bureau
4001 Coastal Highway
Ocean City, MD 21842
800-OCO-CEAN (800-626-2326)

Oregon Ridge Park
13555 Beaver Dam Road
Cockeysville, MD 21030
410-887-1815

Patapsco Valley State Park
8020 Baltimore National Pike
Ellicott City, MD 21043
410-461-5005

Patuxent Research Refuge
National Wildlife Visitor Center
10901 Scarlet Tanager Loop
Laurel, MD 20708
301-497-5760

Patuxent River Park
16000 Croom Airport Road
Upper Marlboro, MD 20772
301-627-6074

Pocomoke State Forest
3461 Worcester Highway
Snow Hill, MD 21863
410-632-2566

Potomac State Forest
1431 Potomac Camp Road
Oakland, MD 21550
301-334-2038

Rocky Gap State Park
12500 Pleasant Valley Road
Flintstone, MD 21530
301-777-2139

Savage River Complex
349 Headquarters Lane
Grantsville, MD 21536
301-895-5453

Seneca Creek State Park
11950 Clopper Road
Gaithersburg, MD 20878
301-924-2127

Soldier's Delight Natural Environment Area
5100 Deer Park Road
Owings Mills, MD 21117
410-922-3044

Susquehanna State Park
3318 Rocks Chrome Hill Road
Jarrettsville, MD 21084
410-557-7994

Swallow Falls State Park
c/o Herrington Manor State Park
222 Herrington Lane
Oakland, MD 21550
301-387-6938

Trap Pond State Park
Route 2, Box 331
Laurel, MD 19956
301-875-5153

DELAWARE

Blackbird State Forest
502 Blackbird Forest Road
Smyrna, DE 19977
302-653-6505

Bombay Hook National Wildlife Refuge
2591 Whitehall Neck Road
Smyrna, DE 19977
302-653-9345

Brandywine Creek State Park
P.O. Box 3782
Wilmington, DE 19807
302-577-3534

Cape Henlopen State Park
42 Cape Henlopen Drive
Lewes, DE 19958
302-645-8983

Delaware Division of Fish and Wildlife
89 Kings Highway
Dover, DE 19901
302-739-5297

Delaware Seashore State Park
Inlet 850
Rehoboth Beach, DE 19971
302-227-2800

Fenwick Island State Park
c/o Holts Landing State Park
P.O. Box 76
Millville, DE 19970
302-539-9060
302-539-1055 (summer only)

Holts Landing State Park
Box 76
Millville, DE 19970
302-539-9060

Killens Pond State Park
5025 Killens Pond Road
Felton, DE 19943
302-284-4526

Lums Pond State Park
1068 Howell School Road
Bear, DE 19701
302-368-6989

Nanticoke Wildlife Area
RR 3, Box 205A
Laurel, DE 19956
302-539-3160

New Castle County Department of Parks
and Recreation
Department of Special Services
187-A Old Churchman's Road
New Castle, DE 19720-3115
302-395-5790

Prime Hook National Wildlife Refuge
RD 3, Box 195
Milton, DE 19968
302-684-8419

Redden State Forest
RD 4, Box 354
Georgetown, DE 19947
302-856-2893

White Clay Creek State Park
425 Wedgewood Road
Newark, DE 19711
302-368-6900

Appendix B: Further Reading

Abercrombie, Jay. *Walks and Rambles on the Delmarva Peninsula*. Woodstock, Ver.: Backcountry Publications, 1985.

ADC's Street Map of Baltimore City and County, MD, Alexandria, Va.: Alexandria Drafting Company, 1998.

ADC's Street Map of Carroll County, MD, Alexandria, Va.: ADC of Alexandria, Inc., 1990.

ADC's Street Map of Howard County, MD, Alexandria, Va.: Alexandria Drafting Company, 1998.

ADC's Street Map of Montgomery County, MD, Alexandria, Va.: ADC of Alexandria, Inc., 1993.

ADC's Street Map of Prince Georges County, MD, Alexandria, Va.: ADC of Alexandria, Inc., 1991.

Delaware Trails Guidebook. Dover: Department of Natural Resources and Environmental Control, 1994.

Fisher, Alan. *Country Walks near Baltimore*. Baltimore: Rambler Books, 1993.

Fisher, Alan. *Country Walks near Washington*. Boston: Appalachian Mountain Club, 1994.

Gosner, Kenneth L. *A Field Guide to the Atlantic Seashore: Invertebrates & Seaweeds of the Atlantic Coast from the Bay of Fundy to Cape Hatteras*. Boston: Houghton Mifflin, 1979.

Harding, John J., and Justin J. Harding. *Birding the Delaware Valley Region*. Philadelphia: Temple University Press, 1980.

Hikes in Western Maryland. Vienna, Va.: Potomac Appalachian Trail Club, 1997.

MacKay, Bryan. *Hiking, Biking, and Canoeing in Maryland*. Baltimore: Johns Hopkins University Press, 1995.

Maryland and Delaware Atlas and Gazetteer. Freeport, Me.: DeLorme Mapping, 1993.

Peattie, Donald Culross. *A Natural History of Trees of Eastern and Central North America*. Boston: Houghton Mifflin Company, 1991.

Phillips, Claude E. *Wildflowers of Delaware and the Eastern Shore*. Hockessin, Del.: Delaware Nature Society, 1978.

Sutton, Allan. *Potomac Trails*. Golden, Colo.: Fulcrum Publishing, 1997.

Sutton, Ann, and Myron Sutton. *Eastern Forests*. New York: Alfred A. Knopf, 1985.

Taber, William S. *Delaware Trees: A Guide to the Identification of the Native Tree Species*. Dover: Delaware Department of Agriculture and Forest Services, 1995.

Trails of the Mid-Atlantic Region. Washington, D.C.: National Park Service, 1990.

Willis, Nancy Carol. *Delaware Bay Shorebirds*. Dover: Delaware Department of Natural Resources and Environmental Control, 1998.

Appendix C: Hiking Organizations for Maryland and Delaware

Abbotts Mill Trail Club
RD 1, Box 12413, SR 36
Greenwood, DE 19950

American Discovery Trail
P.O. Box 20155
Washington, DC 20041-2155

Anacostia Headwaters Greenway
4112 30th Street
Mount Rainier, MD 20712-1834

Annapolis Amblers
539 Shore Acres Road
Arnold, MD 21012-1903

Appalachian Trail Conference
P.O. Box 807
Harpers Ferry, WV 25425

Audubon Society of Central Maryland
7166 Winter Rose Path
Columbia, MD 21045-5134

Baltimore Blaze Stoppers
6904 Beech Avenue
Baltimore, MD 21206-1209

Baltimore Walking Club
8426 Pleasant Plains Road
Baltimore, MD 21286

Capital Hiking Club
6519 Bannockburn Drive
Bethesda, MD 20817

Chesapeake and Ohio Canal Association
P.O. Box 366
Glen Echo, MD 20812

Columbia Parks and Recreation
Association
10221 Wincopin Circle, Suite 100
Columbia, MD 21044-3410

Delaware Greenways Inc.
P.O. Box 2095
Wilmington, DE 19899

Delaware Outing Club
117 Dallas Avenue
Newark, DE 19711-5125

Delaware Wild Lands Inc.
303 Main Street
Odessa, DE 19730

Diamond State Trekkers
11 N. Railroad Avenue, B
Wyoming, DE 19934-1043

Footprints Only
201 W. Padonia Road, Suite 600
Lutherville, MD 21093-2115

Fort Ritchie Volksmarchers
Building 834, Outdoor Recreation Center
Cascade, MD 21719

Frederick Flatfooters
6803 Falstone Drive
Frederick, MD 21702-9478

Freestate Happy Wanderers
8548 Pineway Court
Laurel, MD 20723-1238

Friendly Trails Wandering Club
5457 Enberend Terrace
Columbia, MD 21045

Great Greenbelt Volksmarchers
4617 Lincoln Avenue
Beltsville, MD 20705

Greenbelt Parks
6565 Greenbelt Road
Greenbelt, MD 20770

Maryland Volkssport Association
1343 Huntover Drive
Odenton, MD 21113-2122

Mason-Dixon Wobblers
10886 Rock Coast Road
Columbia, MD 21044-2734

Metropolitan Branch Trail
4112 30th Street
Mount Rainier, MD 20712-1834

Mountain Club of Maryland
8442 Each Leaf Court
Columbia, MD 21045

National Handicap Sports
451 Hungerford Drive, Suite 100
Rockville, MD 20850-4151

The Nature Conservancy
260 Chapman Road, Suite 201D
Newark, DE 19702

North Central Railroad Trail
P.O. Box 50
Glen Arm, MD 21057

Outdoor Education Association
5110 Meadowside Lane
Rockville, MD 20855-1812

Piedmont Pacers
2102 Woodview Road
Finksburg, MD 21048-1118

Potomac Appalachian Trail Club
118 Park Street SE
Vienna, VA 22180

Seneca Valley Sugar Loafers
10513 Neckleby Way
Damascus, MD 20872

Sierra Club, Catoctin Chapter
12 E. 3rd Street
Frederick, MD 21701-5311

Sierra Club, Potomac Chapter
1116 West Street, Suite C
Annapolis, MD 21401-3657

Star Spangled Steppers
809 E. Farrow Court
Bel Air, MD 21014-6903

Walter Reed Wandervogel
146 Fleetwood Terrace
Silver Spring, MD 20910-5511

Wanderbirds Hiking Club
6806 Delaware Street
Chevy Chase, MD 20815-4166

Washington Women Outdoors
P.O. Box 345
Riverdale, MD 20738-0345

Wilmington Trail Club
P.O. Box 1184
Wilmington, DE 19899

Appendix D: Hiker's Checklist

Always make and check your own checklist!
If you've ever hiked into the backcountry and discovered that you've forgotten an essential, you know that it's a good idea to make a checklist and check the items off as you pack so that you won't forget the things you want and need. Here are some ideas:

Clothing
- [ ] Dependable rain parka
- [ ] Rain pants
- [ ] Windbreaker
- [ ] Thermal underwear
- [ ] Shorts
- [ ] Long pants or sweatpants
- [ ] Wood cap or balaclava
- [ ] Hat
- [ ] Wool shirt or sweater
- [ ] Jacket or parka
- [ ] Extra socks
- [ ] Underwear
- [ ] Lightweight shirts
- [ ] T-shirts
- [ ] Bandana(s)
- [ ] Mittens or gloves
- [ ] Belt

Footwear
- [ ] Sturdy, comfortable boots
- [ ] Lightweight camp shoes

Bedding
- [ ] Sleeping bag
- [ ] Foam pad or air mattress
- [ ] Ground sheet (plastic or nylon)
- [ ] Dependable tent

Hauling
- [ ] Backpack and/or day pack

Cooking
- [ ] 1-quart container (plastic)
- [ ] 1-gallon water container for camp use (collapsible)
- [ ] Backpacking stove and extra fuel
- [ ] Funnel
- [ ] Aluminum foil
- [ ] Cooking pots
- [ ] Bowls/plates
- [ ] Utensils (spoons, forks, small spatula, knife)
- [ ] Pot scrubber
- [ ] Matches in waterproof container

Food and Drink
- [ ] Cereal
- [ ] Bread
- [ ] Crackers
- [ ] Cheese
- [ ] Trail mix
- [ ] Margarine
- [ ] Powdered soups
- [ ] Salt/pepper
- [ ] Main course meals
- [ ] Snacks
- [ ] Hot chocolate
- [ ] Tea
- [ ] Powdered milk
- [ ] Drink mixes

Photography
- [ ] Camera and film
- [ ] Filters
- [ ] Lens brush/paper

Miscellaneous
- [ ] Sunglasses
- [ ] Map and a compass
- [ ] Toilet paper
- [ ] Pocketknife
- [ ] Sunscreen
- [ ] Good insect repellent
- [ ] Lip balm
- [ ] Flashlight with good batteries and a spare bulb
- [ ] Candle(s)
- [ ] First-aid kit
- [ ] Your FalconGuide
- [ ] Survival kit
- [ ] Small garden trowel or shovel
- [ ] Water filter or purification tablets
- [ ] Plastic bags (for trash)
- [ ] Soap
- [ ] Towel
- [ ] Toothbrush
- [ ] Fishing license
- [ ] Fishing rod, reel, lures, flies, etc.
- [ ] Binoculars
- [ ] Waterproof covering for pack
- [ ] Watch
- [ ] Sewing kit

About the Authors

David Lillard is executive director of the Blue Ridge Center for Environmental Stewardship and former president of the American Hiking Society, a national organization serving hikers and hiking organizations. A Delaware native, he grew up walking the stream corridors, railroad beds, and farm fields that were once common in northern Delaware. He is a trail volunteer with the Potomac Appalachian Trail Club and a member of several grassroots hiking groups. His books include *Exploring the Appalachian Trail: Hikes in the Virginias.*

Chris Reiter is the managing editor of Blue Ridge Press and the former editor of American Hiker, the magazine of the American Hiking Society. He was born in Wilmington, Delaware, and began hiking and camping on boyhood trips to Cape Henlopen and Virginia's Blue Ridge. Currently living in West Virginia, he is a frequent visitor to the woods, beaches, and marshes of southern Delaware. He writes frequently on hiking, conservation, and natural history.

American Hiking Society

American Hiking Society is the only national nonprofit organization dedicated to establishing, protecting and maintaining foot trails in America.

Establishing...

American Hiking Society establishes hiking trails with the AHS National Trails Endowment, providing grants for grassroots organizations to purchase trail lands, construct and maintain trails, and preserve hiking trails' scenic values. The AHS affiliate club program, called the Congress of Hiking Organizations, brings trail clubs together to share information, collaborate on public policy, and advocate legislation and policies that protect hiking trails.

Protecting...

American Hiking Society protects hiking trails through highly focused public policy efforts in the nation's capital. AHS affects federal legislation, shapes public lands policy, collaborates with grassroots trail organizations, and partners with federal land managers to protect the hiking experience. Members become active with letter-writing campaigns and by attending the annual AHS Trails Advocacy Week.

Maintaining...

American Hiking Society maintains hiking trails by sending volunteers to national parks, forests and recreation lands; organizing volunteer teams to help affiliated hiking clubs; and publishing national volunteer directories. AHS members get involved, get dirty and get inspired by participating in AHS programs like National Trails Day, America's largest celebration of the outdoors; and Volunteer Vacations—week-long work trips to beautiful, wild places.

Join American Hiking Society...

Be a part of the organization dedicated to protecting and preserving the nation's footpaths, our footpaths, the ones in our backyards and our backcountry. Visit American Hiking Society's website or call to find out more about membership. When you join, Falcon Publishing will send you a FREE guide as a special thank you for contributing to the efforts of American Hiking Society.

American Hiking Society
1422 Fenwick Lane
Silver Spring, MD 20910
OR CALL: (888) 766-HIKE ext. 1
OR VISIT: www.americanhiking.org